REPORT ON THE FINDINGS AND STATEMENTS

ON THE QUESTION OF THE

ORDINATION OF WOMEN

BY

DOCTRINAL REVIEW COMMITTEE
OF THE GENERAL ASSEMBLY
OF THE CHURCH OF GOD IN CHRIST, INC.
BISHOP GEORGE D. MCKINNEY, Ph.D., D.D.
GENERAL BOARD MEMBER, CHAIRMAN

Submitted to Bishop Frank Ellis, Chairman
General Assembly

April 1999 Memphis, Tennessee

Published by George D. McKinney

Report on The Findings and Statements on The Question of The Ordination of Women
Copyright © 2021 by George D. McKinney

ISBN 978-0-9909199-7-1

Contributing authors:
Elder Charles Quillen, Elder Charles Stevenson, Bishop Clarence Sexton,
Elder A. Hunt, Dr. Joseph Clemmons, Elder James Holton, Dr. D. Williams,
Dr. Oliver Haney, Jr. Elder Sherman Davis, Elder James Stovall,
Dr. Robert Asberry, Elder James Parson, Jr., Lt. Col. Dianna James,
Mother Parthenia Crudup, Bishop W. Hamilton, Elder Walter Bogan,
Bishop William James, Bishop Wesley Sanders, Elder Jessie Denny,
Dr. Norman Harper, Elder Clyde Young, Dr. Aliene Gilmore, Supt. Carl Howard,
Dr. Thomas A. Body, Mrs. Michele Jacques-Early, Elder Steven Johnson, and
Bishop George D. McKinney, Jr. Ph.D.

Cover and interior design by Traci Wooden-Carlisle

Printed in the United States of America

DOCTRINAL REVIEW COMMITTEE MEMBERS

OF THE GENERAL ASSEMBLY

OF THE CHURCH OF GOD IN CHRIST, INC.

Elder Charles Quillen, Elder Charles Stevenson, Bishop Clarence Sexton, Elder A. Hunt, Dr. Joseph Clemmons, Elder James Holton, Dr. D. Williams, Dr. Oliver Haney, Jr. Elder Sherman Davis, Elder James Stovall, Dr. Robert Asberry, Elder James Parson, Jr., Lt. Col. Dianna James, Mother Parthenia Crudup, Bishop W. Hamilton, Elder Walter Bogan, Bishop William James, Bishop Wesley Sanders, Elder Jessie Denny, Dr. Norman Harper, Elder Clyde Young, Dr. Aliene Gilmore, Supt. Carl Howard, Dr. Thomas A. Body, Mrs. Michele Jacques-Early, Elder Steven Johnson, and Bishop George D. McKinney, Jr., Ph.D.

TABLE OF CONTENTS

REPORT ON THE FINDINGS AND STATEMENTS

ON THE QUESTION OF THE

ORDINATION OF WOMEN

By

DOCTRINAL REVIEW COMMITTEE
OF THE GENERAL ASSEMBLY
OF THE CHURCH OF GO IN CHRIST, INC

Introduction

After 20 years of educating female students in our seminary, the Church of God in Christ is in need of theological direction concerning the full ordination of women. Further, the Presiding Bishop and General Board have authorized the limited ordination of women for special ministries. Following this action, several bishops have participated in the ordination and appointment of women pastors. These actions are taken in light of the interpretation of Part I-women in ministry-church manual pages 144-146.

"The Church of God in Christ recognizes that there are thousands of talented, Spirit-filled, dedicated and well-informed devout women capable of conducting affairs of a church, both administratively and spiritually. Such women are mentioned in the New Testament, Romans 16:1-2, 'I commend unto you Phoebe our sister, which is a servant of the church which is at sin Cenchrea: that ye receive her in the Lord, as becometh saints, and that ye assist her in whatever business she hath need of you: for she hath been a 'succorer' of many, and of myself also. Romans 16:3, 'Great Priscilla and Aquilla my helpers in Christ Jesus'. Aquilla and Priscilla had a church in their home. Acts 9:36 now there was at Joppa a certain disciple named Dorcas: this woman was full of good works and home deeds which she did Acts18: 24-28, Priscilla is equally gifted with her Husband as an expounder of the way of God, and instructor of Apollos. Acts 16:14 Lydia of Thyatira, a seller of purpose, whose hospitality made a home for Paul and a meeting place for the infant church.

It is evident in the New Testament and in the writings of the Apostolic Fathers that women, through the agency of two ecclesiastical orders were assigned official duties in the conduct and ministrations of the early church. Their existence as a distinct order is indicated in 1 Timothy 5:9-10 where Paul directs Timothy as to the conditions of their enrolment. No widow should be enrolled under 60 years of age, having been the wife of one man. She must be 'we reported of good works, a mother having brought up children, hospitable, having used hospitality to strangers, Christ-like in loving service, have washed the saint's feet.'

Other special duties mentioned by the Church Fathers included prayer and fasting, visiting the sick, instruction of women, preparing them for baptism, assisting in the administration of this ordinance, and taking the communion.

Many of the duties of the widows were transferred to the deaconesses by the third century, an order which in recent history has been restored to its original importance and effectiveness.

The Church of God in Christ recognizes the scriptural importance of women in the Christian Ministry, (Matt. 2:1; Mark 16:1 Luck 24:1; John 20:1), the first at the tomb on the morning of Christ's resurrection; the first to whom the Lord appeared (Matt. 28:29, Mark 16:9, John 20:14) the first to announce the fact of resurrection to the chosen disciples (Luke 29:9, 10:22), etc., but nowhere can we find a mandate to ordain women to be an Elder, Bishop or Pastor. Women may teach the gospel to others (Phil. 4:3; Titus 2:3-5; Joel 2:28), have charged of a church in absence of its Pastor if the Pastor so wishes, (Romans 16:1-5) without adopting the title of Eder, Reverend, Bishop or Pastor. Paul styled the women who labored with him as servants or helpers, not Elders, Bishop, or Pastors.

Therefore the Church of God in Christ cannot accept the following scriptures as a mandate to ordain women preachers: Joel 2:28; Gal. 5:28-29; Matt. 28:9-11. The qualification for an Elder, Bishop, or Pastor is found in 1 Timothy 3:2-7 and Titus 1:7-9. "We exhort all to take heed."

Chief among our concerns is whether or not the church is in line with Biblical and theological principles allowing such a full and complete ordination.

In 1992, the Honorable Chairman of the General Assembly, Bishop Frank Ellis, acting on behalf of the General Assembly of the Church of God in Christ commissioned the Doctrinal Review committee to investigate the issue of the "Ordination of Women." The DRC is composed of Bishops, Superintendents, Pastors, Evangelists, Scholars, and Laity. The committee includes men and women from every region in our nation. (See the attached roster of DRC membership). The unquestioned dedication and loyalty of the committee members to the Church are fuller indicated by the fact that the committee held meetings in Memphis (3), Dallas (2), Atlanta (1), and San Diego. Each attending committee member paid his/her own expense (travel, hotel, food, etc.) There was the sacrifice of valuable time as well as a financial sacrifice because there was a willingness to serve our great Church. The responsibility was accepted with fear and trembling because of our love for God and His Church. The committee was unanimous in the position that a proper review of any doctrine required good biblical exegesis as a foundation for making a light decision.

For more than 100 years God has shown favor to the Church of God in Christ as an agency for spiritual and social change in the life of our nation. Through Bishop C.H. Mason's involvement, we were in the heart of the great Azusa Revival of 1906 that changed the spiritual landscape of America. During two World Wars, the Church of God in Christ was consistently loyal to the nation, while at the same time fulfilling its prophetic role of advocating for Peace and Justice. When Blacks immigrated in large numbers from the rural South to the North, East, and West, the churches and storefronts served as a refuge and a center of help and hope. Further, the church rose to the challenge of representing the Kingdom of God during the devastating depression years and the turbulent upheavals of the Civic Rights Movement. Some spiritual observers believe that months ahead, at the close of the millennium there may be challenges and changes, turbulence and troubles of greater magnitude than any in this century. Therefore, at the close of the millennium, it is appropriate that the Church examines both its doctrines and practices in light of Scripture. By Divine Providence, the people from all over the world have come to our cities, where our Church the Church of God in Christ is firmly planted and established.

The Church of God in Christ today has its greatest opportunity to evangelize the nations and minister to the masses who are at our doorsteps. Everyone who is saved or ordained by God must be enlisted in this urgent harvest of souls.

The Church Is Not Directed by Cultural Issues

The Church of God in Christ-like every other organization or organism finds itself surrounded by any number of influential factors that will determine not only its destination but the quality of existence day-by-day. Life must be based on following the main directive-fulfilling the will and purpose of God. As a church then we must recognize why God had called us what he expects from the daily expressions of our lives.

The church as the baptized body of believers has its main reason for existence the proclamation of the gospel of love that God has infused in our hearts. That love has its main objective, the returning of God's creatures and creation back to a state of defense. Thus, the church must openly Face the issue of the ordination of women and their role in the ministry of the church.

The purpose and direction of our lives both collectively and individually are mandated by the revelation of God as found in the scripture. We must find those Basic Principles of truth: That firstly revealed the mind of God and secondly, are not changed by the influences of our changing cultures and traditions. The purpose and direction are not to be determined by outside influences, "we are in the world but not of the world."

Cultural factors of course are not to be ignored but they will be brought under the regulatory influence of the word of God. God's word becomes relevant to the events of our cultural advances, but the basic principles of truth never change. We must always keep in mind the adaptability of the word and its unchanging characteristics.

The church must remember that God's revelation of Himself, His purpose, and His will has from the beginning, been progressive in nature. Each generation has been chosen by God for a specific purpose of accomplishment. Each generation moves forward to new heights and deeper depths of the knowledge of God. The foundation of the revelation of God has been laid (Christ Jesus) but we are granted the privilege to receive a clearer version of God's will. This clearer version does not do away with cover up or destroy the foundation but allows us to build upon that foundation that is able to sustain us and take us higher in our knowledge of Him. Thus, the church must not allow changing customs and traditions to effect change in our relationship to God's purpose and will for our lives.

The church must maintain its faith in the revelation of God. The church must not allow cultural issues to dictate the direction of our endeavors to do the will of God. The church must view all cultural issues and changes in light of the truth God has given to us in the scripture.

Headship vs. Anarchy

All that God has done and will do is ordered by the master plan in the mind of God. There is unmistakable evidence of the orderliness of the purpose of God in creation as we know it. This becomes quite evident that in creation God has placed men in the position of headship and thus he must accept the responsibility of the position. God made mankind the dominant power of creation when he said, let him have dominion over all the works of creation. This position of headship makes man accountable to God for all of his decisions; man becomes God's ruling representative, the crown of creation, the representative of all mankind, the one who must learn to show forth the love of God as he accepts the responsibility God has given him. It is the love of God that allows man to exercise His leadership without manifesting a spirit of domination or supremacy. This was fundamental to the teachings of Jesus who sought to show the extent of God's love exemplified in man who had been created in the image and likeness of the father. There must, out of necessity, be order and purpose to all that God does for without order (headship) there would be anarchy. Since God is not the God of confusion, we must seek to know his order of things if man is not the appointed head then we must ask two questions: (1) who has been given the position of headship and (2) What are the duties and responsibilities assigned to the designated individuals?

Is There Justice?

The Old and New Testament clearly reveal that God is a God of righteousness and justice, Micah 6:8, Luke 3:8-14, and Mark 12:29-31. The Church of God in Christ and every Bible-believing assembly agree that the church is obligated to conduct its affairs under biblical authority and standard of justice and righteousness. The church's commitment to righteousness requires that all of its doctrines, teachings, and practices promote and encourage the development of right relationships with God and man. With regard to ordination, the biblical mandate to do just Micah 6:8 has urgent implications. The church's authority to ordain, to loose, to bind, to forgive sins, etc, is delegated authority from the Lord of the church. Such awesome delegated authority must not be exercised irreverently or arbitrarily since the church is accountable to the God of Justice. All power and authority rest with God who calls and ordains workers for his ministry.

Questions:

1. Does gender-based ordination wrongfully deny the church's blessings and affirmation to women who testify that they are called?

2. To Is there a parallel between the church's practice of gender-based organization and the historical practice of race-based ordination?

The Challenge We Face

It is a fact that the Church of God in Christ has met a theological crisis of significant scope in its hundred-year history. In 1906, the doctrinal question of receiving the baptism of the holy ghost was an issue. In 1907, the speaking in tongues prompted a deep divide and eventual split, and in 1919, the challenge of the baptismal formula plunged Pentecostals into a theological struggle. Now the role of women in the ministry has brought the Church of God in Christ to another point of theological inquiry.

The role of women in the Church of God in Christ has been traditionally one of support in the ministry. It is clear that women are seeking full ordination and inclusion within the ranks of the clergy. Considering that from this organization's inception the leadership has welcomed the full expression and input of women in the life of the church, it should not be difficult to establish evidence of women's contributions. To properly examine that role would not diminish or negate the contribution of women but should bring greater clarity to the picture, and thereby help in our decision about full ordination.

Our founder, Bishop C.H. Mason was genuine in his approach and empowerment of women in ministry. Mason's policies were examples of Paul's exhortations to help those women who labor in the ministry (Phil 4:3). Though it is clear that Paul said in the aforementioned "he also stated in 1 Timothy 2:11, "I do not permit a woman to teach or to have authority over a man, but to be silent." C.H. Mason hardly considered or enforced this saying when it comes to the function of women. Women were never relegated to second-class status, rather than Mason demonstrated liberal and tangible commitment to women. Basically, our committee is supportive of being faithful to the origins and positions of our church. Women have always been afforded an opportunity and essentially the church has flourished through their participation. Therefore, the committee stands in affirming the realities of those contributions. Just as women labored alongside

Bishop Mason, they have yet to distinguish their perpetual place in the life and ministry of the church.

The committee must raise the question of how does one balance scriptures that seemed to limit women with the evidence of their contemporary and his Stuart contributions in the ministry? Possibly Bishop Mason understood and distinguished the Pauline comments as either timely or timeless. The definition of a time-centered comment and a timeless comment is important to our interpretation of the role of women. Equally important is the difference between policies and theological principles, and the difference between cultural concerns and Christ's will as significant indicators of women's possible role. Consider the countless women who labored with their husbands to establish churches! In foreign fields and lonely outposts, women have buried the dead, served communion, and preached sermons. Their contributions have certainly been enhanced with the advent of the seminary. COGIC women serve as Chaplains in the military, in hospitals, in prisons, and in other institutions. The church has provided special ordination to allow their service. Is their ordination and contribution any less valid because they are women? The organization has granted special ordination in spite of what 1 Timothy 2:11 states and we are better for having done so. It is generally held that special ordination did no violence to the scripture.

Our investigation leads the committee to believe that further examination, discussion, and prayer concerning the full ordination of women is merited. Proper examination must be done to ensure a valid and reasonable decision can be made it must be done in order to clarify whether or not the voice of the Lord is encouraging women's role in ministry during these days. It is an accident that we are considering women's roles in ministry. The discussion could easily be about the authority of apostolic appointment or any number of other critical doctrinal subjects. What is significant is the advancement of the church and the facilitation of the Kingdom of God?

Every argument, pro or con, should be considered in the matrix of our decision. To give full credence to the religious and vocational experience of women in the ministry, the church must employ both prayerful effort and divine revelation. Our experience has taught us that revelation is not subservient to tradition, limited by understanding, indifference, prejudice, or fear. Therefore, the General Assembly task might very well be determining a progressive understanding of God's and continuing revelation.

The evidence of Mother Roberson, Dr. Mallory, Mother Coffee, and Mother Anne Bailey should support the continued contribution of women in our ministry. Hopefully, by proper evaluation, we have an opportunity to merge facts, principles of tolerance, and faith together and then grant a proper hearing for making a decision on the full ordination of women.

CURRENT BELIEFS AND PRACTICES

REGARDING

WOMEN IN MINISTRY

CHURCH OF GOD IN CHRIST
Memphis, Tennessee

A HISTORICAL REVIEW OF WOMAN IN MINISTRY THE NEW TESTAMENT AND THE EARLY CHURCH

(Questions on the Validity of True Women in Ministry)

Prepared by Superintendent

Norman O. Harper

Committee Member

For

Bishop George McKinney

Chairman of Doctrines & Reviews Committee

General Assembly Church of God in Christ

November 10, 1993

The Four Gospel Writer's Perception of Women

Since the members of the Christian community claim to be followers of Jesus in some way, it is logical that the scriptural accounts of the attitude of Jesus toward women should play a major role in shaping their views. The writers of the four Gospels have provided Christians with the memory of the life of Jesus. In studying these books, it is possible or probable that the Gospel writers were not trying to give us a completely objective, accurate, and detailed account of Jesus' work on Earth. Rather, they selectively used stories and teachings to make a statement about the meaning of Jesus' life for men and women. As these the gospel writers (Matthew, Mark, Luke, and John), followed Jesus, could it have been that their perception stemmed from their own intolerance predicated on misogyny that was prevalent back in the day?

No Respect of Person

Over the period of 30 years of Bible study, I have often wondered with amazement how (4) writers who were so close to the events and activities of Jesus delivered to us somewhat different interpretations. Though they are similar in nature, there were differences in timing and scenic descriptions. This can be construed as something minor in substance, however, it is to point out the human nature that bears inherent flaws. ***The bottom-line question is; were these men writing under the authority of the spiritual truth of Jesus' attitudes towards women or did they interject their own prejudices.*** Throughout biblical history, we find such behavior. This separatism racism and nepotism was illustrated in Acts 10:1-5 where Peter who was a Jew preached to Cornelius who was a Gentile. A racial partition had kept these factions at odds for centuries. Jesus even encountered this brand of racism in St. John 4:9 as he journeyed through some area and finding a woman at Jacob's well. Due to years of fighting, she could not understand why Jesus who was a Jew would ask her for a drink of water. Traditionally, Jews had no dealings with the Samaritans. There are many other Bible references with which we can find examples of this behavior. Could women have been victims of similar atrocities in the New Testament?

The Culture of That Day

The cultural context in which the first Christians lived and wrote tended to devalue women as church leaders. The question is whether or not this auction was predicated by their own ignorance and fear. In the early church's portrayal of Jesus, this perspective was never conveyed. Jesus never treated women as inferior to men. His words were filled with positive images of women and he defended their equality and full humanity many times in his ministry.

Women Disciples

Women were clearly counted among those who were taught by Jesus and who traveled with him as "disciples". This fact alone suggests his positive attitude toward women. In one instance Jesus appointed and sent forth seventy disciples (St. Luke 10:1). However, it was not mentioned whether they were male and/or female.

Women's Contribution To The Early Church

There were numerous women dedicated who clearly made substantial contributions to the establishment of the early church. Paul refers to women who have been his Co-workers in the evangelization of the Hellenistic world. In Romans, the 16th chapter, he commends Mary, Tryphena, Tryphosa, and Persis for having "labored hard" in the Lord. In the same chapter, he pays tribute to the outstanding missionary work of Priscilla and her husband Aquilla. In Phil. 4:2 Euodias and Syntyche are described as women who have worked or contended side-by-side with Paul. There is no indication in these passages that women were in leadership roles; for Paul referred to them as "Coworkers", "Helpers", etc. One could only speculate something different.

The house churches were crucial to the success of the early mission efforts since they provided support and substance to the growing Christian congregations. They were the places in which the lord's supper was celebrated and the gospel was preached. It is recorded that women provided the facilities for some groups. In Acts

16:14, for example, Lydia was a successful businesswoman who offered her home to the church. Today, the church where I serve as pastor (Kelly Lake Church of God in Christ) began in the living room of Mother Ruby Allen, who presently serves as our church mother. However, this act of conviction and kindness did not catapult her to the position of elder or pastor.

The Recommendation of Paul

In Romans, the 16th chapter, Paul sends recommendations of a friend, Phoebe. He encouraged the Christians at Rome to receive her in the Lord, as becometh saints. He further beseeched them to assist her in whatsoever business she had need of them. Phoebe had been a "Succor" of many and to him. However, he'd never insinuated that she was a Leader of any congregation; although it has been documented that women in the early church did "Oversee" certain groups until an apostle assumed the leadership role.

Summary

I am a product of the traditional and conservative church. Thus, I was taught that women should not teach nor ***usurp*** authority over men, but to be silent. I grew up in a church where women were not allowed to stand in the pulpit unless they were cleaning it. These images contributed greatly to my "right-wing" view on female leadership within the church. However, after having nurtured my imagination by viewing the scripture from another perspective, I am not as candid about the limitations of women in the ministry. Please know that I haven't abandoned my conservative beliefs. However, I am re-examining the church's doctrine with much objectivity.

Frankly, the approach, which I have adopted, recognizes that the Christian tradition is intertwined with the male interpretation of the roles that women should play in the Christian church. In surveying various religious articles, collaborating with other interests and people, and of course steadying the scripture, I have concluded that the following questions should be addressed.

1. Is it possible that men who actually wrote and interpreted the Bible were prejudice against women?

2. Is the Bible the true and infallible word of God as it pertained to women?

I am thoroughly convinced that the church by way of the General Assembly needs to review, Re-evaluate, and Reassess its Doctrinal position. Furthermore, I am delighted that this committee (Doctrine and Review) is serving to propel the Church of God in Christ into this ***Catechism***.

"Women in the Epistles"

Romans 16:1, 2

Phoebe

a. A sister in the faith.

b. Held the function as "deaconess" at the church in Cenchrae.

c. She was a "servant"

    1. "DIAKONAS translated:

    2. Deacon (three times).

    3. Minister (twenty times).

    4. Servant (servant times).

NOTE: "DIAKONAS" refers to one who labors in the dust or on running through the dust. A servant who is an active volunteer laborer on active duty to a person for another.

d. She was a "succourer."

e. A "deaconess" (Servant) is a minister of the New Testament in the Spirit. (2 Cor. 3:6)

NOTE: The word "deacon or deaconess" originally meant "table waiter" in classical Greek, Paul views "deacons or deaconess" as being responsible for the Gospel and ministry of the Word of God. Physical needs here cannot be separated from spiritual needs. (Acts 6,7) Stephen cares for food distribution and preaching.

f. He was a "servant" a "minister" of the Gospel according to the gift of God's grace given unto her by the effectual working of His power. Eph. 3:7

g. She was received and honored in the Lord, treated hospitable, and was helped in her ministry.

h. She was commended for her methodology in service even by Paul.

In Summary

Phoebe is a minister of the church at Cenchreae, her position as "deaconess" is in the masculine, thus no linguistic or theological grounds can be distinguished between male and female as we consider her as "minister" substantiating this text found in Gal. 3:28 "in Christ *there is neither male nor female.*"

In our understanding, Paul assumes in his considerations of this woman by his presentation of her, that there is would be no problems of accepting her as a minister, for she was honored and aided by the Romans. This would thus lead you to believe that Phoebe with not an *isolated phenomenon.*

Phebe's ministry produced recognized fruit, as a clear sign of the call of God as he blessed and increased her ministerial efforts. Her ministry was not confined, she ministered beyond her own congregation. She was known throughout the world, to the Greeks, Romans, and the barbarians, this implies that she propagated the gospel everywhere. It is believed that she was the one who took Paul's letter to the Romans as she ministered even unto him.

Romans 16: 3-5

Priscilla

a.   Was part of a couple singled out as playing a major role in Paul's ministry. 1Corinthians 16:19

b.   She was called a fellow worker co-worker a term of equality, also used by Paul and Apollos in 1 Corinthians 3, 5. In Phil. 4:2, 3 Euodia, Syntyche, Clemente were called "True Yokefellows a term of equality, making Euodia and Syntyche who are women equal with Clement, who of course is a man.

c.   Priscilla along with her husband had a church in their home, risking their lives for Paul and the sake of the gospel.

d.   There is no indication from the text that Priscilla was ever treated as inferior to Aquilla in ministry. She is even named first. The implications are that she shared in task, title, suffering, church building, and recognition.

Romans 16:6

Mary

a.   All say greet Mary she is a hard worker among you, the Romans.

b.   Paul admonishes the church in 1Thessalonians 5:12 to respect those who labor among you. And are over you in the Lord.

c.   Among you in Galatians 4:11 is translated over you in the revised standard version of The Bible, it is implied that Mary is possibly overseeing responsibilities in her ministry of hard work.

Romans 16:7

Junius

It is an unresolved issue as to whether Junius is a masculine contradiction of June I anus or the feminine junior. In the original language, the spelling for either is possible. What must be considered however is that the phrase 'they are men of note'. The word men is not in the original Greek text, but was inserted by the translators. This opened up the idea of consideration as to whether Paul was relating to a woman, or even possibly a husband-wife a team

Consider the text in contacts, genius a king's men, a fellow prisoner, and a Jewish suffer for the faith was in prison with Paul. The implications are that Julius was also an apostle, converted before Paul's conversion, possibly among the first converts after Christ's resurrection.

The Role of Women In The Church

What is the Christian view of the highly controversial view of women in the 12th century? First, the question can only be settled by an appeal to the scripture.

What does the scripture say? There are a number of ways how not to settle this issue. It is not determined by social convention because Christians are called not to conform to this world. We should reject it and not conform to it. We should not decide with emotional prejudices because Christians believe in reason, and we should be suspicious of hidden irrational motives, whether the motives are fair on the one hand by men or desire on the other hand by women.

We should not settle it by ecclesiastical traditions. Especially when this tradition does not claim to be based on scripture but rather on defective biology. Aristotle's view is that girls are imperfect males, accidentally produced by the farthest inadequacy or by the malign influence of a moist sound wind. So, he called women, second-classed souls, incapable of receiving the sacraments of the ordination. Meaning, incapable of being ordained priests in the Catholic Church. So the ecclesiastical traditions of that kind are not to guide us. Nor, are we to be guided by ecumenical relations. This is, not to be guided by what other churches are doing.

If you want to know the present situation, it is that Roman Catholic and Orthodox churches have no women priests in their churches. With regards to Lutherans, Denmark and Norway have them. Finland has none. Sweden now has, but with great controversy. The church of Scotland accepted women in the ministry in 1966, in England since 1917, and Methodists and Baptists more recently.

In the church in England, there are only two women presbyters. They were both ordained a few years ago in Hong-Kong. One is Chinese and the other is from London.

We are not to settle the matter from practical means. For instance, ordaining women because there is a shortage of men for the ministry these days.

20

We are not to settle it by state pressure. It's a grave warning of what has happened in Sweden. To give a brief historical sketch, in 1946, the government's pointed out a committee, who the majority said there was no valid reason against the Ordination of women to the Lutheran priesthood. Five years later in 1951, all the Swedish New Testament professors and lecturers in Swedish universities signed a declaration that in their view-the ordination of women would imply a step away from faithfulness to the truth of the scripture and cannot be reconciled with the conclusions of careful research into the New Testament teachings. In 1957, the church summoned by Parliament, rejected the Royal bill, professing the ordination of women on biblical grounds by 62 to 37. After that, there was a violent public protest and very strong campaigning in the press. The following year, in 1958, the government called another senate Khama whose elected members as a result of enormous propaganda, were all in favor of ordination. The bill was passed 69-29. That was a swinging one year as a result of state pressure. Some pastors resigned, others, opposing the new law were passed over for senior appointments.

Today, no pastor can become Bishop unless he is willing to ordain women. Now that is state pressure. It is not the right reason for coming to this conclusion. The only reason, the only guide must be a theological principle as set forth in scripture.

Now please notice in 1 Timothy 2, beginning at verse 8, purports and contends. In the King James version, I will direct in the Jerusalem Bible, a good example of a call giving direction to the church. Just as in verse 12, he begins, I permit no woman to teach, etc. Here is an authority to prohibition. So quite clearly, Paul believed that he had the authority to issue such directions and prohibitions and expected them to be obeyed.

We're anxious to see what the teaching of the scripture or application of scriptures is today and we're not calling in question the fundamental facts that Paul writes with apostolic authority.

Secondly, in appealing to scripture, we avoid the superficial folly of making scripture contradictory. We assume since scripture is God's word that it possesses

21

an inner consistency and harmony. We should not dismiss the teachings of apostle Paul with the ignorant slander. It is to Paul's pen that the noblest teachings of women, not only in The Bible but the whole of human literature. It is Paul – the same Paul who gives instructions about feminine dress; feminine conduct, who else were teachers sexuality, the creation of God, that marriage is the institution of God, that the prohibition of marriage is the doctrine of demons. 1 Timothy 4:1-3, that relations between husbands and wives reflect the relations between Christ and the church and that in Christ, there is neither male nor female; thus asserting the equality of the sexes centuries before his time.

Thirdly, this is a more difficult question. In the interpretation of the scripture, which we appeal, we must discern between eternal truth, permanently valid, on the one hand, and its contemporary, cultural expression on the other.

ORDINATION OF WOMEN IN MINISTRY

Prepared by

Dr. A. L. Hunt Sr.

Ordination of Women in Ministry

For Commission of the Doctrinal Review

March 17, 1994

Summary

Since there are no scriptures that say that a woman may not be ordained, nor do they say a woman can or cannot pastor, it is my opinion that women are helpers and can help a pastor a church with the assistance of a man. When it comes to usurping authority, they should have a male co-pastor to counsel and discipline the male parishioners in certain areas.

There are many ways in which a woman can beat a man in skills, careers, talents, and even in physical strength. Now as far as ordaining women, The Bible does not address that issue. Based on biblical teachings concerning women, Paul said in Phil. 4: 2, 3, "I beseech thee Euodias and each Syntyche, that they be of the same mind in the Lord. And I entreat thee also, true yokefellow, help those women which labored with me in the gospel." We should also note 1 Corinthians 12:27 – 31; "Now ye are the body of Christ and members in particular. And God hath set some in the church, first apostles, secondarily prophets, thirdly teachers, after that miracles, then gifts of healing, helps, governments, diversities of tongues. Are all apostles? Are all profits? Or all teachers? Are all workers of miracles? Have all the gifts of healing? Do all speak in tongues? Do all interpret? But covet earnestly the best gifts" and yet shew unto you a more excellent way."

Since we are a multi ministry church, based on the scripture, 1 Corinthians 12:27-31, the Megachurch style is to have several pastors in one church with a senior pastor. The senior pastor has oversight over the entire church. Other associate pastors who are given charges and are accountable to the senior pastor may minister in such areas as; Minister of Music, Minister of Education, Minister of Evangelism, Minister of Recreation, Minister of Visitation, Youth Ministry, Follow-up Ministry, and many others.

Ephesians 4:11-13 says, and he gave some, apostles; and some, profits; and some, evangelists; And some, pastors and teachers for the perfecting of the saints, for the work of the ministry, for the edifying of the body of Christ; Til we all come in the unity of the faith, and the knowledge of the Son of God, unto a perfect man, and to the measure of the stature of the fullness of Christ.

I do feel that women can be ordained with restrictions or limitations. The scripture points out the ministries of the church. It does not differentiate between ordaining one particular ministry and not ordaining the other. Where do we draw the line? It does say there are different ministries. I, therefore, accept the fact that we have limitations in our ministries, both male and female.

Paul said I Timothy 2:12, "But I suffer not a woman to teach nor to usurp the authority over the man." Yet, we might note in Acts 18:26 that Priscilla taught Apollos, an eloquent man and mighty in the scriptures. Therefore, I am convinced that this scripture is more cultural than perpetual or eternal in its application. We also note in Matthew 28:5-10 that a woman by the name of Mary Magdalene was sent by Jesus himself to give a message to his chosen and leaders. Again, we have here, a woman teaching and telling men what to do, following the command given here by Jesus Christ. Therefore, we should note that what is perpetual here is the authority that God gave man over the woman. We should take note that a woman can teach a man or give messages to a man as given to them by God, according to the scriptures.

WOMEN IN MINISTRY

From the Pastoral Epistles

Submitted by:

Dr. A.L. Hunt

The Pastoral Epistles

Paul Hastings to add that women are not denied all adornment, but that the greatest I said a woman possesses is a devout and godly life. He makes it clear that he speaks only for Christian women, those professing godliness Khama whose standards must always be higher than those of non-Christians. There is particularly stress here and elsewhere in the pastorals on the necessity for good works, probably because current speculations tended to divorce doctrine and practice. The idea of good works as an adornment is suggestive, for a life of selfless devotion to others may well enhance the appearance. A woman's adornment, in short, lies not in what she herself puts on, but in the loving service she gives out.

That women should learn in silence is in full accord with 1 Corinthians 14:34, 35, although in the latter cases the reference is specifically to public worship. It may be that Paul's present scripture is to be taken with the same proviso, and was designed to curb the tendencies of newly emancipated Christian women to abuse their newfound freedom by in decal correctly lording it over men. Such excesses would bring disrepute on the whole community, as had probably happened at Corinth, and called for firm handling. When taking part in public worship the women's share is to learn, or at least to listen quietly (Moffat). The equality of the sexes, so much at the forefront of modern thought, received little recognition in ancient times. Not only was the prevailing Greek attitude against it, but Hebrew thought was equally unsympathetic. The entire subjection mentioned by Paul related primarily to the public worship as it was then in Acts, the reserve must be exercised in deducting universal principles from particular cases. The idea, however, of women's subjection is not only engrained in the conviction of the mass of mankind which would not in itself be a justification for it but also appears to be inherent in the divine constitution of the human race. Paul mentions this latter aspect in verse 13.

A woman is apparently encouraged to learn yet not allowed to teach. There have been local reasons for this prohibition of which we know nothing. It is noteworthy that no such specific injunction is found in 1 Corinthians, although 1Corinthians 4:34, 35, forbids a woman to be heard in church. If the present prohibition is restricted to public teaching (as seems most probable) it accords perfectly with the 1 Corinthians passage. Paul cannot be accused of being a woman-hater, as is sometimes alleged, on the strength of his evidence, since he acknowledges some women among his fellow laborers, such as Priscilla (Romans 16:3-5) and Euodias and Syntyche (Phil. 4: 2,3). The prohibition may have been due to the greater facility with which contemporary women were falling under the influence of imposters.

Rabbinic prohibitions were much more severe than Christian sense a woman, although fear radical I permitted to read the Torah in public and, was in practice not allowed to teach even small children. The teaching of Christian doctrine, nevertheless, is confined by Paul to the male sex, and this has been the almost invariable practice in the subsequent history of the church.

In public meetings, Christian women must refrain from laying down the law to men and hence are enjoined to silence. It may be that Paul has married women mainly in mind and that man should here be understood as the husband, although this would not be so relevant if church meetings are mainly in view. Indeed, the concluding injunction to silence could not apply to the Christian home and the whole verse must therefore relate to the community.

In 1Corinthians 11:9 Paul had already made use of the argument that the priority of man's creation places him in a position of superiority over women, the assumption being that the original creation, with the creator's own imprimatur upon it, must set a precedent for determining the true order of the sexes. Their relationship, as Simpson points out, was not competitive but can be cordoned and counterpart.

Another reason why women must submit to men is that Adam was not deceived, but the woman. Whereas Eve was deceived or beguiled, Adam sinned with his eyes open. But as Paul says, the serpent deceived the woman, the woman did not deceive the man but persuaded him. Logically this should make Adam more culpable, but Paul is concerned primarily with the inadvisability of women teachers and he may have in mind the greater aptitude of the weaker sex to be led astray in concluding the Word, wherein the transgression, are well rendered in becoming a transgressor, the Greek perfect expressing an abiding state. That Paul did not absolve Adam from responsibility in the transgression is evident from Romans 5:12 where the entry of sin into the world is attributed to Adam, as a representative of man, and Eve is not even mentioned.

From the allusion to Eve, Paul seems to pass to women in general, by making a statement she shall be saved in childbearing which must rank among the most difficult expressions in the whole of the Pastorals.

1. Moffatt translates the words woman will get safely through childbirth, understanding them as conveying to women encouragement in their natural sphere. This is certainly in accordance with the Genesis story which pronounces on Eve the due that in sorrow she shall conceive, adding the assurance of safe delivery if the conditions are observed. It is probable that the duty of child-bearing is emphasized to offset the unnatural abstinence advocated by the false teachers.

2. Chrysostom Text: the verb 'save' in its spiritual sense, but to avoid the manifest absurdity of making the statement said just that; childbearing is a woman's means of salvation as if unmarried or childless women are excluded, he understands the word childbearing as equivalent to child nurturing and supplied the children as the subject of the verb. But this would make women's salvation a matter of good works of a particular kind and it is inconceivable that Paul meant this.

3. Another equally improbable suggestion is that the words should read as in 1Timothy 2:15 she shall be saved by means of the childbearing. For if that were the writer's intention, he would hardly have chosen a more obscure or ambiguous way of saying it. That Paul would have left the words the childbearing without further definition is highly improbable. The Greek

article in general describes the whole process of childbearing, rather than definitive of one particular instance.

4. Scott proposes a fourth possibility, taking the words to mean she will be saved even though she must bear children, that is to say, she shall be linked with man in salvation, in spite of the penalty for her misdemeanor imposed on her. Scott concludes, "the writer, in fact, is making a sort of apology for what he has said about women." This view has the advantage of showing Christian women the way in which the original curse upon their race is mitigated by Christian salvation, but it imposes an unnatural meaning on the Greek preposition dia.

In this verse the verbs change from singular shall be saved to plural if they continue and it can only be assumed that the latter part of the verse refers to Christian women in general. Indeed, it is not too much to claim that the former part of the verse must be interpreted in the light of the latter half. Christian women are exhorted to continue exercising a quartet of Christian virtues - faith, charity (love), holiness adjectives, faithful and loving, and the holy as well as unassuming. Greek preposition often implies that woman's proper sphere, as contrasted with the teacher's office, is in the manifestation of these Christian graces, a sphere in which she has, in fact, shone more eminently than man.

The Role of Women in the Church

By Dr. A. L. Hunt

The highly controversial view of the woman's role in the church in the 20th century can only be settled by an appeal to the scripture.

There are a number of ways how not to settle this issue. It is not determined by social convention because Christians are not to conform to this world. We should not decide by emotional prejudices because Christians believe in reason and should be suspicious of hidden irrational motives - fair on one hand to men, or desire on the other hand by women. We should not settle it by Ecclesiastical traditions that women should not be ordained because considered by Aristotle's view, they are second-class souls, incapable of receiving the sacrament of ordination. We are not to be guided by ecumenical relations that are guided by what other churches are doing.

What does the scripture have to say? Actually, we have no scriptures that say a woman can or cannot be ordained, or pastor. I am of the opinion that women are helpers and can help pastor a church with the assistance of a male co-pastor, which can counsel and discipline the male parishioners when needed which will safeguard the usurping authority over the man as mentioned in I Timothy 2:12. I also feel that this scripture is more cultural than perpetual. If taken literally, a woman could not teach Sunday school, Bible classes, or conduct revivals where men are present. We cannot take one part of this verse and make it perpetual and the other part to be used at our own convenience or wishes.

Scripture supports Paul using women who labored with him in the gospel. Phil. 4:2-3 says, I beseech thee Euodias and beseech Syntyche, that they be of the same mind in the Lord. And I entreat thee also, true yokefellow, help those women which labored with me in the gospel, with Clement also, and with my fellow laborers, whose names are in the Book of Life." You may also note in Acts 18:26 where Priscilla and Aquilla taught Apollos, an eloquent man, mighty in the scriptures. However, the Bible clearly states in Matthew 18:19, 20 "that where two or three

31

are gathered together in my name, there am I in the midst of them." It is not the size of the group, the type of building, but whenever we gather in the name of the Lord, we're the Church. The church is an assembly of the saints.

In interpreting scripture, we must discern between eternal truth, permanently valid on the one hand, and its contemporary, cultural expression on the other. We should note that what is perpetual here is the authority that God gave man over the woman. We should take note that a woman can teach a man or give messages to a man given to them by God, according to the scriptures.

Women in Ministry

As far as I know, no blood has yet been spilled over the role of women in ministry. However, much ink has found its way into print on the subject. What follows is not a repeat of biblical and cultural insight into the continuing debate. Many articles and books are available for these purposes.

In a nation and world moving toward fair and equal opportunities and treatment of minorities in the workplace, the place of women in the church evokes a variety of responses. On the one hand, there are churches where women cannot serve on church boards, teach a mixed-sex class, or be on the paid staff in a "ministry" position. There are other churches where women may work as licensed or ordained ministers and missionaries.

Policies vary widely. In some evangelical churches, women serve but do not officiate at Communion. Others have women deacons and elders and there are some where women serve as evangelists and pastors.

For many years women have enrolled in theological seminaries including the evangelical schools. Their number has grown in recent years.

Beyond their major presence in most local churches, women have made and continue to make noteworthy contributions in teaching, serving on homeland and world mission fields, and in pastoral work often with little recognition or support. They also serve in parachurch and specialized in ministries.

I do not know if or when women will have greater access to the pulpits and boardrooms of the church. Nevertheless, women like men, are part of the people of God and must heed their calling for their own sake and that of the body of Christ.

For now, consider these possibilities:

1. Affirm women in ways that communicate that they are not inferior or second-class Christians. Show and demonstrate that the Lord needs them and that all God's people must carefully discover, and develop their gifts and dedicate themselves to live as word Christians.

2. Many churches would profit from having a woman serve as Director of Women's Ministries on their ministry staff. Training, counseling, organizing, working to develop ministries for and through women of all ages are among the tasks that need to be done in equipping saints for their ministries in and beyond the gathered church.

3. Some churches will benefit from having a woman as an Associate Pastor to work with the youth of all ages in Christian education. Enlisting, training, and coordinating volunteers is a growing concern in churches. I recall a pastor and denominational executive whose strong preference was for a woman rather than a man to serve in the associate role because of the opportunity for a different perspective and complementary ministry giftedness. The Associate Pastor often is a generalist and serves in a variety of ministerial functions.

4. One post needed in many churches is a Director of Senior Citizen Ministries. This could be combined with a visitation or membership care role.

5. The woman in ministry may have a broader parish or community missionary role. Caring for the residents of the community includes evangelism, healing and helping, and requires flexibility and a wide range of skills including community organization.

6. There will be some churches in our culture that will call a woman to pastor their congregation.

Examine again the resources on the role of women in the scriptures and the history of the church. Listen to what others are saying and consider what stance the Lord would have you and your church take.

Probably there will be a combination of tasks assigned to a woman on a church staff. The woman minister should be visible from time to time on the church platform so that her ministry might take on the importance that it truly should have. The times are changing. It is never easy to be ahead or behind change. Sometimes the best man for the job is a woman.

Report on The Findings and Statements on the Question of the Ordination of Women

Clifford V. Anders

Ministries Today Article Women in Ministry

A History of Women's Roles in the Pentecostal and Charismatic Movement

By Vinson Synan

On November 11, 1992, the world was shocked by the news from Britain that had nothing to do with wars, the economy or the troubled affairs of the royal family. The headline news: The Anglican Church had voted to allow women to be ordained as priests of the Church of England. This action, as reported by the Times magazine, amounted to "a second reformation" that was "sweeping Christianity."

Leading the pro women's forces was the Archbishop of Canterbury, George Carey – an acknowledged charismatic – as well as the 500,000 charismatic members of the English church. Only a week after the Anglican bombshell, the American Roman Catholic bishops voted to shelve a pastoral letter that, under pressure from the Vatican, completely rejected the idea that women could ever be ordained to the Catholic priesthood. Times also stated that feminism is emerging as "The most vexing thorn for Christianity."

The role of women in ministry is currently a subject of hot debate in many sectors of the church. While most Protestants have opened the way for woman's ordination, the lines are clearly drawn in Roman Catholic and Orthodox world, as well as among many fundamentalists who still hold vigorously to traditional views that exclude women from leadership in public pastoral ministry.

Adding confusion to the scene has been the rise of militant feminism that, from a non-biblical base, calls for women's equality in all areas of life, including the ministry. The motive and spirit behind this militant stance, rejected by the majority of charismatics, has caused many to question anew the role of women in the church ministry and leadership.

KEEPING SILENCE

For almost 1,800 years, this debate did not exist. Both Eastern and Western churches held to the idea of an all-male priesthood in which women were to "keep silence in the churches" (1Cor. 14:34) and not "usurp the authority over the man"

(1 Tim. 2:12). This tradition was so pervasive that women's voices were not only absent from the public liturgies of the churches, but they also were excluded from the church choirs (young boys sang the soprano and alto parts).

To be sure, in past centuries women who felt called to the religious life could enter convents, become nuns, and spend their lives in prayer and devotion. Yet they receive the sacraments from male priests who alone could model the New Testament ministries of Jesus and the apostles.

Although women could not be priests, many became great saints or even, like St. Theresa of Avilla, a "doctor of the church."

Meanwhile, the development o an increasing devotion to the virgin Mary gave women a sense of importance-not only in the church, but in the plan of salvation and daily intercessory prayer.

The Protestant reformers ultimately rejected the Catholic doctrines regarding Mary, yet, generally speaking, they continued the traditional view of women in ministry. Neither Luther nor Calvin permitted the ordination of women. Indeed, even radicals such as the Anabaptists agreed with the Catholics and Reformers on this point. Traditional Baptists to this day will not ordain women to the ministry.

It was only in the 1700s when evangelical revivals under John Wesley and George Whitefield began to sweep across England and America, that the traditional views of women in ministry were first challenged.

Wesley's attitudes were almost certainly influenced by his mother Susannah, who spent hours each week teaching basic Christian doctrine to her children, and who preached to over 200 persons weekly in prayer meetings that she conducted in her husband's parish. Later, when Wesley's Methodist societies began to flourish, he appointed women as class leaders, explaining that since "God uses women in the conversion of sinners, who am I that I should withstand God?"

With the spread of evangelical revival to America, the role of women in ministry increased. Under revivalist Charles Finney, women were allowed to pray to and to speak in public worship. As president of Oberlin College, Finney admitted women as students-making Oberlin the first co-educational college in America. In fact, it was a former student of Finney, Antoinette Brown, who was the first woman to be ordained in America. This took place in 1853 in the Congregational Church in South Butler, New York.

The actions of Wesley and Finney led later historians to conclude that in most great spiritual awakenings, women are accepted as ministers in the early stages-but often are later bypassed in favor of male leadership when the revival begins to institutionalize.

THE DEBATE

The biblical debate over what the Bible says about a woman's place in ministry has filled volumes. Opposition to women in public ministry is usually based on the apostle Paul's statements in 1 Corinthians 14, "Let your women keep silent in the churches, for they are not permitted to speak" (vv.34-36, NKJV), and I Timothy 2, "I do not permit a woman to teach or to have authority over man." (vv.11-12). Without references to other scriptures, these passages seem to forbid women to prophesy, teach, preach or even say the Lord's prayer or sing hymns aloud in church worship services.

Defenders of women's ministries, on the other hand, begin with a charismatic hermeneutic based on Peter's Pentecost sermon in which he quotes from Joel 2: "And it shall come to pass afterward that I will pour out My Spirit upon all flesh; you sons and daughters shall prophesy... Also on My menservants and maidservants, I will pour out My spirit on those days" (vv. 28-29). An appeal is also made in Galatians chapter 3, where Paul states that in Christ "there is neither Jew nor Greek, there is neither slave nor free, there is neither male nor female; for you are all one in Christ Jesus" (v. 28). All other scriptures are then interpreted in the light of these overarching promises of an all-inclusive ministry in the last days involving both men and women.

A number of Bible passages do, in fact, describe women in important ministries in the early church. Phoebe was a deacon of the church of Cenchrea who

Paul said, "had been a helper of many and of myself also," (Rom. 16:2). The word here in Greek is "deacon" ("minister") – not "deaconess" as it is often translated.

Furthermore, Philip the evangelist had our daughters who prophesied (Acts 2:19). Indeed the list of "apostles" in Romans 16:7 includes Junia, whose famine name indicates that she was in all probability a female apostle.

THE HOLINESS MOVEMENT

One of the first women to point out the scriptural argument for women's ministry in the church was Phoebe Palmer, an important 19th Century Methodist leader in the Holiness movement. In her book, The way of Holiness, which appeared in 52 editions by 1867, Palmer pointed to the foregoing scriptures and concluded that women had as strong a warrant for ministry in Scripture as did men.

Standing with Palmer and Hannah Whitehall Smith, author of The Christian's Secret of a Happy Life (187), who played a prominent role in the British Keswick "Higher Life" movement. Because of Palmer and Smith's fervor, both the Holiness and Keswick movements took pioneering positions favoring women's ministries.

Other Holiness movements and churches, agreeing with this new theology, began to license and ordain women in ministry. One of the firsts was the Wesleyan Methodist Church, which ordained its first woman in 1863. When former Methodist William Booth organized the Salvation Army, he immediately recognized women as ministers equal to men. In the Salvation Army, both husbands and wives were "commissioned" (ordained) as ministry teams. When the Church of the Nazarene and other Holiness churches were organized after 1895, almost all of them made provision for women to be ordained and serve as evangelists and pastors.

Another pioneer was A.J. Gordon, the Baptist pastor who worked closely with D.L. Moody and other "Higher Life" leaders near the end of the century. In his book, The Ministry of Women (1888), Gordon closed with Psalm 68:1: The Lord gives the command; the women who proclaim the good tidings are a great host" (NASB).

THE PENTECOSTAL MOVEMENT

When the Pentecostal movement developed after 1901, it continued and radically enhanced the place of women in ministry. Although primarily preoccupied with the gifts of the Spirit, Pentecostalism also strongly emphasized the imminent rapture of the church. Because time was short, everyone was needed to save as many as possible before the second coming. Female ministers flocked to the standards of new ministry-minded denominations such as the Church of God, the Pentecostal Holiness Church and the Assembly of God. In these churches, women were given unprecedented opportunities to evangelize, teach, pastor, and serve as missionaries.

The long list of female ministers in the Pentecostal movement includes Agnes, whose glosssolalic experience in Topeka, Kansas on January 01, 190,1 led Charles Parham to formulate the Pentecostal doctrine of tongues as the "initial evidence" of baptism in the Holy Spirit.

When the Azusa street revival broke out in Los Angeles in 1906, pastor William Seymour was aided by several female ministers including Lucy Farrow, Jenny Moore (his future wife) Claire Lum and Florence Crawford. When Crawford left Los Angeles in 1909, she founded one of the earliest Pentecostal denominations in America – Apostolic Faith – with headquarters in Portland, Oregon.

Other women who have spread the Pentecostal fire after Azuza Street include Rachel Sizelove in Missouri, Mary Burgess in New York City, Ethel Goss in Texas, and Ellen Hebden in Toronto, Canada. Added to this list was holiness leader Maria Woodworth-Etter, who became a Pentecostal soon after Azuza Street and held some of the largest evangelistic crusades in America until her death in 1924. One Pentecostal evangelist Katie Campbell of Virginia, justified her ministry by noting, "A woman brought sin into the world; they ought to help take it out again."

Not long after the death of Woodworth-Etter, the most famous and important female minister of the century came on the scene: Aimee Semple McPherson. Born in Canada to Salvation Army parents, Aimee soon became a Pentecostal and, following a stint as a missionary in Hong Kong, founded the International Church of the Foursquare Gospel in 1923. After building a massive Angelus Temple in Los Angeles, "Sister" Aimee became a celebrity of the first magnitude, at times dominating the headlines of the nation's newspapers. After her death in 1944, the Foursquare Church continued as one of the leading Pentecostal denominations in America and around the world.

The next major female preacher in America was Kathryn Kuhlman, who began her ministry in Missouri in 1923. After preaching across the nation with moderate success, she settled in Pittsburgh, Pennsylvania, in 1947, where she experienced a remarkable national healing and evangelistic ministry until her death in 1976. After the rise of the charismatic movement in the mainline churches after 1960, Kuhlman enjoyed a massive following among both Catholic and Protestant neo-Pentecostals. Kuhlman often said she was given her healing ministry because somewhere some man had refused to obey the call of the Lord.

Not all Pentecostals have equally embraced all women's ministries, however. From its beginnings in 1897, the Church of God in Christ, for example, has allowed women to evangelize but not to be ordained and serve as pastors of local churches. As a result, female ministers such as Earnestine Reems of Oakland, California, have had to leave the denomination in order to pastor. Interestingly, the COGIC's longstanding policy was recently challenged by Bishop O.T. Jones of Philadelphia, who shocked the church in 1991 when he ordained 15 women and began to assign them as pastors in his diocese.

THE CHARISMATIC MOVEMENT

Unlike the Holiness and Pentecostal movements before it, the advent of the charismatic movement did not usher in significant breakthroughs for women in ministry. The new charismatics – participants in already established churches – were more intent on bringing renewal to their ranks than on championing "side issues" such as women's ministries.

Furthermore, the infiltration and rise of the radical feminist movement in mainline churches caused a conservative backlash among many charismatics. The

1970 publication of The Christian Family by Larry Christenson, a key leader in the Lutheran renewal, promoted a traditionalist view of women in ministry.

Other independent charismatics influenced by the shepherding/discipleship movement, as well, took a hard-line stance against women in public ministry.

Nevertheless, a number of women rose to ministry prominence in the 1980s. These have included Agnes Sanford, Aimee Cortese, Anne Giminez, Marilyn Hickey, Iverna Tompkins, Freda Lindsay, Ruth Carter Stapleton, Roxanne Brant, Rita Bennett, and Frances Hunter. Many of these women were – and continue to be – major speakers at large charismatic rallies. Some, such as Giminez and Hickey, have been featured on national TV programs.

CATHOLIC CHARISMATICS

The Catholic charismatic movement developed after 1967, during a time of conservative reaction to many of the liberalizing trends that were dividing the church – including the demand of radical feminists for the ordination of women to the priesthood. In general, Catholic charismatics stood apart from such militant efforts and supported the traditional view. Influential charismatic communities such as the Word of God in Ann Arbor, Michigan, and the People of Praise in South Bend, Indiana, also took a traditional stand on a woman's place in the home and in ministry.

At the same time, virtually all Catholic charismatics recognized the important role played by Elena Guerra, the Italian nun whose letter to Pope Leo XIII led to a major encyclical on the Holy Spirit in 1897.

Furthermore, many outstanding Catholic women took leadership roles in the renewal – women such as Jane Gallagher Mansfield, Dorothy Ranaghan, Josephine Massyngberde Ford, Judy Tydings, Edith Difato, and Nancy Kellar.

THE THIRD WAVE APPROACH

Since about 1980, a charismatic movement called the "third wave" (evangelicals who manifested spiritual gifts but who disdain labels "Pentecostal" or "charismatic") has given birth to hundreds of o congregations in America. A leading example of this movement is the Association of Vineyard Churches founded by John Wimber. The Vineyard's position on women in ministry may be typical of most third-wave churches.

According to Jerry Ward, pastor of Oklahoma City Vineyard, the issue has by no means been settle within the Vineyard movement. Although some women have been ordained in the southeast region, the practice "has not been generally accepted," Ward says. As of 1992, women are not allowed to exercise pastoral oversight in Vineyard churches, though "women's giftedness in ministry is fully utilized." Women are most often used in husband and wife teams that minister in small cell groups.

WHERE ARE WE NOW?

In 1990, the Assemblies of God adopted a position paper reconfirming the church's historic stand in support of a significant role for women in ministry. Yet some recent observers such as Edith Bumhofer, an Assemblies of God historian, believe that the prominence of female ministers as experienced in the flush of early Pentecostalism seems to be fading into history.

Paradoxically, while the number of licensed and ordained women in major Pentecostal denominations has increased, the percentage of female pastors has diminished over the years. As of 1991, the Assemblies of God counted 4,604 women with ministerial credentials, the most of any denomination in the United States. This amounts to 15 percent of all ministers in the American A/G church. Of these, some 322 are listed as "senior pastors."

The percentage of women ordained in the International Church of the Foursquare Gospel has held steady a about 40 percent for several decades (37 percent in 1992). The percentages of ordained and license women ministers in the Pentecostal Holiness Church (17 percent) and the Church of God (Cleveland, Tenn.; 15 percent) still exceed those of any of the mainline Protestant denominations. But recent surveys indicate that fewer women are serving as pastors in these churches than ever before.

So what does the future hold for women who feel called to minister in the church? Plenty, if current trends are any indication. According to the Association of Theological Schools, 18,103 women were enrolled in American theological seminaries in 1991, accounting for 30.1 percent of all theology students. These women constitute the largest unused pool o ministerial potential in the nation.

But will they be used? Pentecostals and charismatics crossed that bridge almost a century ago by opening the door for anointed women to minister in the power of the Holy Spirit. In the future, much will depend on discerning leaders who are able to separate the voice of valid and balanced biblical teaching on women's ministries from the shrill cry of the militant feminist whose agenda is usually anything but spiritual.

Vison Synan is a professor of history at Oral Roberts University and director of the Holy Spirit Research Center on the ORU campus. He also serves as chairman of the North American Services Committee. – Ministries Today Article Volume January/February 1993.

HISTORY OF WOMEN IN THE PENTECOSTAL MOVEMENT

1996 PCCNA National Conference
Memphis, Tennessee, October 1, 1996

History of Women in the Pentecostal Movement
Cheryl J. Sanders, Howard University School of Divinity

On the whole, the Holiness-Pentecostal movement in the United States has made a distinctive contribution to the historical evolution of religion in America by involving blacks, women, and the poor at all levels of ministry. There are well over 100 church bodies listed in the Directory of African American Religious Bodies which can be identified as Holiness or Pentecostal. These churches were led by black Christians around the turn of the century who "came out" of the black Baptist and Methodist churches, seeking "the deeper life of entire sanctification" and Spirit baptism; "Their initial concern was not so much to start a new denomination as to call the existing ones back to the wells of their spirituality."[1] What the Holiness and Pentecostal churches have in common is an emphasis upon the experience of Spirit baptism. Although some of these churches have adopted the sexist and racist norms of white mainline Protestantism, others have produced compelling models of cooperation between male and female leaders.

Church historian Susie Stanley uses the term "stained-glass ceiling" to describe barriers to women's leadership and advancement in Christian denominations with a long history of ordaining them. At the beginning of the present century, the ordination of women was accepted virtually throughout the Holiness movement. And when Pentecostalism emerged shortly thereafter, "it carried through this theme and was perhaps even more consistent in the practice of the ministry and ordination of women."[2] Compared to mainline denominations which began ordaining women only in recent years, the Holiness movement has a "usable past."[3] Women in five Wesleyan-Holiness denominations – Church of God (Anderson, Indiana), Church of the Nazarene, Free Methodist Church, Salvation

Army, and the Wesleyan Church – currently constitute twenty-five percent of the clergy in their denominations, whereas women comprise seven percent of the clergy in thirty-nine other denominations that now ordain women.[4]

In 1978 Pearl Williams-Jones surveyed five major Pentecostal bodies and categorized them with respect to their treatment of women's ministry and leadership.[5] The first category, consisting of churches who insist upon the subordination of women in ministry roles, actually comprises the overwhelming majority of black Pentecostals: the Church of God in Christ, the Church of Our Lord Jesus Christ of the Apostolic Faith, and the Bible Way Church of Our Lord Jesus Christ, World Wide. The second category, churches that grant women positions of authority equal to men, includes the Pentecostal Assemblies of the World and the Mount Sinai Holy Church of America (which was founded by a woman, Bishop Ida Robinson).

In general, over the course of the twentieth century, there has been a dramatic and substantial decline in women's ecclesial leadership in the Holiness and Pentecostal churches. Stanley cites statistics showing that the proportion of women clergy in the Church of the Nazarene fell precipitously from twenty percent in 1908 to one percent more recently, and, in the Church of God (Anderson, Indiana), from thirty-two percent in 1925 to fifteen percent. As early as 1939, a Church of God publication set forth a radical theological and ethical commentary upon the decline of women preachers:

> The prevalence of women preachers is a fair measure of the spirituality of a church, a country, or an age. As the church grows more apostolic and more deeply spiritual, women preachers and workers abound in that church; as it grows more worldly and cold, the ministry of women is despised and gradually ceases altogether. It is of the nature of paganism to hate foreign people and to despise women, but the spirit of the gospel is exactly the opposite.[6]

In this view, the rejection of women's ministerial leadership represents a worldly loss of focus upon the egalitarian spirit of the Christian gospel. Not surprisingly, the reestablishment of barriers to church leadership by most of the

Holiness-Pentecostal groups on the basis of sex in the early decades of this century coincides with their increased complicity with prevailing mainstream practices of racial separation and segregation.

The story of the 1906 Azusa Street Revival, which marks the beginning of Pentecostalism as an international movement, offers a model of cooperative ministry and empowerment among the sexes, where authority and recognition are granted to either sex based upon the exercise of spiritual gifts. The early Pentecostal movement was led by William J. Seymour, a man whose own life's story reflects practically all major facets of the denominational racism experienced by black Christians in the United States.[7] Born in Louisiana in 1878, Seymour was raised as a Baptist, as a young man joined a local black congregation of the Methodist Episcopal Church in Indianapolis, Indiana, and next was drawn to the Evening Light Saints, a name widely used at the time for the Church of God (Anderson, Indiana).

After joining the Holiness movement, Seymour came under the influence of a black woman pastor in Houston, Texas, Lucy Farrow. He attended her church in 1903. Significantly, she was the first to expose Seymour to the practice of speaking in tongues:

> He heard a woman pray aloud in a language, or what seemed to be a language, that no one there could understand. Seymour was touched to the core. As a man of prayer himself, he could sense that this woman had somehow attained a depth of spiritual intensity he had long sought, but never found. These experiences changed Seymour's life. After the meeting, he asked Lucy Farrow, the woman who had spoken in the strange tongues, more about her remarkable gift.[8]

Farrow introduced Seymour to the white Pentecostal pioneer, Charles Fox Parham, who ran a Bible School in Topeka for missionaries where she had worked as a "governess." When Seymour enrolled in Parham's classes in-3-Houston, he was subjected to the indignity of having to sit in a hall where he could hear the classes through the doorway, in keeping with Southern "etiquette." Seymour accepted Parham's advocacy of speaking in tongues, but rejected his racist prejudices and polemics.

Seymour's work with women ministers continued. He was invited by Neely Terry, a Holiness woman from Los Angeles, to pastor a Holiness congregation in California which had been founded by Julia W. Hutchins. Seymour traveled to Los Angeles bearing the message that speaking in tongues was the necessary evidence of the Pentecostal experience, but Hutchins rejected his preaching and locked him out. He found refuge in the home of Richard and Ruth Asberry on Bonnie Brae Street, where he conducted several weeks of prayer meetings. When on April 9, 1906, Seymour finally manifested the tongue-speaking experience he had promoted in his preaching, a revival broke out and crowds began to gather at the Bonnie Brae Street residence and in the streets. He leased a vacant building at 312 Azusa Street in Los Angeles from the Stevens African Methodist Episcopal Church (where several persons worshipping with him had formerly been members), a two-story wooden structure located in a poor black neighborhood in Los Angeles, near some stables and lumberyard. Within a few days more than a thousand persons were trying to enter the small mission building, and the Azusa Street Revival was underway. The core group consisted primarily of black female domestic workers, but over three years, from 1906 to 1908, the Revival drew persons of every race, nationality, and culture. In Seymour's own words, "the work began among the colored people. God baptized several sanctified women with the Holy Ghost, who had been much used of Him."[9]

On the surface, this account of the Azusa Street Revival presents an all too familiar image of a black man leading a congregation of black women that seems less than empowering from the vantage point of gender. The Revival resulted from the partnership of women and men unified by their desire to experience the spiritual empowerment of speaking in tongues. Seymour was largely mentored, guided, and offered a context for ministry by women. Women were involved in every aspect of his spiritual development: moreover, women were willing to follow his tongues doctrine and experience its full effects as a public witness. In this light, the locus of empowerment was not the cooperation of men and women with each other as an end in itself. Rather, the people were spiritually empowered by their ability to respond to charismatic leadership, a process facilitated by the willingness of one man to welcome the participation and preaching of women. And when the desired spiritual manifestations came forth among this humble gathering, the experience of corporate charismatic empowerment drew attention from all parts of the world.

Seymour eventually encountered some negative experiences with white women in the Revival who did not share his perspective on racial unity. When Parham visited Azusa Street at Seymour's invitation in October of 1906, he denounced the Revival as a "darky camp meeting."[10] The two white women who helped him to publish the periodical, Apostolic Faith, with an international circulation of 50,000 subscribers, effectively destroyed Seymour's publication outreach ministry by taking both the periodical and mailing list to Portland, Oregon, where one of them founded another evangelistic organization. In his book "Fire From Heaven", Harvey Cox notes how Seymour's disillusionment with white Pentecostals affected his understanding of the gift of tongues:

> Finding that some people could speak in tongues and continue to abhor their black fellow Christians convinced him that it was not speaking in tongues but the dissolution of racial barriers that was the surest sign of the Spirit's Pentecostal presence and the approaching New Jerusalem.[11]

Seymour saw the breaking of the color line as a much surer sign than tongue speaking of God's blessing and the Spirit's healing presence, signifying that the charismatic ideal of cooperation with the Spirit had become compromised in practice by the forces of racism. Once the whites defected, the Azusa Street Mission became almost entirely black.[12] The denominations which took the lead thereafter to spread the Pentecostal doctrine and practices, e.g., the Church of God in Christ and the Assemblies of God, were organized along racial lines and generally assigned subordinate roles to women.

White racism ultimately undermined and destroyed the vision of racial equality promoted by the early Pentecostals. Interracial cooperation could not be sustained within the charismatic leadership structures where cooperation between the sexes had been so conspicuous (at least temporarily). As a result, Seymour revised the doctrines, discipline, and constitution of his Apostolic Faith Movement to recognize himself as "bishop" and guarantee that his successor would always be "a man of color."[13] However, after Seymour died in 1922, it was a woman of color who assumed the leadership of the Mission – his widow, Jennie Seymour. As is often the case after the death of charismatic leaders, the mission located at Azusa Street did not last very long thereafter. The building was demolished in 1931, and the land was lost in foreclosure in 1938, two years after Jennie Seymour's death.[14]

That a man led this movement is perhaps unremarkable; that he was so heavily influenced by women's spiritual leadership is hardly unprecedented. What is highly unusual here, however, is the immediate interracial and international impact produced by this tiny core group of black women and men. Together they exercised charismatic gifts in a manner that would alter the course of church history throughout the twentieth century. Today Pentecostalism has become the dominant expression of Christian worship in many major urban centers, claiming some 410 million adherents worldwide.[15]

The largest denomination of the Holiness-Pentecostal tradition, the Church of God in Christ (COGIC), does not permit the ordination of women but has the most powerful Women's Department of any black denomination.[16] Despite this restriction, women have exercised ministerial leadership in numerous ways, serving as evangelists, worship leaders, and religious activists, and sometimes having charge of churches in the absence of a male pastor. The distinctive leadership orientation of the COGIC women led to levels of female empowerment and male-female cooperation and that would prove vital to the success of the denomination throughout the twentieth century, in contrast to the Azusa Street Mission which failed after the death of Seymour. Cheryl Townsend Gilkes has offered this general observation regarding the importance of the establishment of structures of female "influence" as a determining factor in the survival of black religious movements:

Although many denominations were formed between 1895 and 1950, those that survived and flourished were those with strong Women's

Departments. Structures of female influence enabled denominations with charismatic male founders to grow after those founders died; other denominational movements with high visibility but no structures of female influence almost disappeared.[17]

The Women's Department of the COGIC was formed shortly after the beginning of the Azusa Street Revival. Bishop Charles H. Mason, a former Baptist minister who with C.P. Jones founded the COGIC as a Holiness denomination, participated in the Revival and received the gift of speaking in tongues. As a result, a split occurred with Jones and the COGIC became Pentecostal under Mason's leadership in 1907. Around the same time, Mason recruited Lizzie Woods Roberson from a Baptist academy to organize the Women's Department as its "overseer." What is unusual about this development is that Mason was divorced, and thus did not have a wife to appoint to this position, as normally occurred in other black denominations where the women's organizations are led by the wives of ecclesial leaders:

> This historical "accident" generated the model of a nearly autonomous women's organization. Mason not only recruited Mother Robinson to head the women's work but also on her advice appointed women's overseers along the same jurisdictional and district lines as the male overseers who later became bishops. The title "overseer," a literal translation of the Greek word usually translated as "bishop," was used in the early days of the church for both men and women leaders in the church. Such usage implied that the founders of the COGIC and other denominations initially envisioned a church organized in parallel structures of both male and female overseers.[18]

The adoption of the terminology associated with episcopally governed churches reflected both the Baptist roots of their leadership and a Presbyterian tendency toward "more or less sharing power between the laity and the clergy."[19] Gilkes has determined that these black church women transformed their autonomy into a form of power best described as "influence," and "created a pluralist political structure in an episcopally governed church where pluralism was never intended."[20] This autonomous, parallel structure more closely resembled the dual sex political systems characteristic of some West African societies than the patriarchal episcopal polities or European origin. The women employed distinctive leadership styles and methods that promoted broader-based participation:

> The women's methods of leadership have evolved in direct contrast to the authoritarian style demanded by the nature of episcopal polity: hierarchical, individualistic, and dominating. In comparison, women's leadership tends to be consensus-oriented, collective, and more inclusive, involving larger numbers of people in decision-making.[21]

The emergence of the COGIC Women's Department was timely in view of the plight of black women in church and society during the first decade of the twentieth century. First, the spiritual and professional focus of this organization of black women produced significant affirmations of black female personhood:

> In the face of cultural assaults that used the economic and sexual exploitation of black women as a rationale for their denigration, the Sanctified Church elevated black women to the status of visible heroines-spiritual and professional role models for their churches.[22]

A second factor is a professionalization of Christian education (in contrast to the concurrent marginalization of Christian education by Baptist and Methodist denominations), which enabled women to use their roles as educators and the "educated" as a source of power and career opportunity. Thirdly, the Women's Department presented "professional" role models for black working women, at a time when employment opportunities for black women were primarily restricted to domestic service at low wages; thus, "Higher education and work were identified as legitimate means of upward mobility for black women, and they were encouraged to achieve economic empowerment through white-collar employment."[23] An important consequence of this emphasis upon higher education and professional employment was the financial empowerment of women, whose numerical dominance in the churches, in turn, created a situation that clearly contradicted the ethic of male domination and control.[24]

As a general rule, these churches rejected cultural norms and organizational models that imitated white patriarchy. For both the Holiness and the Pentecostal churches, holiness was the premier ethic and guide for liturgy, preaching, and polity:

> Church members could not advance ideologies of patriarchy that contradicted standards of holiness since "holiness" was the most important achieved status in these churches - and status not humanly granted. Biblical debate concerning women was confined to structural norms, not the nature, quality, or character of women per se.[25]

The positive affirmation of women's nature, quality, and character sets these churches apart from other Protestant and Catholic traditions whose exclusion of women from leadership is grounded in the rejection of the full humanity of women. As a result, even where structural prohibitions have been in effect, women nevertheless found ways to exercise their gifts of ministry and leadership to the benefit of the entire church body. For example, women evangelists and revivalists founded churches, so they were included in church histories. In addition, male church leaders often reported in their spiritual biographies that they became converted in response to the ministry of female preachers and revivalists. Thus, it was not gender but spiritual gifts that qualified individuals to be acknowledged and honored in Holiness and Pentecostal circles; "the person and congregational accounts passed down in written records and oral tradition placed a high value on the contribution of women and men to the most important goal of the church-salvation and holiness."[26]

Following Gilkes's analysis, the model of leadership developed by the COGIC Women's Department is a dialectical one, based on a tradition of protest and cooperation.[27] On the one hand, this dialectics is driven by the women's struggle against structures and patterns of subordination based on sex, and on the other, by their determination to maintain unity with black men in the face of racism and discrimination in the larger society, and in response to internal power struggles among male leaders within the denomination. Because cooperative and egalitarian norms govern this dialectical model, the structural exclusion of women from certain positions in the church is partially offset by the maintenance of various spaces and spheres for women to exercise their spiritual gifts and leadership.

Although the prevailing norms of racial and sexual exclusion eventually were brought to bear upon various Pentecostal denominational structures, these churches nevertheless provided important opportunities and role models for women's spiritual and social empowerment. The shifting patterns of inclusion and exclusion in these churches have been governed by two primary factors, namely, the egalitarian doctrine of the Holy Spirit on the one hand, and the impact of racist, sexist, and elitist societal norms on the other. Pentecostal leaders of today, both male and female, can recover and reclaim the inclusive impetus of the early twentieth century, as the Spirit guides the church into the twenty-first century.

Endnotes

1. William C. Turner, Jr., "Movements in the Spirit: A Review of African American Holiness/Pentecostal/Apostolics," in Wardell Payne, ed., Directory of African American Religious Bodies (Washington, D.C.: Howard University Press, 1991), 248.

2. Donald W. Dayton, "Yet Another Layer of the Onion, Or Opening the Ecumenical Door to Let the Riffraff In", The Ecumenical Review, Vol. 40, No. 1 (January 1988), 106.

3. Susie Cunningham Stanley, quoted by Timothy C. Morgan, "The Stained-Glass Ceiling," Christianity Today (May 16, 1994), 52.

4. Stanley, Feminist Pillar of Fire: The Life of Alma White (Cleveland: Pilgrim Press, 1993), 2.

5. Pearl Williams-Jones, "A Minority Report: Black Pentecostal Women," Spirit, vol. I, No. 2, (1977): 31-44.

6. Charles E. Brown, "Women Preachers," The Gospel Trumpet (May 27, 1939), 5.

7. This account of Seymour's role in the Azusa Street Revival is adapted from several sources. See Joseph Colletti, "Selected Historical Pentecostal Sites in the Los Angeles Area," (Pasadena, California: David J. du Plessis Center for Christian Spirituality); Leonard Lovett, "Aspects of the Spiritual Legacy of the Church of God in Christ: Ecumenical Implications" in David T. Shannon and Gayraud S. Wilmore, eds. Black

Witness to the Apostolic Faith (Grand Rapids: Wm. B. Eerdmans, 1985, 1988); Cecil M. Robeck, Jr., "Azusa Street Revival" and "Bonnie Brae Street Cottage," and H. Vinson Synan, "William Joseph Seymour," in Stanley M. Burgess and Gary B. McGee, eds., Dictionary of Pentecostal and Charismatic Movements (Grand Rapids: Zondervan, 1988); and James S. Tinney, "William J. Seymour: Father of Modern-Day Pentecostalism," in Randall K. Burkett and Richard Newman, eds., Black Apostles (Boston: G.K. Hall, 1978).

8. Harvey Cox, Fire From Heaven (Reading, Mass.: Addison-Wesley, 1995), 49.

9. William J. Seymour, quoted in Ian MacRobert, The Black Roots and White Racism of Early Pentecostalism in the USA (London: Macmillan Press, 1988), 48.

10. Turner, 251.

11. Cox, 63.

12. Cox, 64.

13. Synan, 781.

14. Robeck, 35.

15. Cox, xv.

16. Cheryl Townsend Gilkes, "'Together and in Harness': Women's Traditions in the Sanctified Church," in Micheline R. Malson, Elisabeth Mudimbe-Boyi, Jean F. O'Barr, and Mary Wyer, eds. Black Women in America: Social Science Perspectives (Chicago: University of Chicago Press, 1990), 229. This article was originally published in Signs, vol. 10, no. 4, Summer 1985.

17. Gilkes, 237.

18. Gilkes, 237.

19. Gilkes, 229.

20. Gilkes, 240.

21. Gilkes, 240.

22. Gilkes, 225.

23. Gilkes, 225.

24. Gilkes, 235.

25. Gilkes, 231.

26. Gilkes, 231.

27. Gilkes, 242.

Pentecostal Women in Ministry:
Where Do We Go from Here?

Presented by Sheri R. Benvenuti

Pentecostal women who are called to ministry walk a fine and often precarious line. We, on the one hand, are not radical feminists who demand certain fights, suspicion patriarchal hierarchy as the greatest of all human evils or refer to God as "she" at every turn. However, on the other hand, we are not simply passive about our call to ministry. We do notice the "man's world" in which we must function, and we understand that the "female," too, helps make up what we know about the image of God. We are not women who wish to displace men, nor do we view women who are not called to ministry as being in any way inferior. We are women who simply and humbly ask that we be given room to be obedient to the Lord who has called us. We are certainly not the first generation of Pentecostal women who have pursued such an opportunity.

When one reads about some of the great women in our history such as Aimee Semple McPherson, Alice Belle Garrigus, Maria Woodworth-Etter, Marie Burgess, Kathryn Kuhlman, and Mae Eleanore Frey, it is encouraging to know that these extremely gifted women ministered with great success at a time in history that did not make life easy for them. Their call to preach seemed to supersede everything else in their lives, motivating them to pay a difficult price to fulfill God's will. Their faithfulness is of great encouragement to every Pentecostal woman in ministry today.

However, there is some disappointment at the present state of women in ministry in our Pentecostal fellowships. While there are indications that a few of our denominations are experiencing a small increase in the total amount of women who serve in those fellowships[1], the figures reveal that there will be a slow upward climb ahead for women who are called to serve.

I must confess that I have a vested interest in the issue of women in ministry, not only from an academic perspective but also from a personal point of view. I have been a Pentecostal minister for the last twenty-five years. During this time the discussion of Pentecostal women in ministry has come to the point where much work has been done both biblically and historically to redefine the opportunity for women in ministry positions. However, my experience still causes me to resonate with the great Assemblies of God evangelist, Mae Eleanore Frey who once said, "... for God-fearing, intelligent, Spirit-filled women, upon whom God has set his seal in their ministry, to have to sit and listen to men haggle over the matter of their place in the ministry is humiliating, to say the least."[2] In addition to this difficult personal situation for women, there is also the greater reality of a world desperately needing every anointed person to preach the gospel, while the Church busies itself with an unending doctrinal debate over who is qualified to minister in what position. We are, in a sense, watching the house burn down while arguing about which fire truck to use. The time has come for Pentecostal women in ministry to leave the arena of debate and simply be who they are and do what God has called them to do.

In view of the need for practical solutions which will work to encourage women in this endeavor, the historical context from which we function is vitally important for Pentecostal women in ministry simply because it not only sets precedent for what we do but also because history has a way of teaching some invaluable practical lessons. With this in view, there are at least three important needs that can be identified to justify a place for Pentecostal women in ministry.

The Need for Pentecostals to Return to Their Roots

The moment this statement is made, one must assume that Pentecostals have indeed strayed from their initial identity. The fact that the participation of women in ministry is even an issue within the context of Pentecostalism suggests this to be true. There are at least two things that have contributed to this change from the early days of Pentecostalism. First, as Pentecostal denominations began to formalize their structure, women who were active in every type of ministry position were simply left out of denominational leadership roles. Up to this point, in fact, there is little to suggest that women doing the work of the ministry, holding positions as pastors, teachers, and evangelists, were even questioned in the validity of their function. Men and women of that day seemed to be grounded in the understanding that because God chose women to participate in the New Testament Holy Spirit baptism experience, it was only logical that they, too, should carry the message of the gospel. In the words of Mae Eleanore Frey, "God Almighty is no fool--I say it with all reverence--Would He fill a woman with the Holy Ghost--endow her with ability--give her a vision of souls and then tell her to shut her mouth?"[3]

In their insightful article concerning this idea, Charles H. Barfoot and Gerald T. Sheppard hold that in those early days, three factors were responsible for the equality of the sexes in Pentecostal ministry:

1. The importance of "a calling."

2. The confirmation of the call through the recognition of the presence of ministry gifting in the person by the community.

3. The community's eschatological belief that they were experiencing the "latter rain" in which "your sons and your daughters will prophesy."[4]

Barfoot and Sheppard suggest, however, that "as routinization and regimentation of community relationships set in, reactions did occur against the [Pentecostal] movement's prophesying daughters."[5] One vital reaction to which Barfoot and Sheppard refer involves the whole question of authority. That is, should women in ministry have positions of authority over men? As Pentecostal fellowships moved from the pioneer phase of their development into the formalization of church structure, a shift began to take place in the minds of the early framers of these groups. Where once women were free to function in any ministry gift, now some were unable to fulfill their call by being relegated to newly defined "feminine" roles, while others paid a great price to remain true to their call. That the idea of authority should be at the center of the discussion not only determined the path that early Pentecostalism was to take, but was a direct reversal of the position taken by the early pioneers of the movement.

In early Pentecostalism, authority was never the issue; rather, servanthood was always the focal point of one's ministry calling. Even the manner in which the church services were conducted suggested that early Pentecostals fully believed that the Holy Spirit himself held absolute authority, and the Spirit anointed whomever he chose to serve the body of believers. Frank Bartleman describes those early days:

> Brother Seymour was recognized as the nominal leader in charge. But we had no pope or hierarchy ... The Lord Himself was leading ... We did not honor men for their advantage, in means or education, but rather for their God-given 'gifts...' The Lord was liable to burst through anyone. We prayed for this continually. Someone would finally get up anointed for the message. All seemed to recognize this and gave way. It might be a child, a woman, or a man.[6]

While deconstruction of structural organization is not what is called for, what is necessary is a return to the biblical, and early Pentecostal, understanding that all authority is defined by the degree to which one serves. That is to say, for the Pentecostal, authority is not derived through position alone, as some may assert, but rather is found in the individual who serves the body of Christ through the power of the Holy Spirit. With this understanding, the gender of the individual in question becomes irrelevant, for no one ever debates which gender is qualified to serve.

The second contributing factor is what Cecil Robeck calls "the 'evangelicalization' of Pentecostals."[7] While Pentecostals have achieved a sense of acceptance and respectability through their relationship with the National Association of Evangelicals, "as evangelical values have been adopted by Pentecostals, the role of women in ministry has suffered."[8] Pentecostal denominations have traditionally allowed women much greater freedom in ministerial roles than their evangelical counterparts. A return to our Pentecostal roots, in this case, would mean a return to the theology and experience that make us who we are: a diverse, yet unified group of individuals who are each empowered by the Holy Spirit to function in ministry gifts.

Each of the women who were involved in ministry in the early days were women who were incredibly and undeniably gifted. These were women who reaped a great harvest. Many people were converted, many were healed, denominational boundaries were broken, and men, women, and children received the outpouring of their own personal Pentecost. Edith Blumhofer asserts that:

> In the early Pentecostal movement, having the "anointing" was far more important than one's sex. As evangelistic bands carried the full gospel across the country, women who were recognized as having the anointing of the Holy Spirit shared with men in the preaching ministry ... A person's call--and how other believers viewed it--was far more important than [ministerial credentials].[9]

For a Pentecostal, one's call to ministry is confirmed by the gifting. While denominational ordination is an important factor in validating one's call, it is simply that, a validation of the ministry one is already doing through the empowerment of the Holy Spirit.[10] Consequently, women in ministry who are Pentecostals should be just that, Pentecostals. They should be encouraged to pray for the sick, preach, teach, evangelize, and do the work of the ministry, understanding that their validation comes through the gifting of the Spirit, as well as the corresponding ordination of the Church.

The Second Important Necessity is The Need for Role Models

There is no greater example of the necessity for women to have role models than that found in the life and ministry of Aimee Semple McPherson. After 10 years of grueling evangelistic work, McPherson decided to settle down in Los Angeles in 1921. She purchased property near Echo Park, designed and built Angelus Temple, dedicating the new building on January 1, 1923. By the time she was thirty-three years old, Aimee Semple McPherson had established the first Christian radio station in the United States, a 5,300 seat auditorium in which thousands of people were saved and healed, a Bible College, and ultimately a denomination, all of which are still in operation today.[11] The International Church of the Foursquare Gospel now has well over 1.9 million members, with over 31,000 churches and meeting places in 72 countries around the world.[12]

While McPherson was uniquely gifted and greatly used by God, she did not exist in a vacuum. Other influential women had begun to pave the way for her, providing many models to follow and, as a result, a certain level of acceptance for women in ministry that she otherwise may not have enjoyed. The number of women providing a legacy of leadership in the Pentecostal movement were numerous. Among those women already addressed, such as Maria Woodworth-Etter, who by the end of 1885, was drawing an estimated 25,000 people to her camp meetings. Also active in the Movement was Marie Burgess, who after having been baptized with the Holy Spirit in 1906 under the ministry of Charles Parham, began preaching in Illinois, Ohio, and Michigan, eventually founding the great Glad Tidings Hall in New York.

McPherson herself was not unaware of the impact she would have upon women in ministry, and in fact, encouraged other women to follow her lead. In a lecture to one of her Bible School classes, she stated:

> This is the only church, I am told, that is ordaining women preachers. Even the Pentecostal works, in some cases, have said, "no women preachers." But I am opening the door, and as long as Sister McPherson is alive, she is going to hold the door open and say, "Ladies, come!"[13]

She was evidently true to her word, for by 1944, the year of her death, women accounted for 67% of the ordained clergy in the denomination which she founded, the International Church of the Foursquare Gospel. Following her death, however, a change in the number of ordained women began to occur. By the late seventies, the figure had dropped to 42%.[14] By 1993, the number of ordained women had decreased to approximately 38% [15] While this ratio is relatively high compared to other Pentecostal denominations, it must be noted that a great percentage of these ordained women are wives of ordained pastors who do not necessarily function in legitimate church leadership roles, with only a handful of these women functioning as senior pastors of a congregation.

Even more interesting is the lack of women found within corporate leadership in the denomination. Because all executive offices are appointed, using senior pastors as the pool of possible candidates, coupled with the fact that there are few female senior pastors in the denomination, of the 34 executive council members, only are women, with two of these women serving in traditionally female roles as Assistant Secretary and Director of Women's Ministries. Further, of the 166 divisional representatives, none are female.[16] While there may be other contributing factors, the lack of women in high-profile positions has surely made a strong contribution to the decrease of women who hold senior ministry positions within the Foursquare Church. Could it be that the absence of a powerful example such as Aimee Semple McPherson has contributed to this decline?

This phenomenon has not gone unnoticed by some of the leaders in the denomination. In fact, in February of 1995, the International Church sponsored the first National Women's Leadership Conference in Fort Worth, Texas. The 900 women who were in attendance strongly responded to the theme of the conference: Catch the Vision: Create a Legacy. These women obviously believe that it is not only important for Pentecostal women in ministry to fulfill their call in the present, but that by doing so, they will also create greater opportunity for future female leadership as well by modeling Spirit-empowered ministry for the next generation of women.

The Need for Affirmation

Pentecostal women who are called to ministry have need of affirmation from three specific sources. Harvey Cox, in his *Fire From on High*, has noticed the high value Pentecostals have put on "direct revelation." In his chapter that concerns Pentecostal women in ministry, Cox says of a testimony he heard:

> It went a long way in answering my question about how so many women win the right to preach in a church which, at least technically, forbids it. It clearly demonstrated why Pentecostals, who take the authority of the Bible very seriously but also believe in direct revelation through visions, have opened a wider space for women than most other Christian denominations

have. What the Bible says is one thing, but when God speaks to you directly, that supersedes everything else.[17]

While it is true that Pentecostal women in ministry have had a tendency to base the validity of their ministry on "the call" experience alone, one must consider that the call itself requires a scriptural basis. Women must first function in ministry with the validity of their call resting in scripture, not in spite of it. Pentecostals must hold to the truth that gender bias runs in direct opposition to the entire message of the gospel. While it is true that in the old fallen order, sex discrimination is practiced, redemption in Christ has set us free from the practice of using gender as the criteria for determining positions of leadership within the Church. Paul declares that "there is neither Jew nor Greek, slave nor free, male nor female, for you are all one in Christ Jesus" (Gal. 3:28). Paul declares this rather radical statement within the context of a discussion with the Galatians concerning the futility of their attempts to satisfy the Old Testament law (particularly circumcision) by their own works, while continuing to maintain that they are living by grace. In Paul's view, circumcision, specifically a male rite, had fulfilled its purpose in the Old Testament. In the New Testament, however, the old rite has been replaced by the rite of baptism, in which all believers--male and female, slave and free, Jew or Greek--can participate. Stanley Grenz says of this passage in Galatians that,

> Paul indicates that the transition from circumcision to baptism has destroyed the significance of the distinctions between persons which formerly were used to establish social hierarchies. These include appeals not only to ethnic heritage (Jew and Gentile) and social status (free and slave) but also to gender differentiation (male and female). Therefore the hierarchy of male over female introduced by the Fall is now outmoded ... [18]

For Pentecostals to live according to any hierarchical structure which exalts one race, one social group, or one gender over another is to bring ourselves under a bondage that was never purposed for us in Christ. That is not to say that organization is not necessary, it certainly is. However, we must live according to the New Testament injunction to "be subject to one another out of reverence for

Christ" (Eph. 5:21). All human relationships within the context of the community of God must always be guided by equal submission.

Further, looking to scripture as the foundation for ministry means that the "problem passages" must be wrestled through, using all of the academic tools available. My personal experience has been that once these issues were dealt with, in a manner true to hermeneutical principles that provided solid answers, I felt a confidence in my ministry that had not been experienced up to this point. In addition, not only is it important for the Pentecostal female minister for her own benefit to understand that she is functioning in ministry because of a scriptural foundation (not in spite of it), this knowledge will also serve to neutralize opposing doctrine, thereby opening a greater opportunity for women in official ministry positions.

Secondly, women are entering Bible Colleges and Seminaries in staggering numbers. In fact, according to 1993 statistics, 25-30 percent of the students enrolled in seminary degree programs in the United States are women.[19] Clearly, women are sensing the call of God to full-time ministry; as a result, they are responding to their call by pursuing formal education. It is vital, then, that our Pentecostal colleges offer education concerning women in leadership within the context of the Pentecostal distinctive. However, this education must not be in any way limited to women or to the subject of women in leadership but should encompass both historical and Biblical analysis arising from a Pentecostal tradition. In short, young Pentecostals need to be taught the distinctions of their Pentecostal heritage and identity, which include the scriptural validation of ministry for women. This effort will not only give female students great confidence in their call through proper understanding and equipping but will also serve to inform our young male Pentecostals, as well, preparing them to deal with the reality of the female ministers they will surely encounter in their ministries.

Last, the call of God, in addition to the act of ordination for female Pentecostals, becomes a moot issue unless ministry opportunities are available to women. Today, I can not look across my desk at a young female who is about to graduate with a degree in Pastoral Ministry and confidently say to her that there will be a position open to her in the local church for which she has been called and trained. For example, in the Assemblies of God in 1993, 15.2% of credentialed ministers were females, but 40.2% of that number were 65 years or older. And, only 1.06% of all credentialed ministers were female senior pastors. Further, there are some Pentecostal denominations that do not yet allow women full ordination. Because women who are called to ministry cannot be disobedient to the will of God for their lives and must be true to their calling, this lack of opportunity within the Pentecostal ranks will, I fear, cause many of our brightest and best ministers to defect to non-Pentecostal denominations where their fire and zeal is most welcomed, regardless of their gender.

Therefore, our Pentecostal fellowships must be willing to give equal opportunity to those women who are called to ministry, not merely allowing them the more traditional female roles in the church, but recognizing the possibility that no position in church/servant leadership is gender restricted.

Conclusion

Today, Pentecostals find themselves asking what it means to be truly Pentecostal. With a new appreciation for education rising within their ranks, young Pentecostals, both male and female, are beginning to notice that in the early days of the Movement, Pentecostals were involved in the women's suffrage movement, were conscientious objectors, and were vitally involved in many areas of social reform. Further, some are now calling for an abandonment of much of the evangelical theology which is diametrically opposed to the original Pentecostal experience, while at the same time holding to a form of biblical literalism, which is in effect, having the result of the development of a Pentecostal hermeneutic which is more in line with the Pentecostal experience.

Ideally, as women become more assured in their calling to ministry, more confident in their gifting by the Holy Spirit, and are affirmed in who they are biblically and historically through the process of education and ministry opportunity in their fellowship, these women will rise to the occasion.

"If women are no less capable than men of piety, zeal, learning, and whatever else seems necessary for the ministry, then why should the church not draw on the huge reserves which could pour into the priesthood if women were here, as in so many professions, put on the same footing with men?"[20]

Why, indeed?

1. For specific statistics on two Pentecostal fellowships, the Assemblies of God, and the Church of God, refer to "The Contemporary, State of Women in Ministry in the Assemblies of God" by Deborah M. Gill, and "Perfect Liberty to Preach the Gospel: Women Ministers in the Church of God" by David Roebuck in Pneuma: The Journal of the Society for Pentecostal Studies 17/1 (Spring 1995) 25-36.

2. Mae Eleanor Frey, "Selected Letters of Mae Eleanore Frey," Comp. by Edith L. Blumhofer, Pneuma 17/1 (Spring 1995) 78.

3. Ibid. 77. 9

4. Charles H. Barfoot and Gerald T. Sheppard, "Prophetic Vs. Priestly Religion: The Changing Role of Women Clergy in Classical Pentecostal Churches," Review of Religious Research 22/1 (September) 4.

5. Ibid. 4.

6. Frank Bartleman, What Really Happened on "Azusa Street"? (Northridge, California: Voice Christian Publications, 1966) 32-34.

7. Cecil M. Robeck, Jr., "National Association of Evangelicals," in Dictionary of Pentecostal and Charismatic Movements, Stanley M. Burgess and Gary B. McGee, eds. (Grand Rapids: Zondervan, 1988) 635.

8. Ibid. 635.

9. Edith Blumhofer, The Assemblies of God: A Popular History (Springfield: Gospel Publishing House, 1985) 137.

10. Refer to the ordination of Paul and Barnabas in Acts 13. Both men were already leaders in the church at Antioch when "the Holy Spirit said, 'Set apart for me Barnabas and Saul for the work to which I have called them.'"

11. Rolf K. McPherson Interview, San Dimas, CA. October, 1992.

12. 1995 Ministry Report, International Church of the Foursquare Gospel.

13. Class Notes on the Book of Acts, LIFE Bible College, Los Angeles, N/D.

14. Barfoot and Sheppard, 15.

15. 1993 Ministry Report, International Church of the Foursquare Gospel.

16. 1995 Ministry Report, International Church of the Foursquare Gospel.

17. Harvey Cox, Fire From Heaven: The Rise of Pentecostal Spirituality and the Reshaping of Religion in The Twenty-first Century (Reading, Massachusetts: Addison Wesley Publishing Company, 1995) 131.

18. Stanley J. Grenz and Denise Muir Kjesbo, Women in the Church: A Biblical Theology of Women in Ministry (Downers Grove: InterVarsity Press, 1995) 178.

19. Gordon A. Wetmore, "God-Called Women," The Seminary Tower 49/1 (Fall 1993)

20. Paul K. Jewett, The Ordination of Women (Grand Rapids: Wm. B. Eerdmans Publishing Co., 1980) 14.

RETAINING PRESENT POSTURE

DOCTRINAL REVIEW COMMITTEE ON

"WOMEN IN THE MINISTRY"

A Woman's View of Women in Ministry from the
Traditional View

Women's View of Women in the Ministry

Feminist View

Feminist Interpretation of the Bible

Opening Statement

It is indeed a privilege for me to be able to take a stand for the prevailing teaching of the Great Old Church of God in Christ, as it relates to the position of women in ministry. The Church of God in Christ recognizes the call of God on the lives of both male and female, the diversity of ministry and the unity and individuality of those called to be workers together with Him. Yet in the midst of the operation of the affairs of the church, God has always had and still maintains the established order as per His revealed plan and purpose. That order calls for men to be the authorized head of the church both in title and position.

Doctrinal Review Committee Report

A Biblical answer to the question: "Who Calls to the Ministry and how a person is called?"

All saved persons are "saints by calling," but not all are called to the Ministry. A call to the Ministry is a Divine "call", for God calls whomsoever He wills. Jesus said to His disciples: "Ye have not chosen Me, but I have chosen you and ordained you that ye should go and bring forth fruit, and that your fruit should remain" (St. John 15:16). Christ called "unto Him whom He would" (St. Mark 3:13-14). The Lord said of Paul: "He is a chosen vessel unto Me, to bear my name before the Gentiles and kings and the children of Israel" (Acts 9:15).

The Lord burdens the heart of an individual, impresses him personally and gives him that holy urge to be used by Him. Paul said "necessity is laid upon me. Yea, woe is unto me if I preach not the gospel" (1 Cor. 9:16).

The call to the Ministry frequently comes in an atmosphere of spirituality when one is enjoying fellowship with God through reading and meditation of His word and prayer. It comes through fervent supplication to know the will of God for one's life.

The Call may come in various ways and under different circumstances. Let's look at just a few out of many: "The God of glory appeared unto him" (Abraham) and a definite call was given him, with the promise of his own blessing and, through him, to all the families of the earth (Acts 7:2; Gen. 12:1-3). In Exodus 3-4, God convinced Moses that He knew what He was doing in calling Moses. God gave Joshua a commission and then granted him a vision of the One who had commissioned him (Joshua 1:1-9; 5:13-15). Gideon was not convinced of his call and commission until the Lord had wrought two miracles on his behalf (Judges 6:11-24). Isaiah had a vision, a call, and a commission, and responded by saying: "Here am I, send me (Isaiah 621-13). With Peter, the miracle of the great catch of fish served to provide the circumstances under which his call and commission came (St. Luke 5:1-11).

Although God calls to the Ministry whomsoever He wills, it is Biblically clear that the Pastoral or Overseeing Ministry is limited to men (1 Timothy 3:1-2; Titus 1:5-9). Pastors, Bishops, or Elders must be the husband of one wife.

Our church today must not turn from the righteous requirements for Pastors, Elders, and Bishops which God has set forth in the original revelation of the apostles. we must not get off course by Ecclesiastical Politics. There is plenty of room and opportunity for women in ministry in our great Church, I thank God for the wonderful women who have done and are doing great work for the Master. We must not allow the Feminist Movement and the secular world to dictate our course. We must stay with the Word of God that God's Blessings and favor will continue to be with the grand old Church of God in Christ.

Honorably Submitted,

Supt. C. A. Stevenson

To: Doctrine Review Committee

Subject: A Defense for the Official Doctrinal Manuel of the Church of God in Christ

From: Supt. Sherman Davis, Jr.

There seems to be a preponderant of evidence that says God's order and role for the woman in the church is different from that of the man. However, I do not feel that man is superior to the woman. In Christ "There is neither Jew nor Greek (no ethic difference), There is neither bond nor free (status nor social rank), there is neither male nor female (biological difference) for ye are all one in Christ Jesus." Gal. 328

Yet, I definitely believe their roles are different. 1 Cor. 11:3 "But I would have you know that the head of every man is Christ, and the head of the woman is the man and the head of Christ is God." Could it be that from the beginning it was not so? Matt. 19:8 and by design, "…Adam was first formed and then Eve. And Adam was not deceived, but the woman being deceived was in the transgression." I Timothy 2:13, 14.

Let us consider the following statements used to support women preachers.

1. "Women are more in number in our congregations; therefore they should be able or ordained to preach." I do not believe that statement justifies a change in our manual. When did God use numbers as a criterion for His work? Deut. 7:7 "The Lord did not set His love upon you, nor choose you because ye were more in number than any people; for ye were the fewest of all people.

2. "Women are more dependable than men." I don't feel that statement is any more valid than the prophet Elijah's statement when he felt that he alone was left to do God's will.

3. Women are already preaching, why not ordain them."

    Surely, we could not sanction something in violation of God's word.

I would like to close with excerpts of Ben Kinchlow's forward to "Maximized Manhood."

"There is a very interesting phenomenon occurring in twentieth-century America from birth to late teens, a child's overwhelming perception of authority figures in nearly 100% female, with an occasional male making a genera ineffectual appearance.

In the hospital, female nurses are responsible for almost every aspect of childcare. At home, the mother is usually the dominant authority figure. And, 90% of the teachers in grade school are-you go it-women. The first police person a child meets is more than likely a female crossing guard.

When the child goes to the movies, the grocery store, department stores, fast food restaurants, vacation bible school, or Sunday school, who sells the tickets, takes the orders, collects the money, shows you where to sit, tells you about God? (Except in many churches where a man preaches to a congregation consisting of mostly women.) (Not long for us if some have their way. Mine) Who tells you what to wear, cleans up your room: who spends the money, pays the bill? In other words, who's really in charge? Is it any wonder that today's young man is making every effort to demonstrate that he's a real man-like mom."

THE SPECIAL COMMISSION ON WOMEN IN THE MINISTRY IN THE CHURCH OF GOD IN CHRIST

AT

Charles Harrison Mason

Theological Seminary

24th Founder's Week Celebration

February 22-24, 1994

"Resolved that the Church of God in Christ should maintain its present position regarding

Women in the Ministry."

Presented by

Pastor James Stovall

First Jurisdiction, Southern California

In the wisdom of the Holy Spirit, the forefathers of the Church of God in Christ laid the foundation of our great church. This foundation far exceeded the expectations of those who asked God for guidance and insight in the establishment of this great work. God was about to open the windows of heaven and "pour out of his spirit."

To speak on behalf of the position of the church concerning the ministry of women is not a difficult task, for we believe that all of the doctrines and teachings of the church are based on the "Principles of Truth" that allow us not only to know God but to understand God's purpose in our daily lives. One might say that there is no clear-cut statement in the Scripture, or clarion call delineating the position, but this is not true. God's position is clear, and His truth changes not. The revelation of His principles doesn't change. Man has been called to occupy the position of headship from the very beginning. This positional stance of man is the subject of concern today as it relates to women in ministry. The unfolding of this position has been the topic of revelation from the time of creation.

Every generation has been chosen by God for a specific purpose and accomplishment. Each generation moves forward to new heights and greater depths of the knowledge of God which equips us to be fruitful in every good work. The generation that was chosen by God to establish our great church was endowed with the wisdom of the Holy Spirit that allowed them to lay a foundation that has weathered the changes of time for more than 75 years.

God's order for men and women is spelled out in the book of Genesis. Male and female were created in the mind of God, but it was the male that was formed first from the dust of the earth and the female who was formed from the rib taken from the side of man.

She was to be a help meet for him. One who was compatible physically, emotionally, and spiritually. The woman was to compliment all the activities of the man. God states, "it is not good for man to be alone." The completeness of man is found in the woman and the completeness of the woman is found in the man. The relationship as formulated in God's perfect creation was a union motivated and maintained by love.

The establishment of this relationship of shared (complimentary) existence was in force until the fall, which was facilitated when Adam, the federal head of all generations, transgressed God's law in the Garden of Eden.

Sin, as it became more pervasive in successive generations, was exacerbated by man's inability to comprehend God's purpose for His creation; that of giving glory to God in his prescribed order of leadership. The quest for equality has become the by-word of our day. This drive for equality that has manifested itself with respect to social, political, and economical rights and privileges, has now manifested itself in the church. God has placed man in the position of authority. The quest for equality of the sexes in the areas of "title and position" in the administration of the church, violates the order ordained and maintained throughout all of scripture. God is the head of Christ. Christ is the head of man and man is the head of the woman. The leadership position and "title" have been reserved by God for man who must answer to God.

We must not allow the social and cultural principles of egalitarianism to change the God-given order of church administration.

We must remember that we are a chosen generation, a peculiar people, chosen to maintain the position of male leadership which was a type of the relation of Christ and the church.

We must remember that the church cannot determine its direction by the philosophies and ways of the world.

We must be prepared to offer spiritual gifts unto God that are acceptable only through Jesus Christ.

The success of the Church of God in Christ depends on this generation being willing to hold on to God's order of authority both in position and title.

VIEWS OF WOMEN IN MINISTRY

The Traditional View
The Feminist View
Feminist Interpretation of the Bible

Submitted Mrs. P.T. Crudup

Women In The Church: Biblical Data Report

Introduction

I. Woman at Creation

A. Woman has personal equality with man as an image-bearer of God (Gen. 1:27-28; 5:1).

Allowing for biological distinctives a woman has the same human nature, qualities, and abilities as a man. Maleness and femaleness, though distinct, are fully harmonized (Gen. 1:28; Ps. 8:4-8; 1 Cor. 11-12).

B. Woman has a distinctive role function within this equality (Gen. 2:18).

The priority of the male in creation reflects God's appointed order for His creation not male superiority. Man has the responsibility of headship (cf. 1 Cor. 11:37; Eph.5:21), and woman has the responsibility of being a "fitting helper" (Gen. 2:18). Each supplies what is lacking in the other. They are complementary because they are distinct.

II. Woman at the Fall

The superiority of males over females is first mentioned in Scripture as an inevitable consequence of sin, not as an inherent quality or right. In the post-Fall order of things God said man would exploit woman's natural "helpmate desire" toward him, or more probably, he would retaliate in the face of her "desire"

(cf. Gen. 4:7) to dominate and lead him in order to dominate and subjugate her (Gen. 3:16b). The subjugation of either women or men is a symptom: of mankind's fallen nature (cf. e.g., pagan religions).

III. Women in Old Testament Times Until the Time of Jesus

A. Women served in the doorway of the Tabernacle (Exod. 38:8; 1 Sam. 2:22).

The same word (saba) is used for their work as that of the Levites. These women were probably widows who devoted themselves to the service of God.

B. Miriam, a prophetess, and all the women with her gave public praise to God (Exod. 15:20-21).

Apparently, she also had some leadership roles along with Moses and Aaron (Mic. 624).

C. Deborah was a prophetess and also a judge in Israel (Judg. 4-5).

She and Barak sang a song of praise for God's deliverance which is recorded for both men and women to read (Judg. 5).

D. Hannah prayed in the house of the Lord, and her prayer of thanksgiving was recorded for both men and women to read (1 Sam. 1:9-2:10),

E. Huldah was a prophetess who prophesied before the high priest and the men of King Josiah (2 Kings 22:8-20; cf. 2 Kings 22:3 with Jer. 1:2).

F. Many women sang in the temple choirs (1 Chron. 25:5-7; Neh. 7:66-67).

G. Many women had an important part to play in proclaiming the Lord's Word (P5. 68:11):

H. Though a few women served as civil rulers-in Israel (e.g., Deborah) there is no record of a female priest or high priest.

I. The prophet Joel predicted that one day "your sons and daughters will prophesy" (Joel 2:28-32; cf. Acts 2:16-18).

J. The Virgin Mary's praise to God is recorded for both men and women to read (Luke 1:46-55).

K. Anna was a prophetess who served in the temple night and day with fasting and prayers (Luke 2:36-38).

IV. Women in the Ministry and Teaching of Jesus

A. A loyal group of women accompanied Jesus and served Him on His ministry tours (Luke 8:1-3; Matt. 27:55; Mark 15:41).

B. In contrast to normal custom and rabbinic standards, Jesus spoke with a Samaritan woman and revealed to her the nature of true worship (John 4:7-26).

C. Jesus cared equally for the physical infirmities of women (Mark 1:29-31; 5:25-34)' and He drew attention to the devotion of an unnamed poor widow to teach a lesson in discipleship (Mark 12:41-44).

D. He permitted Mary, Lazarus' sister, to sit at His feet and learn-a privilege granted only to men at that time (Luke 10:42).

E. Women who had been healed by Jesus praised God publicly in the synagogue (Luke 13:13).

F. In a male-dominated culture, He redressed legal situations which were weighted against women (cf. Matt. 19:9-10; Mark 10;11-12).

G. Though Jesus had both male and female disciples, all twelve original apostles were men (Matt. 10:1-4: Mark 3:13-19).

H. He entrusted women with the high privilege of carrying the news of His resurrection to His twelve disciples (Mark 16:6-8; Luke 24:11). This was a remarkable thing in that culture since a woman's testimony was not legally valid in order to establish a fact. No wonder the disciples had a hard time believing them!

I. Mary Magdalene was one of the first people to see Jesus as the risen Lord (John 20:11-18).

J. Jesus' charge to evangelism and discipleship, given to the apostles, applies to the church at large with reference to all believers, men and women (Matt. 28:19-20; Mark 16:15-16; Acts 1:8).

V. Women in the Life and Ministry of the Early Church

A. The Holy Spirit fell on men and women on the Day of Pentecost (Acts 2:1-4).

B. Women prayed with men (Acts 1:14; 12:12).

C. Women had various ministries of hospitality, service and good works (Dorcas, Acts 9:36; Mary, the mother of Mark, Acts 12:12; Lydia, Acts 16: 14-15).

D. Priscilla and Aquilla took Apollos aside and explained to him the way of God more accurately (Acts. 18:26-28).

E. The Holy Spirit used women as His prophetic mouthpiece (Philip's four daughters were prophetesses, Acts 21:8-9). Overall, it appears that women took as active a part in the life and ministry of the church as men.

VI. Women in the Ministry and Teaching of Paul and Peter

A. Paul affirms the personal equality of man and woman in the new creation by stating that in Christ there is "neither male nor female" (Gal. 3:28).

A woman obtains salvation by faith exactly as a man does (Eph. 2:8-9; 1 Pet. 1:18-19). and both are co-heirs of the grace of Life despite some physical limitations a woman has as one who has "the weaker [feminine] vessel [body]" (1 Pet. 3:7).

Like a man, she is indwelt by the Holy Spirit (Rom. 8:9b), and her body also serves as a sanctuary of the Holy Spirit (1 Cor. 6:19-20).

In the New Testament, the headship-submission relationship relates to the home and the church. All women are not subject to all men.

K. 'Paul's list of elder qualifications indicates that the office of elder/pastor is limited to men, and this office with its commensurate authority is conferred by the local church (1 Tim. 3:1-7; Titus 1:5-9; 1 Pet. 5:1-4).

Consequently, the directing/ruling function of the local church is reserved for men. There are no examples of "ordained" women elders in the Scriptures, nor are they encouraged to seek such an office. Nevertheless, elders may delegate certain responsibilities to various church members, both men and women.

L. Whether the office of deacon is open to women is debated. The primary passage which raises this issue is I Timothy 3:11. There are three major interpretations of this verse:

1. The women mentioned are unmarried assistants to male deacons (Robert M. Lewis, "Women" of I Timothy 3:11," Bib Sac. 136 (April-June, 1979): 167a175).

2.   The women mentioned are the wives of male deacons (Charles Ryrie, The Role p. 2; Women p. 32 the Church. p. 91; C. K. Barrett, The New Clarendon Bible, p.61).

3.   The women mentioned are a select group of female deacons within the church (James Hurley, Man and Woman in Biblical Perspective, and the majority of commentators). The second and third views seem more probable, and both handle the data adequately. Whether or not they held the office of deacon in New Testament times, it is clear that women fulfilled many of its functions (cf. I Tim. 2:10; 5:9-10; Acts 9:36). Phoebe may have been a recognized deacon of the church in Cenchrea (Rom. l6:1-2). If So, this would indicate that both men and women served in this office.

However, since she was probably a wealthy social leader in the city, she may have been simply an unofficial patroness of the church.

M. since the function of teaching is a spiritual gift and not an offlce of the church, it is available to both men and women (Rom. 12:7; 1 Cor. 12:28-29).

The question, however, is not whether a woman may teach but whom she may teach and in what setting. Three Pauline passages speak to this issue: 1 Corinthians 11:2-16; 14:26, 34-36; and I Timothy 2:9-12. The interpretation and application of these passages continue to evoke considerable debate in evangelical circles. It is generally agreed that these verses primarily refer to activities within the context of corporate worship.

1.   1 Corinthians 11:2-16; 14:26.

2.   On two occasions Paul mentioned specific situations in which a woman may speak in corporate worship (1 Cor. 11:5 and 14:26).

3.   In 1 Corinthians 11, Paul instructs a woman to have a sign of authority on her head (1Cor 11:10) when she prays and prophesies in order to show submission to those in authority.

4.   1 Corinthians 14:34-35

5. In light of 1 Corinthians 11:5 and 14:26, it is reasonable to suggest that 1Corinthians 14:34-35 does not mean that women are to be absolutely silent at all times during corporate worship. Of several interpretations of this passage, two of the most common are also the most probable.

   a. Paul's prohibition is against women speaking out to teach men in corporate worship (cf. I Tim. 2:11-12; George Knight, The New Testament Teaching on the Role of Men and Women, pp. 36-37).

   b. Paul's prohibition is against women evaluating the utterances of the prophets in corporate worship since this evaluation would involve an exercise of authority which would go against the requirement of submission to male headship (1 Cor. 11:2-6; 1 Tim. 2:11-15; cf. James Hurley, Man and Woman in Biblical Perspective, pp. 188-194). Both interpretations have merit, but the latter one fits the context of 1 Corinthians 14:26-35 better. As shown above, the Law did not prohibit prayer and praise by women in public worship. Consequently, Paul's reference to the Law (14:34) is probably a reference to the creation account and God's established creation order as it is now to be exhibited in the local church.

1. I Timothy 2:9-15

In verses 9 and 10 Paul directed that a woman's dress and behavior should be appropriate when she engages in corporate worship so that in attitude, appearance, or conduct she does not give the impression that she rejects God's established order of male headship in this sphere.

In verse 11, he asserted that women are to receive instruction in corporate worship with a quiet and submissive spirit. If they do this, they will have less problem obeying Paul's command in verse 12 to neither teach nor have authority over a man in public worship. This is not Paul's narrow opinion or an over-reaction to a local church problem at Ephesus (of. Douglas Moo, "I Timothy 2:11-15: Meaning and Significance" Trinity Journal 1 NS (1980):62-83).

The reason for Paul's prohibition is twofold:

a. Adam was formed before Eve (2:13)-a reference to God's established order in creation and the principle of headship (Gen. 2:21-22).

   1. There is a proper kind of order of leadership in the new creation as well as in the old, prior to and following the 'Fall'.

b. Eve was genuinely deceived by Satan; whereas Adam was willfully disobedient to God's command (2:14).

   She acted on her own initiative and was deceived. Paul did not wish Eve's error to be repeated in the church. Thus, a woman--no matter how gifted or capable--is not "to have authority" (not just "to usurp authority," KJV) that properly belongs to a man in this sphere. This is simply God's established order. Paul did not mean that a woman is inherently less intelligent.

N. The Scriptures indicate that a woman may participate actively in corporate worship, but she is not to teach or engage in activities in which she has authority over a man or men in this sphere.

She may minister in church services or church-related meetings so long as her primary purpose is not to have the authority that befits the office of elder/pastor. It is debated whether this prohibition regarding teaching the Scriptures or Bible doctrine extends beyond the confines of corporate worship or church-related meetings.

There are numerous spheres of leadership and ministry that are appropriate for women, limited only by situations where a woman would assume "headship" authority over a man or men. Such spheres include Christian education. outreach and evangelism, specialized pastoral ministries, church administration, a music ministry, a prayer ministry, a service ministry, and a writing ministry.

Perhaps two biblical guidelines would be helpful in evaluating particular situations:

a) Does our interpretation or application of a biblical passage in a given situation affirm woman's personal equality with man?

b) Does our interpretation or application of a biblical passage in a given situation affirm woman's responsibility of willing submission to man's headship responsibility in the home and church?

A WOMAN'S VIEW OF WOMEN IN MINISTRY FROM

THE TRADITIONAL VIEW

Acknowledgments

I am deeply indebted to the librarian at Catholic University for the assistance given me in the selection of current journals and for permission to reproduce copies of the periodicals concerning the ministry of women; to my son, Elder Carlton L. Crudup for allowing me to use the many volumes of his accumulated library on Black Theology and women in the ministry in the Black Church; also to my son, Elder Warren Crudup, Jr. for typing and using the church computer produce this document; lastly, to the Women's Department of the Church of God in Christ who submitted my name to be a part of the Doctrinal Review Committee on Women in the Ministry.

A Woman's View of Women in Ministry

1. A woman is an adult female person.

2. Tradition: (a) an inherited, established, or customary pattern of thought or action. (b) the handing down of beliefs and customs by word of mouth or by example without written instructions.

3. A view is the (a) act of seeing or (b) examining inspection; (c) a way of looking at something; (d) extent or range of vision.

4. Ministry: the office, duty or function of a person engaged in or giving aid to; serving as a minister in religion; fulfilling needs in the many areas of ecclesiastical duties.

From the <u>Church of God in Christ Official Manual</u>, pp. 144;

"Women in the Ministry"

The church recognizes the capabilities of women who are talented, Spirit-filled, dedicated, knowledgeable in administrative and spiritual affairs of the church. Also, they were devout continuing in fasting and prayer ministries. They were engaged in the visitation ministry, the training or teaching ministry to perform special duties in preparation and assisting in the ordinances of the early church – later called deaconess. The Church of God in Christ recognizes the scriptural importance of women in the Christian ministry.

Evaluation Summary:

Women (1) may preach the gospel to others and (2) have charge of a church in the absence of its pastor, if the pastor so wishes.

Servants or Helpers

Therefore, take heed, the Church of God in Christ cannot accept a scriptural mandate to ordain women preachers.

A WOMAN'S VIEW

Matthew 23:11, Matthew 20, 26: But he that is greatest among you shall be your servant.

Church women have established important legacies in their respective denominations.

Regardless of the level of office or specific activity, they have brought to bear their historical role model that contradicts and criticizes the expectation for behavior and attitudes that culture defines as appropriate.[1] The church is of importance to women. Their call by God defies obstacles. Somehow the obstacles serve as incentives for new depths and higher spiritual experiences. While the denominations' positions on the proper role of women vary, women are central to these churches; survival and growth through community outreach ministries, street meetings, cottage prayer meetings, door to door canvassing, feeding the hungry, and most of all, very expressively informing their listeners, "It's holiness or hell."

The recent article in People Magazine featuring DeLeon Richards represents only one item in the uncounted contributions members of Pentecostal churches have made to popular culture. "A little girl eight years old, a member of the Church of God Christ told the awed reporter, "God gave me the voice and told me to use it."[2] The spiritual authority that his child's statement represents is an important resource in a society that seeks to destroy the individual spirit as well as the body and community.

Churches such as the Church of God in Christ proffered social roles that carried titles of respect, dress codes, and institutional authority to travel throughout the south. The "Women's Department" is a strong force in the church. Through the training of females of all ages, it provides many avenues for grooming women in the ministry. Mrs. Lizzie Woods Roberson was the first organizer and leader, originally called m, of the Women's Department of the Church of the God in Christ. She was recruited because of her educational position at a Baptist Academy.[3] The Church of God in Christ was proud of the fact that they had recruited Arenia C. Mallory to head Saints Industrial Academy since she was a "protege of Mary McCleod Bethune." She was recruited by our founder, Bishop Charles H. Mason. The Church of God in Christ under the leadership of Mother Roberson, Dr. Mallory, Mother Coffee, Mother Anne Bailey and now Mother Mattie McGlothen, has grown and become a model for other churches to follow. The great leaders taught, traveled, and made great sacrifices. Great were the roles played by the female constituents who left their comfort zones and traveled to foreign countries, carrying the gospel of Jesus Christ to uncivilized and underdeveloped places. The women in Home and Foreign Missionary Work helped these persons to survive. Foreign missionaries organized different auxiliaries among the nations, preached, taught, baptized, and served as pastors until the natives could assume these roles. They did construction work. They toiled beyond their physical capacity, all because they responded to the call of God to go and spread the good news of salvation.

In the words of Dr. Lucille Cornelius, describing the role of women in the Church of God in Christ after the death of Bishop Mason and by extension the role of women in other denominations, "The women stuck together and held the church in harness until the brethren could find their identity in the form of leadership that we must have in this time.[4] These servants of God should never be undervalued. Many times the contributions made by the women of the church have been overlooked and ignored. We need a closer evaluation of the work of our great church. If we can only say one thing about women in the sanctified (C.O.G.l.C.) we should be able to say that they are prophets in this tradition. They have maintained the faith as delivered to the "saints" and it stands available to anyone at a point of personal or collective crisis. In their persistent refashioning of tradition in the context of the continuous crisis of black experience, women are responsible for the care and cultivation of tradition. Women have in a number of circumstances, provided the discerning voice that distinguishes between spirituality and "show."

I am proud to be a woman in the ministry of the Church of God in Christ. My entire life has been in the Pentecostal church. I have very high esteem and appreciation for the loyalty, endurance, and achievements of those who have excelled beyond traditional views. Many of our female seminarians as well as other missionaries have joined in other fellowships and received ordinations, yet they remain in the Church of God in Christ. Also, many are given provisional ordination within the church but cannot identify as being fully ordained. They are excluded from the ordained brotherhood.

My view of women in ministry from the traditional view. "It's time for reevaluation." There is a growing corps of women who are preparing themselves educationally for ministries in the wider community which require the endorsement of the parent church organization. For them is the challenge of obtaining credentials (ordination) to pursue these opening areas of opportunity.

---

1 Bonnie Thornton Dill, "The Dialectics of Black Womanhood, " Signs Journal of Women, Culture and Society, vol. 4, no.3 (Spring 1979) 543-55.

2 DeLeon Richards, " People Magazine," October 14, 1985, vol. 23, no. 16, p. 51.

3 Pleas, Fifty Years of Achievement, p. 36.

4 Lucille Cornelius, The Pioneer History of the Church of God in Christ, COGIC Publishing House, 1975.

WOMEN IN THE MINISTRY

"A Formal and Personal Inquiry"

One of the most pressing quests of every person is the search for personal identity. For women, it is a particularly intricate task because there are so many forces from outside ourselves telling us what the answer should be. Recently, most of us have felt that we had an option or a right to our own reality, as an integral part of God's creation, and an appointed place in the divine image. We have an inheritance as daughters of God.

As Christians (men and women alike) we are to follow the Gospel of our Lord and Savior, as written in Matthew, Mark, Luke, and John. The Hebrew Scriptures are a historical account of the building of a people's faith. It is the first part of the journey, the arduous painful climb up the mountain toward mature knowledge of God. Through the Exodus, the Law, history, wisdom literature, and the prophets, the Hebrew people struggled to know the greatness and compassion of God, but they were often mistaken.

Then Jesus came, with the eternal word of love, the proclamation of the new reign of God. Jesus showed us signs and wonders – signal events that exemplified His message. He acted and spoke in an entirely new way to relate to himself and to His neighbor. In His transfiguration, we were all promised transformation.

After Christ's resurrection, we began the long walk down the mountain. We stopped to build churches along the way as shrines to Christ's appearance. We, like Paul, and others talk about what Jesus said and did, and we try to make sense of it all. We misinterpret and make mistakes, we mishear and misunderstand. Even the canonical epistles are only attempts to explain the truth that we have already seen in the person of Jesus Christ.

Christ is the one to whom we women must look for the final answers about who and what we are. In doing so, we need to look especially at Jesus' relationships with other women. Read and reread the story again, and again. Women are lifted up, affirmed, accepted, healed, and encouraged. Women were taught and loved. Jesus talked with women and debated with women. Jesus allowed women to worship and adore him with their tears, and their love. With him, we have a place of honor.

Like Mary Magdalene, we were the first recipients of the power of Christ's resurrection. Through our love and faith, we can know Christ's message firsthand. We have been commissioned in the person of Mary to speak the word of forgiveness and new life. What happened to Mary Magdalene in church history is a warning to any woman who is called to speak this kind of truth. Her announcement of the same "Good News" that Jesus enacted in his relationships with women, will make her very threatening to those who do not want to hear. Mary obviously did not care what others thought, an attitude that people are not accustomed to seeing in a woman. She had no fear of what the authorities would do to her as a mourner at the foot of the cross, or as a solitary visitor to the tomb. She simply did what love bade her do.

In the story of Ruth and Naomi, God has reached beyond the limits of patriarchy to show women how to be strong. If there is no divine judgment against the male system in this story, there is at least divine instruction of women in using their God-given skills to adapt and survive within it. These women are more than sweet, gentle victims who were rescued by their distant relative. They are strong, capable, intelligent, and realistic. As women, we can learn much from the example of Ruth and Neomi, and that is how to work within the system, oppressive as it might be, to gain the status that we want and deserve. And also, to look within ourselves for the strength that God has given us to work in the ministry. As modern-day women, we are challenged in these same ways. How do we incorporate positive, God-given strengths in a healthy and productive way?

For the first seven years of my married life, I stayed at home and raised my children. It had been drilled in me since childhood, that my role in life was to raise my children and make a happy home for them and my husband. I also thought that this was God's plan for me as a woman. My college degrees were "just-in-case" insurance, protection for me if my husband left me or died, and I found myself on my own. For most of my life I have stayed within the bounds of acceptable behavior for women in the Church. But after many years of working in the church and taking leadership roles, I can no longer ignore the fact that I have a calling on my life to minister to those that do not know Christ as their personal savior.

I found I had a void in my life and a compelling desire to search the Word of God and share it with others. I sincerely feel that each individual is unique. Being unique denotes a responsibility not to accept as a matter of course established, restrictive policies regarding women in the ministry, even though they are sanctioned by the Church in which we are members.

As a Christian woman who represents the Father, I am a woman of intelligence and inner strength. I understand my own need, and how to achieve in a positive and socially productive way to accomplish what God has called me to do. He will make a way. After all, I am a daughter of the Father. A godly woman called by God will work to reach those that are in need of hearing about Jesus Christ and His saving power. As theologian Matthew Fox says, gifts that we are given are meant for creative purposes. If they are not used creatively, they will become destructive. Scripture has given us a more subtle picture of Christian women working in the ministry. It is the picture of one who works within the extremely patriarchal culture to ensure the survival of herself and those closest to her but also is committed to changing that culture to enable full utilization of her gifts in God's ministries.

Women who desire to serve God by working in the church with such ready-made ministries as religious education teachers, choir directors, ushers, etc.; are tempted to accept these ministries as the only available options. However, the danger in accepting ready-made ministries forces one to adapt and diverts focus on unique God-given gifts. We must not violate ourselves by accepting alternatives to what God would have us to do in His ministry.

However, in order to know God's will for our life, we must first get acquainted with ourselves. We need to focus on the questions, who am I? What do I want to become, what am I doing or can do to become the person God would like me to be, as the woman in ministry. In becoming acquainted with myself, I realized that the desire to serve God has been in my spirit and very being since 1975. After receiving my first theological degree, I realized that I had been afforded this opportunity because of what God had in his divine plan for my life. My validation for God's call on my life is evidenced through my ability to teach, my capacity for nurturing, my love for home and family, and my insatiable desire to serve God with all my being, and share His love with others.

Women in ministry can succeed in today's world only by using their God-given gifts creatively. We must first recognize the gift, and purposefully direct it into positive avenues of action. Christian women are women of wisdom and are not cruel or unnecessarily judgmental; they are honest in their appraisal of a situation, and will not use their gifts to punish. They will leave justice up to God.

God has spoken to and through women from the very beginning of the faith. Time and time again women have been called to speak, to serve, to direct, and to lead God's people into ways of peace. Today, women are being called by the hundreds, into ordained and lay ministry. God's call of women to the ministry, is being affirmed by congregations, and denominations around the world. Is this any different from what God has been doing for four thousand years?

The wise woman will listen for the voice of God for affirmation of her reality as a woman called to the ministry and one that is created in God's holy image. The wise woman of today will allow God to direct her and instruct her. Something inside of her, her center, her very being, (the Holy Ghost) should let her know the voice of God. A woman of God is one who is innately attuned to the voice of Christ. A godly woman is one whose sensitivity and receptivity is most acute. She is one who stays centered and shares what her soul knows. When she is serene and balanced within herself, the reflection of Jesus in her life can be seen by others.

Women who turn a deaf ear to God's call, and churches that refuse to affirm God's actions are denying much of the tradition of women. They find proof-texts that refer to the dark side of women or to the cultural, patriarchal bias that unfortunately has found its way into our Scriptures. But they cannot refute what history has told us. Scripture is the Word of God; it is not the words of God. Focusing on the literal, specific words is little more than another idolatry. When those words are used to deny the wise woman her rightful place as an inheritor of the divine image, when she falls prey to false patriarchal teaching and biblical interpretation, she may indeed fall victim to the negative force of reality. As a result, her ministry for God will not be what God intended.

God has called all; men and women to His service. Nothing "man" can do will hinder God's call to each of us to work in His vineyard.

Respectfully submitted,

Missionary Patricia A. Allen
Temple Church of God in Christ
Washington, D. C. Jurisdiction

REFERENCES

Millett, C. Ballard. In God's Image: Archetype of Women in Scripture. California: LuraMedia, 1991.

Scripture references are from the Holy Bible, King James Version, Copyright 1976, by Thomas Nelson, Inc.

Feminist Views

Feminism-The theory of political, economic, and social quality of the sexes. Organized activity on behalf of women's rights and interests.

The feminist agenda for bringing about change in the way that the church deals with women in ministry emanate from several observations they have made:

1.   Theology was written primarily by men and therefore is written from the masculine perspective. A rewritten "inclusive" theology in which the feminine perspective is also rendered is needed.

2.   Women have been relegated to a "second-class" citizenship below men who hold the power. The black church has taken a stand against society's racism while at the same time perpetuating a system of sexism within its own community by downgrading the status of its women. An upgrading of women in society and the church is mandated.

3.   The laws and customs which bar women from ordination are sexist and therefore unfair. They must be eliminated.

4.   The Bible, upon which our entire system of faith is based, was primarily written by men from a patriarchal social perspective. God has been "masculinized" and the godly virtues are given a very masculine slant. The role of women in the Bible, with notable exceptions, has been minimized. A Bible in which a God which transcends all sexual stereotyping is desirable.

Feminist views range from moderate to radical, but their consensus is that once a theology inclusive of all people without regard to race, sex, or any other designation is developed, then, and only then, will women be given the equality and status due them.

Christ, Carol P. and Plaskow, Judith, mm, Harper and Row, San Francisco, 1979.

"Introduction" pp. 1-16 (excerpts)

Feminists have charged that Judaism and Christianity are sexist religions with a male God and traditions of male leadership that legitimate the superiority of men in family and society. This new challenge to traditional faiths just confirms the view of some feminists that society has outgrown its need for religion. Other feminists are convinced that religion is profoundly important. For them, the discovery that religion teaches the inferiority of women is experienced as a betrayal of deeply felt and spiritual and ritual experience. They believe the history of sexism in religion shows how deeply sexism has permeated the human psyche but does not invalidate the human need for ritual, symbols, and myth. They believed that religion must be reformed or reconstructed to support the full dignity of women. They believe that religion is a deeply meaningful part of human life and that traditional religions of the west have betrayed women.

"Feminist Criticism of Religion"

It is precisely this sense of injustice that lies at the heart of the first feminist criticism of religion. Most of these criticisms originated in an often inarticulate sense of exclusion from traditional religious practice or theology. Women who felt called to be rabbis, priests, and ministers frequently found themselves barred from these vocations. Orthodox Jewish women who wanted to participate fully in worship were excluded from the praying community and seated behind a screen. Catholic and Protestant women who wanted to serve communion were asked, instead to serve church suppers. Women in every congregation heard phrases such as "God of our Fathers," "men of God," and the "brotherhood, of man" preached from the pulpit. Everywhere they turned, women found signs that read, "For Men Only."

Feminist criticism of religion began with the obvious. Explicit statements of female inferiority or subordination, exclusion of women from ministry, and teachings on marriage and family were scrutinized and deplored. Jewish women examined the traditional View that women are unclean during menstruation and seven days thereafter, and they also asked whether traditional centering of Jewish women's religious lives in the home was sufficient. Christian women questioned Paul's teaching that the Wife must be subordinate to her husband as the church is to Christ, and they rejected the passage traditionally read at weddings that asked the wife to obey her husband but simply asked the husband to love his wife.

The image of God as male was at once the most obvious and most subtle sexist influence in religion. Women who were bold enough to address this issue directly found that nothing aroused the ire of male theologians and churchmen so much as the charge that traditional language about God is sexist. The question seemed to challenge the fundamental core of biblical revelation. Women were told that God transcends sexuality and were advised not to bother with trivial questions of language. Many feminists also failed to recognize the crucial importance of God-language. Mary Daly made the image of God central in the feminist critique of religion in "After the Death of God the Father," published in 1971. The recent resurgence of interest in Goddesses has brought the issue of sexual imagery in God-language to the forefront of feminist thinking in religion.

As the feminist critique of the biblical religion developed, scholars began to recognize that the issues of God-language, exclusion of women in leadership and ritual, and teachings on marriage and family were systematically related to the theological world view of biblical faith. This was most obvious in Christian theology, which is more systematic than Jewish thought. According to Rosemary Ruether, the sexism in the Christian tradition is integrally related to the dualistic and hierarchal mentality that Christianity inherited from the classical world. This is a model for domination because reality is divided into two levels, one superior, and one inferior. Classical dualism became the model for the oppression of women when the culture-creating males identified the positive sides of dualism with themselves and identified the negative sides with the women over whom they claimed the right to rule. When this dualistic pattern of thinking is combined with a symbolic tradition in which God is addressed and in predominantly male language and imagery, the sexism of religious thinkers appears logical and consistent. No longer can sexist statements of theologians be excused as trivial and peripheral slips of men whose thought is otherwise free of sexism.

The formative community that has appropriated the revelatory experience, in turn, gathers a historical community around its interpretation of the vision. This process goes through various stages during which oral and written teachings are developed. At a certain point, a group consisting of teachers and leaders emerges that seeks to channel and control the process, to weed out what it regards as deviant communities and interpretations, and to impose a series of criteria to determine the correct interpretive line. In the process, the controlling group marginalizes and suppresses other branches of the community, with their own texts, and lines of interpretation. Thus, a canon of Scripture is established.

Once a canon of scripture is defined, one can then regard subsequent tradition as a reflection upon Scripture and always corrected by Scripture as the controlling authority. The winning group declares itself the privileged line of true (orthodox) interpretation. However much the community, both leaders and led, seek to clothe themselves in past codified tradition that provides secure access to divinely revealed truth, in reality, the experience of the present community cannot be ignored.

A religious tradition remains vital so long as its revelatory pattern can be reproduced generation after generation and continues to speak to individuals in the community and provide for them the redemptive meaning of an individual and collective experience.

Religious traditions fall into crisis when the received interpretations of the redemptive paradigms contradict experience in significant ways. The crisis may be perceived at various levels of radicalness. Exegetical criticism of received theological and Scriptural traditions can bring forth new interpretations that speak to new experiences.

A more radical break takes place when the institutional structure that transmits tradition is perceived to have become corrupt. They are perceived not as teaching truth but as teaching falsehood dictated by their own self-interest and will to power. The revelatory paradigms, the original founder, and even the early stages of the formulation of tradition are still seen as authentic. It scents necessary to go behind later historical tradition and institutionalized authorities and "return to" the original revelation.

Only by finding an alternative historical community and tradition more deeply rooted than those that have become corrupted can one feel sure that in criticizing the dominant tradition one is not just subjectively criticizing the dominant tradition but is, rather, touching a deeper bedrock of authentic Being upon which to ground the self. One cannot wield the lever of criticism without a place to stand.

The critical principle of feminist theology is the promotion of the full humanity of women. Whatever denies, diminishes, or distorts the full humanity of women is, therefore, appraised as not redemptive. Theologically speaking, whatever diminishes or denies the full humanity of women must be presumed not to reflect the divine or an authentic relation to the divine, or to reflect the authentic nature of things, or to be the message or work of an authentic redeemer or a community of redemption.

The uniqueness of feminist theology is not the critical principle, full humanity, but the fact that women claim this principle for themselves. Women name themselves as subjects of authentic and full humanity. The use of this principle in male theology is perceived to have been corrupted by sexism. The name of males as norms of authentic humanity has caused women to be scapegoated for sin and marginalized in both original and redeemed humanity.

Women, as the denigrated half of the human species, must reach for a continually expanding definition of inclusive humanity--inclusive of both genders, inclusive of all social groups and races. Any principle of religion or society that marginalizes one group of persons less than fully human diminishes us all.

Feminism appropriates the prophetic principles in ways the Biblical writers for the most part do not appropriate them, namely, to criticize this unexamined patriarchal framework. Feminist theology that draws on Biblical principles is possible only if the prophetic principles, more fully understood imply a rejection of every elevation of one social group against others as image and agent of God, every use of God to justify social domination and subjugation. Patriarchy itself must fall under the Biblical denunciations of idolatry and blasphemy, the idolizing of the male as representative of divinity. It is idolatrous to make males more "like God" than females. It is blasphemous to use the image and name of the Holy to justify patriarchal domination and law. Feminist readings of the Bible can discern a norm within Biblical faith by which the Biblical texts themselves can be criticized.

Again, what is innovative in feminist hermeneutics is not the prophetic norm but rather feminism's appropriation of this norm for women. Feminism claims that women 100 are among those oppressed who God comes to vindicate and liberate.

Feminist theology is not asserting unprecedented ideas; rather it is rediscovering the prophetic context and content of Biblical faith itself when it defines the prophetic-liberating tradition as the norm. On one level, this means that feminist theology, along with other liberation theologies, strips off the ideological mystifications that have developed in the traditions of Biblical interpretation and that have concealed the liberating content.

On another level, feminism goes beyond the letter of the prophetic message to apply the prophetic-liberating principle to women. Feminist theology makes explicit what was overlooked in male advocacy of the poor and oppressed: that liberation must start with the oppressed of the oppressed, namely, women of the oppressed. This means that the critique of hierarchy must become explicitly a critique of patriarchy. All the liberating prophetic visions must be deepened and transformed to include what was not included: women.

In the New Testament Paul understood the need to struggle against all traces of ethnocentric religion in the relations of Jew and Greek in the Church. But he was much less able to envision, never mind put into practice, the ideas of equality in Christ between male and female, slave and free.

This expansion of the Biblical message to include the unincluded rests on the assumption that the point of reference for Biblical faith is not past texts, with their sociological limitations, but rather the liberated future. We appropriate the past not to remain in its limits, but to point to new futures. In applying the prophetic principle to the critique of sexism and the liberation of women, we deepen our understanding of social sin and its religious justifications and expand the vision of messianic expectation. By applying prophetic faith to sexism, we reveal in new fullness its revolutionary meaning.

Carol P. Christ, and Judith Plaskow,
Woman Spirit Rising, Harper and Row,

San Francisco, 1979

Saving, Valerie, "The Human Situation: A Feminine View" pp. 24-41. It is, after all, a well-known fact that theology has been written almost exclusively by men. This alone should put us on guard, especially since contemporary theologians constantly remind us that one of man's strongest temptations is to identify his own limited perspective with universal truth.

It is my contention that there are significant differences between masculine and feminine experience and that feminine experience reveals in a more emphatic fashion certain aspects of the human situation which are present but less obvious in the experience of men. Contemporary theological doctrines of love have, I believe, been constructed primarily upon the basis of masculine experience and thus view the human condition from a male standpoint. Consequently, these doctrines do not provide an adequate interpretation of the situation of women--nor, for that matter, of men, especially in view of certain fundamental changes now taking place in our own society.

We know, too, that we can no longer make any hard-and-fast distinctions between the potentialities of men and women as such. The twentieth century has witnessed the shattering of too many of our traditional conceptions of sexual differences for us any longer to ignore the tremendous plasticity of human nature. But perhaps the most telling evidence of all that every distinction between the sexes above the physiological level is purely arbitrary comes from the descriptions given by cultural anthropologists of many primitive societies whose ideas about the behavior appropriate to each sex are widely different from, and in many instances contradictory to, those held in our own tradition.

As for men, Margaret Mead has observed:

> In every known human society, the male's need for achievement
> can be recognized. Men may cook, or weave or dress dolls, or
> hunt hummingbirds, but if such activities are appropriate

occupations of men, then the whole society, men and women alike, votes them as important. When the same occupations are performed by women, they are regarded as less important. In a great number of human societies, men's sureness of their sex role is tied up with their right, or ability, to practice some activity that women are not allowed to practice. Their maleness, in fact, has to be underwritten by preventing women from entering some field or performing some feat. Here may be found the relationship between maleness and pride; that is, a need for prestige that will outstrip the prestige which is accorded to any woman. There seems to be no evidence that it is necessary for men to surpass women in any specific way, but rather that men do need to find reassurance in achievement, and because of this connection, cultures frequently phrase achievement as something that women do not or cannot do, rather than directly as something which men do well.

Many of the characteristic emphasis of contemporary theology--its definition of the human situation in terms of anxiety, estrangement, and the conflict between necessity and freedom; its identification of sin with pride, will-to-power, exploitation, and self-assertiveness, and the treatment of others as objects rather than persons; its conception of redemption as restoring to man what he fundamentally lacks (name, sacrificial love, the I-Thou relationship, the primacy of the personal, and, ultimately, peace)--it is clear that such an analysis of man's dilemma was profoundly responsive and relevant to the concrete facts of modern man's existence. Insofar as modern woman too, increasingly accepted the prevailing values of the age and took on the challenges and opportunities, risk, and insecurities of participation in the masculine world, this theology spoke directly to her condition also. And, since the most striking features of modern culture were but heightened expressions of one aspect of the universal human situation, the adequacy of this theology as a description of man's fundamental predicament seemed assured.

As a matter of fact, however, this theology is not adequate to the universal human situation; its inadequacy is clearer to no one than to certain contemporary women. These women have been enabled, through personal experience and education, to transcend the boundaries of a purely feminine identity. They now stand closer to the juncture of nature and spirit than was possible for most women in the past. They believe in the values of self-differentiation, challenge, and adventure and are not strangers to that "divine discontent" which has always driven men. Yet these same women value their femininity also; they do not wish to discard their sexual identity but rather to gather it up into a higher unity. They want, in other words, to be both women and full human beings.

My purpose, indeed, as far as it concerns women, in particular, is to awaken theologians to the fact that the situation of women, however similar it may appear on the surface of our contemporary world to the situation of man and however much it may be echoed in the life of individual men, is, at the bottom, quite different--than the specifically feminine dilemma is, in fact, precisely the opposite of the masculine. Today, when for the first time in human history it really seems possible that those endless housewifely tasks~-which, along with bearing and rearing of children, have always been enough to fill the whole of each day for the average woman-may virtually be eliminated; today, when at last women might seem to be in a position to begin to be both feminine and fully developed, creative human beings; today, these same women are being subjected to pressures from many sides to return to the traditional feminine niche and to devote themselves wholly to the tasks of nurture, support, and service of their families. One might expect the theologians that they at least not add to these pressures. One might even expect them to support and encourage the women who desire to be both a woman and an individual in her own right, a separate person some part of whose mind and feelings are inviolable, some part of whose time belongs strictly to herself, in whose house there is, to use Virginia Woolf's marvelous image, "a room of one's own." Yet theology, to the extent that it has defined the human condition on the basis of masculine experience, continues to speak of such desires as sin 'or temptation to sin. If such women believe the theologians, she will try to strange those impulses in herself. She will believe that having chosen marriage and children and thus being face to face with the needs of her family for love, refreshment, and forgiveness, she has no right to ask anything for herself but must submit without qualification to the strictly feminine role.

Gayraud S. Wilmore and James H. Cone, Black Theology: A Documentary History, 1966:1979, Orbis Books, N.Y., 1982

Theressa Hoover, Black Women and the Churches: Triple Jeopardy, p.377-387 excerpts.

To be a women, black and active in religious institutions in the American scene is a labor under triple jeopardy. Women constitute a very small number of persons in political office at all levels of the nation's life. Religiously, though they compromise more than 50 percent of the churches' membership, they are by no means at the higher levels of decision-making. In the churches, women are by far the largest supporting groups in our religious institutions, and, in the black church. They are the very backbone. Also, the women were truly the glue that held the churches together. They were present at midweek prayer services, the Monday afternoon missionary services, Sunday morning, afternoon, and evening preaching services.

Judith Hole and Ellen Levine in their book "Rebirth of Feminism" say:

> Feminist activities within the Christian community most often fall into three categories: (1) challenging the theological view of women; (2) challenging the religious laws and/or customs that bar women from ordination; (3) demanding that the professional status and salaries of women in the church be upgraded.

These categories may apply to the total feminist movement in the churches, but do not yet reflect the view of many black women. First, the economic necessity of the black woman's efforts on behalf of her church has not pressured her to the point of accepting the prevailing theological view of women. When she gets a little release from church pressures, she will look beyond her local church and realize that such theological views and practices are operative both in her exclusion from doctrinal decision-making and in her absence from national representation.

Second, in the predominantly black churches women are not excluded from ordination by law, though they may be in practice. In many ways, she has been the most oppressed and the least vocal. She has given the most, and gotten the least. She has shown tremendous faithfulness to the spirit of the church. Her foresight, ingenuity, and "stick-to-itiveness" have kept many black churches open, many preachers fed, many parsonages livable. She has gathered unto herself the children of the community, she has washed them, combed their hair, fed them and told them Bible stories. In short, she has been their missionary, the substitute mother, their teacher. Many leaders of the present-day black church owe their commitment to the early influence of such a black woman.

With such a heritage of strength and faith, black women in the churches today must continue strong in character and faith. They must teach other sisters to work within the "walls" of the church, challenging theological pacesetters and church bureaucrats; they also must ever be aware of their infinite worth, their godliness in the midst of creatureliness, and their having been freed from the triple barriers of sex, race, and church into a community of believers.

Wilmore, Gayraud S. and Cone, James H., Black Theology: A Documentary History, 1966-1979, Orbis Books, N.Y., 1982

Grant, Jacquelyn, "Black Theology and the Black Woman," pp. 418-431.

Liberation theologians assert that the reigning theologies of the West have been used to legitimate the established order. Those to whom the church has entrusted the task of interpreting the meaning of God's activity in the world have been too content to represent the ruling classes.

In examining Black Theology it is necessary to make one of two assumptions: (1) either Black women have no place in the enterprise, or (2) Black men are capable of speaking for us. Both of these assumptions are false and need to be discarded. They arise out of a male-dominated culture that restricts women to certain areas of society. In such a culture, men are given the warrant to speak for women on all matters of significance. It is no accident that all of the recognized Black theologians are men. This is what might be expected given the status and power accorded the discipline of theology. Professional theology is done by those who are highly trained. It requires, moreover, mastery of that power most accepted in the definition of manhood, the power, or ability to "reason." This is supposedly what opens the door to participation in logical, philosophical debates and discussions presupposing rigorous intellectual training, for most of history, outside the "women's sphere." Whereas the nature of men has been defined in terms of reason and the intellect, that of women has to do with intuition and emotionalism. Women were limited to matters related to the home while men carried out the more important work, involving the use of rational faculties. Black males have gradually increased their power and participation in the male-dominated society, while Black females have continued to endure the stereotypes and oppressions of an earlier period. By self-appointment, or by the sinecure of a male-dominated society, Black

113

men have deemed it proper to speak for the entire Black community, male and female.

In a sense, Black men's acceptance of the patriarchal model is logical and to be expected. Black male slaves were unable to reap the benefits of patriarchy. Before emancipation they were not given the opportunity to serve as protectors and providers for Black women and children, as White men were able to do for their women and children. Much of what was considered "manhood" had to do with how well one could perform these functions. It seems only natural that post-emancipation Black men would View as primary importance the reclaiming of their property--their women and their children. Moreover, it is natural that Black men would claim their "natural" right to the "man's world." But it should be emphasized that this is logical and natural only if one has accepted without question the terms and values of patriarchy--the concept of male control and supremacy.

Like all oppressed peoples the self-image of Blacks has suffered damage. In addition, they have not been in control of their own destiny. It is the goal of the Black liberation struggle to change radically the socioeconomic and political conditions of Black people by inculcating self-love, self-control, self-reliance, and political power. The concepts of self-love, self-control, self-reliance, and political participation certainly have broad significance for Black women, even though they were taught that, by virtue of their sex, they had to be completely dependent on man; yet while their historical situation reflected the need for dependence, the powerlessness of Black men made it necessary for them to seek those values for themselves.

Racism and sexism are interrelated just as all forms of oppression are interrelated. Sexism, however, has a reality and significance of its own because it represents that peculiar form of oppression suffered by Black women at the hands of Black men. It is important to examine this reality of sexism as it operated in both the Black community and the Black Church.

If the liberation of women is not proclaimed, the church's proclamation cannot be about divine liberation. If the church does not share in the liberation struggle of Black women, its liberation struggle is, not authentic. If women are oppressed, the church, the church cannot possibly be a "visible manifestation that the gospel is a reality"--for the gospel cannot be real in that context. One can see the contradictions between the church's language or proclamation of liberation and its action by looking both at the status of Black women in the church as laity and Black women in the ordained ministry of the church.

It is often said that women are the "backbone" of the church. On the surface, this may appear to be a compliment, especially when one considers the function of the backbone in the human anatomy. Theressa Hoover prefers to use the term "glue" to describe the function of women in the Black Church. In any case, the telling portion of the word backbone is "back." It has become apparent to me that most of the ministers who use this term have reference to location rather than function. What they really mean is that women are in the "background" and should be kept there. They are merely support workers. This is borne out by my observation that in many churches, women are consistently given responsibilities in the kitchen, while men are elected or appointed to the important boards and leadership positions. While decisions and policies may be discussed in the kitchen, they are certainly not made there.

The conspiracy to keep women relegated to the background is also aided by the continuous psychological and political strategizing that keeps women from realizing their own potential power in the church. Not only are they rewarded for performance in "backbone" or supportive positions, but they are penalized for trying to move from the backbone to the head position--the leadership of the church. It is by considering the distinction between prescribed support positions and the policy-making, leadership positions that the oppression of Black women in the Black Church can be seen more clearly. For the most part, men have monopolized the ministry as a profession. The ministry of women as fully ordained clergy persons has always been controversial. The Black church fathers were unable to see the injustices of their own practices, even when they paralleled the injustices in the White Church against which they rebelled.

The oppression of women in the ministry took many forms. In addition to not being granted ordination, the authenticity of "the call" of women was frequently put to the test. Several Black denominations have begun to ordain women. But this matter of women preachers having the extra burden of proving their call to an extent not required of men still prevails in the Black Church today. A study at Union Theological Seminary in New York City bears this out.

Interviews with Black ministers of different denominations revealed that their prejudices against women, and especially women in the ministry, resulted in unfair expectations and unjust treatment of women ministers whom they encountered.

It is the unfair expectations placed upon Women and blatant discrimination that keeps them "in the pew" and "out of the pulpit."

The failure of the Black Church and Black Theology to proclaim explicitly the liberation of Black women indicates that they cannot claim to be agents of divine liberation. If the theology, like the church, has no word for Black women, its conception of liberation is unauthentic.

There is a tradition which declares that God is at work in the experience of Black women. This tradition in the context of the total Black experience can provide data for the development of a holistic Black Theology. Such a theology will repudiate the God of classical theology who is presented as an absolute Patriarch, a deserting father who created Black men and women and then "walked out" in the face of responsibility. Such a theology will look at the meaning of the total Jesus Christ Event; it will consider not only how God through Jesus Christ is related to the oppressed men, but to women as well. Such a theology will "allow" God through the Holy Spirit to work through persons without regard to race, sex, or class.

Black women have to keep the issue of sexism "going" in the Black community, in the Black Church, and in Black Theology until it has been eliminated. To do otherwise means that they will be pushed aside until eternity.

MOVING TOWARD CHANGE

THE TRADITIONAL VIEW OF WOMEN IN MINISTRY

THE CHURCH OF GOD IN CHRIST

ROBERT LEE ASBERRY

The historical position of the Church of God in Christ on the role of women in the ministry is clearly and comprehensively stated in the official manual.1 A perusal of those pages will demonstrate that the church has never been anti-woman. Rather, the church has recognized from Scripture and church history the vital place that women have had in the ministry.

The critics of the church's traditional position on women in ministry must take a hard look at the word tradition from a biblical perspective. The Greek word "paradosis" means something over (or along) received intact and to be passed on just as it was received in the first place. Paul speaks of his instruction about Christian behavior as a "tradition received of us" and he also urged the brethren to "stand fast and hold the traditions which ye have been taught," whether by our word or our epistle. (2 Thessalonians 3:6; 2 Thessalonians 2:15.)

The word tradition or a form of it is used in Paul's instructions on women in 1Cor.11:2. The King James Version uses the word "ordinance." The NIV uses the teachings which are much too weak. The Greek word, as alluded to earlier, is the plural "paradosis" (traditions), the same as in 2 Thessalonians 2:15 and 3:6. The verb "delivered" in 1 Corinthians 11:2 is parallel to "taught" and "received" in 2 Thessalonians 2 and 3.

Tradition, as used above, is much more formal and important than casual words or incidental expressions of opinions, but rather "the form of sound words" "to be held fast" 2 Tim.1:13. In some spiritual matters, Paul was very rigid. Among these were traditions associated with preaching, ruling, and observance of the Lord's Supper in the Christian assembly (1 Cor. 11:2, 20-22, 34). He set forth a definite "paradosis" ("ordinance", "tradition") and order (the Greek word is "taxis", "a prescribed arrangement" 1 Cor. 11:34). Thus, those who say we should jettison our tradition have no support from Scripture.

As mentioned previously, the Church of God in Christ has never been opposed to women being involved in ministry. The Bible is replete with numerous and lumin0us examples of godly, devoted, and dedicated women who have been used by God to bring about meaningful changes. The Old Testament seems to support the traditional view of the role of women in leadership and ministry. We have the biblical story of Barak and Deborah and Jael in Judges 4 and 5. Deborah does not set a precedent. The judges before and after her were men. There are a few prophetesses mentioned. They are exceptional, and no books of scriptural prophecy came from them. The priesthood was wholly composed of the male descendants of Aaron, the brother of Moses. Every facet of the theocratic system of the Old Testament was presided over by men.

In addition to the above-mentioned women, Miriam, the sister of Moses, is called a prophetess (Exodus 15:20-21; Micah 6:4). Women who were skilled voluntarily contributed their possessions and worked with their hands in constructing the Tabernacle (Exodus 35:21-22, 25-26). Women served in the doorway of the Tabernacle. The same word for service was used for the Levites (Exodus 38:3; 1 Samuel 22:22). Abigail rescued her household by demonstrating great courage and initiative. She gave David wise counsel, calling him back to God, thereby saving him from taking murderous revenge (1 Samuel 9,16). Josiah was sent to Huldah, the prophetess, for God's directions, even though both Jeremiah and Zephaniah, also prophets of the Lord, were living in Jerusalem at the same time (2 Kings 22:11-20). The book of Esther tells the story of a courageous young woman who risked her life and comfortable position to save her people.

As we come to the New Testament, women are very prominent in the ministry of Jesus and the work of the early church. Jesus taught women spiritual truths (Luke 10:38-41; John 4:11:1-44). Women supported Jesus from their private wealth. He allowed women to travel with Him during His public ministry (Matthew 27:552 Luke 8: 1-3). Jesus considered women to be competent witnesses (Luke 24:9-11).

He gave women the responsibility of being the first to testify to His resurrection. He forgave women and offered them new life (John 4:1-42: 8:1-ll). He healed women and men. (Luke 4:38-39; 8:40-56,13:10-17; John 11:1-44; Luke 6:6o10).

A study of the early church will show the varied duties that women performed. Women were present at Pentecost (Acts 2:1-4). Women like Lydia and Priscilla hosted early church meetings. (The book of Acts contains the names of thirty-three women who were involved in some form of ministry). Dorcas was called a disciple, a helper of widows and the poor, and someone who used her homemaking skills (Acts 9). Philip's four daughters were prophetesses (Acts 1238-9). Euodia and Syntyche were women who "contended" at Paul's side for the gospel (Philippians 422-3). The sixteenth chapter of Romans mentions ten women, eight by name, and others are included in general phrases, such as "the house-hold of Stephanos." Phoebe was called a servant. Mary, Tryphena, Tryphosa, and Persis worked hard in the Lord (Rom. 6,12). Rufus' mother was like a mother to Paul (v.13) Obviously, women were active in public worship in the church at Corinth. (1 Corinthians 11:5).

The Old and New Testaments clearly demonstrated the prominent place that women have held in the ministry. Therefore, a balance must be maintained between rigid legalism that has too often characterized male leadership in fundamentalism. On the other hand, one must guard against the casual license that seeks to restructure the Scripture in order to accommodate modern trends. The essence of the debate seems to revolve around headship and submission, prophecy, preaching, and ordination. Also, a distinction must be made between a spiritual gift and an office. The issue or conflict must be resolved on biblical grounds and not by contemporary trends. The Bible is the final authority on doctrine and practice.

We must look at some of the problematic passages that bear upon women in ministry. The prophecy of Joel 2:28-32 as quoted in Acts 2:14-21 has been used to support the notion that women should preach as well as men. There are at least four views on this passage. First, Pentecost fulfillment: The prophecy of Joel was completely fulfilled on the day of Pentecost (J. Alexander, F.F. Bruce, Henderson, Lenski, Young, Allis, Ellison, Pusey). One of the seven arguments against this view is that numerous kinds of people did not prophesy, dream dreams, and have visions on the day of Pentecost. Second, Continuous fulfillment: Joel's prophecy was partially fulfilled on the day of Pentecost and is being fulfilled in the present age and will be finally fulfilled at the Second Advent (Blanc, Freeman, Torrey). One of the five arguments opposing this view is that Joel does not refer to speaking in tongues. Though prophesying was done by a few in Acts, it was not widespread ("on all mankind") and was a gift that was to be done away with (1 Cor. 13:8). Dreams and visions were not exercised extensively in Acts, and are not needed today. To suggest that prophesying, dreams, and visions are for today is to open up the biblical canon for additional revelation. Third, Partial fulfillment: Joel's prophecy was fulfilled on the day of Pentecost and will also be fulfilled at Christ's Second Advent (Pentecost, Walvoord). One of the five arguments opposing this view is that Joel said the outpouring of the Holy Spirit will come after Israel repents, whereas in Acts the order was reversed (the outpouring of the Holy Spirit came on the eleven apostles before the 3,000 repented, Acts 2:4 and 33). Furthermore, the 3,000 who were saved did not prophesy, see visions, and dream dreams: and their repentance did not result in millennial blessings. The fourth view is Eschatological fulfillment: Joel's prophecy was not fulfilled on the day of Pentecost. It was used by Peter homiletically and will be fulfilled at the Second Advent (Gaebelein, Ryrie, Feinberg). The critics of this view say New Testament writers did not always use the normal fulfillment formula.

At this point, I would like to summarize the research of two Old Testament scholars on Joel 2:28-32. Charles Lee Feinberg noted scholar, writer, and teacher. The events set forth are placed chronologically in that time designated as "afterward." According to Hosea 3:5, it is coupled with "in the latter days." The prophet is speaking of the latter days for Israel, a period that covers both the Tribulation period and the reign of the Messiah which follows it. Next, the outpouring is upon all flesh. Despite the differences of opinion, all Israel is included. third, differences of age (young and old), sex (sons and daughters), or position (servants and handmaids) will constitute no barrier nor hindrance to this gift of prophecy was given to a slave. Finally, Feinberg concludes that Peter used Joel's prophecy as an illustration of what was transpiring in his day and not as a fulfillment of this prediction. A recent Old Testament scholar comments by saying, "All inhabitants of Judah, regardless of gender, age, or social status, would experience this outpouring." He further states that the recipients of the Spirit would exercise prophetic gifts, fulfilling Moses' desire that "all the Lord's people" might prophesy under the control of God's Spirit" Numbers 11:29). In conclusion, he gives the following principles: 1. The outpouring of the Spirit on Pentecost was not 'nearly as all-inclusive as that envisioned by Joel. 2. Nothing even remotely similar to the cosmic signs of verses 30-31 took place. 3. Peter was anticipating the soon return of Christ in response to national repentance on the part of the Jews (Acts 3:19-20). The noted evangelical theologian Charles C. Ryrie says, "Is prophesying by both sexes is to be characteristic of the church, then so should be the other things in the passage like "blood, and fire, and vapor smoke,... the sun...turned into darkness." Thus, on the day of Pentecost, the Holy Spirit descended on women and men but the preaching was done by a man, Peter.

Another key biblical passage that has caused much controversy is Galatians 3:28. Evangelical feminists consider this to be one of the key texts in the New Testament. Paul K. Jewett calls this the Magna Carta of Humanity. He considers this to be the last word on Christian liberty. Letha Dawson Sconzoni and Nancy A. Hardesty, leading proponents of the equality of the sexes have this to say in light of this passage, "All social distinctions between men and women should be erased. The spirit of egalitarianism is the impetus behind the evangelical feminist movement." On the other hand, the traditionalists believe that those who espouse this position have not accurately understood the teachings of the Bible. Thus, the meaning of the passage can only be determined by looking carefully at the context and careful exegesis.

The apostle Paul based his teaching on the roles for women from the Creation and Fall narratives of Genesis 1-3. He does this in this passage and others: 1 Corinthians 1137-12; I Timothy 2:11-15: and 1 Corinthians 14:34. Genesis 1:26-28 demonstrates that man and woman are in the image of God. Thus, it would seem like Paul, in Galatians 3:28, is emphasizing the unity of male and female.

If one looks at the context of Galatians 3:28, he/she will discover that Paul is discussing the nature of justification and how one may be included in the Abrahamic Covenant. The entrance into the covenant is by faith and not by works. Faith is the great equalizer. All believers; Jew/Gentile, slave/free, male/female are justified by faith and are made heirs of the promise. In Christ's offer of salvation, there is no distinction. It seems that Paul is arguing that no kind of person is excluded from the position of being a child of Abraham who has faith in Jesus Christ.

The evangelical feminist fails to make a distinction between equality of essence and equality of functions-there is no place in the church for class distinction. There is a place for role differences. In essence, every woman is equal to every man. When it comes to our equality in the kingdom of God, men and women are equal but they do not have the same function. There is a functional difference. No woman should have to ask for equal rights. She has them automatically. She has God ordained equality. Every woman is equal to every man.

There are some basic flaws in the position of evangelical feminists. First, their attempt to reinterpret the Bible leads to ambivalence, bias, conflict, and error. Galatians 3:28 is making a fundamental theological statement about the equality of man and woman in their standing before God and not about how male/female relationships should be conducted in society. Second, there is a distortion of the biblical worldview. God is the source of the very concept of authority and hierarchy (Rom.l3:1). Third, there is a substitution of humanism for a biblical worldview. (Rom.1:18-32).

In 1 Corinthians 11:2-16, Paul has an interesting and perplexing discussion about women praying and prophesying. The passage presents a thorny problem because of the combination of theology and practical exhortation. The issue centers around whether or not the commands are "culturally universal" or "culturally limited." Some religious groups interpret them to be universal and therefore insist on women wearing hats or handkerchiefs. Others see them as relating to the particular day in which Paul lived with certain theological overtones for today.

Since context is crucial to the interpretation of a passage, this section must be placed in a proper perspective. Contextually, 1 Corinthians 11:2-16 begins a section on the proper exercise of Christian liberty in the church service. While a believer is not bound by the law, there are certain things he or she must consider as proper and improper. After a discussion on the concept of head and wearing veils, the apostle addresses the phrase "praying and prophesying."

The mentioning of "praying and prophesying" seems to indicate that women were allowed some service in the public meeting of the church. Some of the more reputable Greek exegetes take the position that this refers to public worship. According to Oscar Cullman, there is a difference between prophecy and preaching. Preaching and teaching, he says, are founded on an intelligible exposition of the Word of God, whereas prophecy is based on προφήτης (revelation).

In the New Testament, the verb form, προφητεύω, is used twenty-eight times and it always has (with the possible exception of John 11:51) the idea of revelation flowing from God. Paul uses it eleven times. He uses it nine times in 1 Corinthians

12:14 and 'two times in 1 Corinthians 14:45. The noun propheteia ($\pi \varrho o \varphi \eta \tau \varepsilon i \alpha$) is used nineteen times in the New Testament. Paul uses it once in Romans 12:6 and five times in 1 Corinthians 12-14. The consistent New Testament idea is that a prophecy is an actual message or oracle from God. The word is not used in the New Testament to refer to the interpretation of an oracle by a skillful interpreter. In short, prophecy in Paul cannot denote anything other than inspired speech. And prophecy as charisma is neither skill nor aptitude nor talent; the charisma is the actual speaking forth of words given by the Spirit in a particular situation and ceases when the words cease.

Another writer who seems to make a distinction between prophecy and preaching is Grudem. He attempts to prove this in several ways. First, he states that the gift of prophecy in the New Testament Church had less authority than apostolic teaching. The Old Testament men were able to speak and write with absolute divine authority, (Deut.18:18-20; Jer.l:9:Num.22:38). In the New Testament, the men who spoke and wrote were no longer called prophets by Jesus. They were called apostles. Paul uses two different construction when talking about apostles and prophets in Eph.4:11. Second, a spontaneous "revelation" made prophecy different from teaching. God brought things spontaneously to a person's mind which he called revelation. Third, no human speech that is called teaching is based on a revelation. Teaching is simply an explanation or application of Scripture. Fourth, those who prophesied in the New Testament Church did not have the same authority as those who taught the word of God. Those who prophesied did not tell the church how to interpret and apply Scripture to life. They did not proclaim the doctrinal and ethical standards by which the church was guided nor did they exercise governing authority in the church. Finally, we read in Acts 21:9 that Philip's four unmarried daughters prophesied. They are mentioned only in passing, but it is interesting to note that there is no record of their speaking with absolute divine authority or any words of Scripture written by them or by any other prophets who were ordinary believers in the local New Testament Church.

The passage in 1 Corinthians 14:33-35 seems to be diametrically opposed to 1 Corinthians 11:2-16. The previous one talks about women praying and prophesying. Here women are admonished to keep silent. Over the years, scholars have attempted to solve what seemed like a contradiction. First, these verses are said to be an interpolation. Second, the activities of 11:5 are merely mentioned, not condoned, and they are disallowed in 14:34. Third, praying and prophesying are not the same activity as speaking or teaching and therefore are allowed by Paul. They do not challenge the authority or leadership of men, so they are not restricted. Fourth, there are two types of service: public service for all and a private service for believers only. Paul allowed women to participate in the latter but not in the former. Finally, the problem of 14:34 deals with a specific difficulty in the Corinthian situation, namely with the tendency of the women' to interrupt the dialogue section of the service with wide, edifying questions. Paul refuses to allow this activity in this situation but does not give a blanket refusal to women's participation in the service.

Obviously, the apostle was not calling for the absolute silence of women. The issue he is addressing is coming together to minister with spiritual gifts. Two interpretations seem to be plausible. First, Paul prohibits women from speaking out to teach men in the assembly and so (14:34) is parallel to I Timothy 2. Second, Paul prohibits women from evaluating the various messages of the prophets in the assembly since this would be an exercise of authority reserved for elders. Allen P. Ross has offered the following solution. He says, "...the woman could speak in the assembly if she did not have the authority to say what she wished, but gave a divine utterance."

THIS IS A GREAT MYSTERY... CHRIST AND THE CHURCH EPHESIANS 5:32

(EDITOR'S NOTE: THE PSALMIST DECLARES IN 'PSALM 119189 THAT
"FOREVER, OH LORD, THY WORD IS SETTLED IN HEAVEN".) OUR MISSION
IS VERY AMBITIOUS; ONE FRAUGHT WITH MANY DANGERS. WHO CAN
SAY WITH ANY CERTAIN'IY THAT HE ALONE "KNOWETH THE MIND OF
GOD". ONLY A FOOL TAMPERS WITH THE SCRIPTURE. PETER. CALLED
THEM "UNSTABLE"; WHO. . ." WREST THE SCRIPTURE TO THEIR OWN
DESTRUCTION"... GOD'S EDICTS ARE IMMUTABLE AND WE ARE NOT TO
DEBATE THEM BUT RATHER OBEY THEM. ABRAHAM, IN HEBREWS 11:8
"BY FAITH...OBEYED GOD; SO. I ENDEAVOR TO STAND ON EVERY WORD
OF GOD WHETHER I UNDERSTAND IT OR NOT.
SO MY COLLEAGUES, HERE'S MY RESEARCH. READ IT PRAYERFULLY, AND
BY ALL MEANS, CRITIQUE IT. LET'S DEBATE THE ISSUES; BUT, OUR
CONCLUSIONS MUST REMAIN TRUE TO THE SCRIPTURE. FOR "THE
SCRIPTURE CANNOT BE BROKEN". . .

W.E. Bogan

12/27/93

God's Basis for His Ordering of Men and Women

We learn from Genesis chapter 2 that man was first created, and then from Adam's rib, God made the woman and brought her unto man to be a helpmeet for him.

1 Corinthians 11:8-12 "For man is not of woman, but woman of man. For also man was not created for the sake of the woman; but woman for the sake of the man. Therefore, ought the woman to have an outward sign of man's authority on her head on account of the angels. However, neither (is) woman without man, nor man without woman in (the) Lord. For as the woman (is) of the man, so also (is) the man by the woman, but all things of God" (Trans). Here is an exquisitely guarded and balanced presentation of the truth of the relationship between man and woman.

The very fact that woman was taken out of man proves her equality with him-She is not his inferior, but his equal, his helpmeet. There is equality, but with it, diversity. Woman was made for man, to be with him at his side. God never intended for woman to be an independent creature apart from man, but that she should be associated with him, and that together they should be one flesh and tuplify Christ and His Bride, the Church. Woman never shines more brightly than when fulfilling the object for which she was created, which primarily was to be man's helpmeet.

However, we must notice the fact that the woman was made of the man indicates that man is her head. This is the deduction which the Spirit of God brings before us in the above quoted verses of 1 Corinthians 11:10. Therefore (in view of her place in creation), because of her place in creation, she should have a covering on her head as a token or symbol of her submission to his authority, that she may show the proper reverence to her head just as do observing angels to their head which is God (1 Corinthians 11:10).

The apostle says, "I would have you know, that the head of every man is Christ; and the head of the woman is the man" (verse 3). Because of this divine order in creation, woman is to recognize man's headship and to have on her head the sign of his authority over her, that is, a covering on her head, especially when she prays or prophesies and when she is in the Assembly (verses.5-10). The angels are to behold God's order in creation and the church.

Our purpose here is not to give a disposition of the wrongness of women being .in church without their heads covered but, I only refer to this now in connection with her place in creation and its consequent recognition of man as the head, which the head covering signifies according to Scripture.

In 1 Corinthians 11:14-15, the apostle refers to nature as further evidence of the distinction between man and woman and of her proper place of subjection. "Doth not even nature itself teach you, that man, if he has long hair, is a dishonor to him? But woman, if she has long hair, it is a glory to her; for the long hair is given to her in place of a veil" (New Trans.) God has given long hair to women and shorthair to man as a distinguishing mark between them. It is natural for women to have long hair and for men to have short hair.

Long hair is generally in Scripture a symbol of dependence, submission, and of that modesty that becomes woman as "the weaker vessel" to which man is to give honor (1 Pet. 3:7). The passage before us in chapter 5 of Corinthians speaks of a woman's hair as her glory.

A woman only manifests the glory and beauty put upon her when she abides in her God-given role of dependence and subjection and maintains her feminine posture. The more feminine woman is, the more beautiful and pleasing to God she is. The more beautiful and pleasing to God she is. The more woman tries to appear like a man and to take his place, the more she loses her true beauty and distinctive uniqueness.

The expression "Doth not even nature itself teach you?" is capable of wide application to our present subject-The natural constitution and temperament of man and woman is quite diverse. God in His wisdom put great differences in the physical, mental, and emotional makeup of man and woman. He has given man generally greater height, strength and in happy contrast has given woman natural grace, gentleness, and mental nimbleness, fitting her especially for the domestic circle-The Creator has most evidently so constituted men and women by nature to fill distinct and separate roles, yet to be supplementary to each other.

Thus we learn from creation and nature that woman has a distinct role from that of man in society, and we shall see that her God-given role in the Church is in harmony with her place in creation and nature. We will find that her place in creation fixes her role in the church as well and that her place in nature is illustrative of her role in grace, or her relation as a Christian woman to God. The two are inseparable. God does not give women or men a role in the church which is contrary to their place in creation and nature.

DIFFERENCES DUE TO CREATION

"God said, Let Us make man in Our image, according to Our likeness, and let them rule over the fish of the sea and over the birds of the sky and over the cattle and over all the earth and over every creeping thing that creeps on the earth. And God created man in His image, in the image of God He created him: male and female He created them. And God blessed them; and God said to them, Be fruitful and multiply and fill the earth and subdue it" (Gen-1:26-28).

"Then the Lord God formed man of dust from the ground and breathed into his nostrils the breath of life, and man became a living being...Then the Lord said, It is not good for the man to be alone. I will make him a helper suitable for (corresponding to) him...but for Adam, there was not found a helper suitable for him. So the Lord God caused a deep sleep to fall upon the man, and he slept; then

132

He took one of his ribs and closed up the flesh at that place. And the Lord God fashioned into a woman the rib which He had taken from the man and brought her to the man. And the man said, "This is now bone of my bones and flesh of my flesh. She shall be called 'woman' because she was taken out of man. For this cause, a man shall leave his father and mother and shall cleave to his wife and they shall become one flesh" (Gen. 2:7,18, 20, 21-24).

"It was Adam who was first created and then Eve" (I Timothy 2:13).

"I want you to understand that Christ is the head of every man and the man is the head of a woman and God is the head of Christ (as man)... for man does not originate from woman's sake, but woman for the man's sake" (1 Cor-11:3, 8-9).

These verses give God's simple order as a result of creation. Man was created before the woman. The woman was created to be the man's helper, to be the perfect complement and companion for him, physically, emotionally, and spiritually. Although not exactly said in Scripture, the woman in fulfilling her role undoubtedly finds her husband to be her perfect complement to round out her life. Each needs the other to be a well-rounded, fulfilled person. Without the other partner, there is a certain emptiness, a certain incompleteness.

Even though men and women equally were created to be representatives of God on earth, being in His "image", and both resembled God ("likeness") in the sense of being creatures with a spirit and thus able to have intelligence and a God consciousness, God's order in creation dictated that the man was to be in charge and his wife was to be his helper. Thus, the man is the "head" of the woman. He is to give direction and control in the family and also is responsible for sustaining the family-These are the three thoughts behind the term "headship".

Does this divine order make the woman a slave, an inferior being, a second-class citizen? No more than being a colonel makes the person personally inferior to a general! The colonel may be a nicer and more brilliant person than the general, yet the colonel recognizes the superior rank the government has given to the general. He thus intelligently, willfully submits himself to the general. in like manner, the Christian woman submits to her husband, even though she may be more intelligent, better educated, or whatever, simply because it is God's ordering.

A major difference between the colonel-general relationship and the husband-wife relationship is the matter of "love." It should remove any thought of slavery or lack of consideration of the wife on the husband's part. In fact, Christianity elevates womanhood: in most countries where Christianity is not prominent, women often are hardly more than slaves. Although the fact still remains that the woman was created to be her husband's unique helper, she was taken from his side, his bosom, to be loved and cherished. She was not taken from his head to rule over him or ever have equality in headship, nor was she taken from his feet to be trampled upon as if her feelings and suggestions were not important. Rather, like two piles of a sheet of plywood, there is to be a cleaving, a joining, a gluing together in the bond of marriage between two individuals so that they become one completely new family unit in love, each one giving strength and substance to the other.

THE FALL - Pt. 1

Having seen from creation that a woman's role is one of subjection to her head and companionship with him, we will now consider what part she had in the fall of humanity in the Garden of Eden, and what role she was given in consequence thereof. From the divine account in Genesis 3, we learn that the serpent tempted Mother Eve. to take of the forbidden fruit and that she was the one who ate it and also gave it to her husband who likewise ate of it (verses 1 and 6). Because of this, God said to Eve, "In sorrow, thou shalt bring forth children; and thy husband, and he shall rule over thee" (Gen. 3:16).

Here We see the first woman, taking the lead and leaving her natural place of dependence. And instead of repelling the serpent's advances, and seeking to help and protection of her God-given head, she acted in independence and was beguiled by the serpent into disobedience of God's Command. God definitely pronounced therefore, that her role was to be one of subordination to her husband.

The Spirit of God refers to this deception of Eve by Satan in I Timothy 2:11-14 and gives it as a reason why women in this present church age are not to usurp authority over the man. There we read: "Let the woman learn in silence with all subjection. But I suffer not a woman to teach, nor to usurp authority over the man, but to be in science. For Adam was first formed, then Eve. And Adam was not deceived, but the woman being deceived was in the transgression."

Here we have two reasons for why a woman is not to teach in the church. One is Adam's first place in creation, implying headship, and the other, that the woman was deceived by the serpent. Adam was not deceived like the woman; he sinned with his eyes open and was more guilty than his wife but it was Eve who was deceived. Such was her part in the fall of humanity, and since she proved herself a bad leader in this respect, in God's wise government she is barred from the place of authority or teaching in the church. Thus, here we get the first and most powerful warning against women taking the lead. It is surely a vivid warning signal at the very start of man's journey across the sea of time.

As another has observed: "When women get out of their place, they appear to be the special prey of the devil. It is a woman in the parable, who introduced the leaven into the three measures of meal. (Mt. 13:33)-type of the introduction of corrupting principles which have permeated the Christian profession. it was a woman-Eve-who was 'in the transgression.'

"They are 'silly woman laden with sins, led away with diverse lusts', who are led captive by evil men in the perilous times of the last days (2 Tim. 3:6). It is a woman-Jezebel-who stands historically in the Old Testament pages as an example of all that is disgusting and wicked; who stands figuratively in Revelation as the example of ecclesiastical corruption and religious depravity of the worst type (I Kings 21; Rev. 2:20).

"In the present day the great majority of spiritualist mediums are women; modern spiritism began with women the Fox sisters in America. It was a hysterical woman, Mrs. White, who by her blasphemous pretensions has been the leader, and largely the inventor, of that wicked system-Seventh Day Adventism.

"Christian Science-which is neither Christian nor scientific-owes its origin to Mrs. Eddy a woman".

This is not indeed to slight woman, for morally she is generally of finer qualities than man and usually exceeds him in affection and devotion to Christ. Nor is it a question here of a woman's ability, for compared with man, she manifests no inferiority of genius, culture, tact, speech, etc. it is only positionally that man is above woman. The point we wish to emphasize here is this: that when a woman departs from her God-given role and sphere of service and takes the place of teaching and leading, she often becomes the special victim of Satan's deceptions and the propagator of his falsehoods and heresies. This is the lesson we should learn from Eve in the Garden of Eden and from woman's subsequent history.

On the other hand, when a woman abides in her God-given place, she is a most effective power for good, and her presence and power in the service of Christ are, under God, vitally essential to the success and continuance of the Church. The Bible is full of examples of godly, faithful, and devoted women who performed great services for God in their divinely appointed spheres.

Gathering up what has been before us, we may summarize it thus: Because Eve was deceived by Satan and took the lead in the act of the first sin, as a consequence, the woman was put in the governmental dealings of God, in a place of subordination to man, and she is to learn in silence with all subjection and is never to exercise authority over man. This is what we've learned about a woman's scriptural role because of her part in the fall of humanity in Eden. And this divinely two appointed status remains unchanged in the present church period of Grace. Furthermore, woman's history has only proven the wisdom and justice of the circumscription of her sphere as imposed by God.

THE FALL - Pt 2

Sadly, the woman (Eve) soon usurped the place of headship which belonged to her husband. She made a vital decision without involving Adam until it was too late. Genesis 3:1-6 records her sad downfall, as well as her husband's. Satan craftily got Eve to question, to think emotionally about what God had said (v 1). The forbidden fruit then quickly became her new center (v.3, cf-2:9) instead of God and her husband. She thus became spiritually "eccentric" – off her true writer. She also weakened and added to God's warning about the forbidden fruit (v.3, cf-2:17)-Satan had her right where he wanted her! He thus boldly contradicted God and told her that God was withholding something good from her (verses 4-5). Verse 6 records her fateful decision and her involvement of her husband who likewise sinned, but willfully, and also fell, bringing sin into the world (Rom. 5:12-19) and its consequence, death. Adam failed in his headship just as Eve failed in her submission to her husband.

When God confronted them with their sin, Adam blamed" God and his wife (v.12) – a common excuse men still use to justify their failure to take responsibility and headship-At least Eve was more honest about it (v.13), although she didn't admit to or confess her real problem of usurping the place of headship. God then pronounced His judgment on them both, but promised that through the woman's seed, a redeemer would come (fulfilled in the Lord's virgin birth), and then reinforced the instructions concerning the place that Eve should have taken as the helper to her husband. God said, "In pain, you shall bring forth children, yet your desire shall be for your husband and he shall rule over you" (Genesis 3:16). Please read that whole third chapter.

This ordering of the sexes, begun at creation, was designed by God for a purpose. it is necessary for the smooth operation of the family, for whenever people work together, there must be a chain of command for the work to function smoothly, even if administered in genuine love.

Differences Due to The Sexes Picturing Christ And His Church

Neither Adam nor Eve nor anyone else in Old Testament times knew that God's ordering of the sexes in creation looked forward thousands of years to show forth to the world and even to angels the truth that God was going to have a. "bride" for that Redeemer who would come through "the woman's seed" – the Lord Jesus Christ-and that "bride" would be "the fulness (completeness) of Him who fills all in all" (Eph. 1:23), just as Eve was to be the fullness or completeness of her husband, Adam.

God has ordained that men and women are to picture Christ and His Church as they conduct themselves collectively in relation to God's Church, fulfilling essentially the same roles as husband and wife. Their proper conduct will show forth "the manifold wisdom of God, (that it) might now be made known through the Church to the rulers and authorities in the heavenly places" (Eph. 3:10).

This unique relationship between Christ and His Church, and its picture as found in the husband-wife relationship, is given us in Ephesians 5:23-33. Please read it all. In verse 23, we see that "the husband is the head of the wife as Christ also is the head of the Church". The time is fast approaching when the Lord's coming for His Church will take place (John 14:1-4, 5) I Thess. 4:13-18) and then He will present to Himself the Church in all her glory" (Ephesians. 5:27).

As we see God's ordering of the sexes in these verses, even in the home environment, we are told that it is a great mystery (something not revealed before in the Bible), "but I am speaking with references to Christ and the Church" (Eph. 5:32).

We thus begin to see how the husband and wife picture Christ and His Church. The man is ordained to be a picture of Christ while the woman is a "type" (picture) of the Church. "As the Church is subject to Christ, so also the wives ought to be to their husbands in everything" (v-24). Christ is the Head of His Church; the Church is to be in submission to Him. The wife, seeing the truth of what she represents, thus willingly becomes submissive to her husband, her head. In like manner (as we will see later) Christ teaches His Church. The Church never teaches Christ, and even this is worked out in picture form in the man-woman relationship.

If by one clever scheme Satan could play havoc with God's plan for both the home and the Church (Assembly), do you think he would hesitate to use it? Of course, he would use it because he hates God and God's people, and he is using it; and with much success! Satan's scheme is to subtly entice both men and women to leave their God-ordained spheres of service and compete with each other instead of complementing each other. Christian counselors claim that such role-reversal is the number one problem in Christian homes.

It is a great privilege to live under a government where 'human rights' are sought for the individual. Those in authority down through the ages have generally tended to suppress the "rights" of some segment of society to promote their personal interests. However, those who govern and those governed have consistently left out an important consideration: what about God's rights over the creatures He has decreed? We who claim to have accepted the Lord Jesus Christ as our Savior and to recognize Him as both Creator and Lord of our lives, have a special obligation to maintain God's rights. Nowhere is this more important than in the home and local assembly regarding His order for the sexes. We of all people must totally reject Satan's scheme to disrupt that order.

There are a host of books by Christian authors on the subject of understanding the temperament, behavior, concerns, fears, wants, and needs of men and women. There is some very practical advice, solid truth, and spiritual help in a number of these books. However, almost every extreme also can be found in them. Thus, if and when we read them, we must be well-grounded in what the Bible really teaches on God's order for the sexes-In fact, we need that knowledge to even function effectively for God in our daily lives. This book is intended as a summary of that Biblical teaching. However, as you read it you are responsible to evaluate every word utilizing the Word of God. "Examine everything carefully; hold fast to that which is good" (I Thess. 5:21, NASB). "They received the Word with great eagerness, examining the Scriptures daily to see whether those things (taught by Paul and Silas) were so" (Acts 17:11).

The big push today is to minimize the differences between men and women. 'Unisex' is proclaimed by action, dress, hairstyle, toys, and in other more subtle ways. However, the fact remains that men and women are different. God created them to be complements of each other. The woman, rather than being a different "man", is the complement of the man physically, emotionally, mentally, and spiritually. Neither one is superior or inferior, just different. God has specially equipped the man and woman to "complete" or "valance out" the other. Satan seeks to minimize these differences by masculinizing the woman and feminizing the man in appearance, thought, and action.

We must conclude from the Scriptures that her role is from that of man's and that it is not scriptural for a woman to do that which is definitely man's work for the Lord. Sometimes Galatians 3:28 is quoted to prove the contrary. "There is neither male nor female, for ye are all one in Christ Jesus". This verse, however, is not speaking about conduct and order in the Church, but is a statement about the redeemed family of God and that there is no difference as to salvation and grace between Jew or Greek, bond or free, male or female. From other passages, we have seen that God's order in creation still abides in the Church.

Galatians 3:28, "There is neither male nor female, for you are all one in Christ Jesus", is a favorite verse of those who advocate equal roles for men and women. Does this one verse negate all the other verses that speak of distinct and different

141

roles for men and women? Of course not! Scripture must be taken as a whole, rightly divided, properly interpreted. "No prophecy of Scripture is a matter of one's own interpretation" (2 Pet. 1:20). Rather, the context of Galatians 3 shows that Christian men and women alike are the elect of God, alike are born of the Spirit, alike heirs of the promises of God. We alike enjoy our spiritual blessings in the heavenlies in Christ.

We alike will have a future of reigning with and serving our blessed Lord in the Lord's thousand-year reign and in the eternal state (Rev. 20:4-6, 22:3-5, etc). Peter tells us that the Christian woman is "a fellow-heir (with the man) of the grace of life" (I Pet. 3:7).

After the coming of the Lord (1 Thess. 4:13-18, etc), men and women will no longer be the "complements" of each other. There will no longer be 'marrying and giving in marriage." Rather, we will be "like the angels in heaven" (Mk. 12:25) in the sense of being complete in Christ and thus no longer needing a husband or wife to be complete. We undoubtedly will know each other and remember our good times on earth together, but we will have a new object in view-Christ and the service He has for us to perform. However, while we are still living on this earth, God has proclaimed a certain order to be maintained by men and women, particularly in the spheres of the home and local assembly (church), and He has even explained to us why He has chosen that particular order. When this order is maintained, the home and assembly have the ability to function as God intended.

THE ILLUSTRATION OF THE HEAVENLY BODIES

God even uses the heavenly bodies to illustrate the same truths. The sun is "the greater light" (Gen. 1:16) and the moon is "the lesser light" that shines during the absence of the greater light. However, the moon has no light of its own but reflects (although poorly at best) the light of the sun to varying degrees. In the same way, the Church reflects Christ, although in an incomplete, dull way, during the night of

His absence from this earth. Genesis 37:9-10 shows us through Joseph's dream that the sun is a picture of the husband, and the moon (depending on the sun, not taking a superior place) pictures the wife. When the moon is directly opposite the sun, fully, as it were, in submission to the ready to be used by the sun, it shines its brightest. Likewise, the Church. Likewise, the wife. At no time is she more glorious as when she is fulfilling her submissive piece as a true helper to her husband. She then clearly proclaims the truth of Christ.

The Places of Men And Women In the Church

I accept the less restrictive View that the woman is not to teach the man and exercise authority over him-In the presence of the man, she always takes the place of a learner, never a teacher, regardless of how much Scripture she knows.

THE MAN IS TO SPEAK

Since the man represents Christ, the Head of His Church" the man is to speak in the meetings of the local church (assembly), but only as the Holy Spirit leads. Liberty to speak does not give you a license to speak whenever one feels like it. The Lord through the Holy Spirit is in charge of His gifts which He has given (1 Cor. 12:11). The Holy Spirit "works" all those gifts (like a puppeteer works the strings of a puppet) so that the desired ministry is given by the available participant.

In relation to the "prophetic" or "open ministry" meeting of 1 Corinthians 14:29-33, we are told just before the instructions that the women are to be silent in the meetings of the assembly, "Let two or three prophets speak" (verse 29). The point to be made is that the men are to speak as. the Lord leads. I Peter 4:10-11 says, as each one has received a special gift, employ it in serving one another as good stewards of the manifold grace of God. Whoever speaks, let him speak, as it were, the utterances of God." What God wants to be spoken at that particular moment.

In connection with woman's part in the fall of humanity in Eden, we have already quoted 1 Timothy 2:11-14 and noted the governmental restrictions put upon women. it will be well for us to have those verses before us in connection with our present phrase of the subject. "Let the woman learn in silence with all subjection. But I suffer not a woman to teach, nor to usurp authority over the man, but to be in silence. For Adam was first formed, then Eve. And

Adam was not deceived, but the woman being deceived was in the transgression".

These verses apply to a wider sphere than that of the gathered local assembly. They speak of proper conduct as between man and woman and would include any public testimony where both sexes are present. They refer to the public teaching of mixed sexes, for then man is at her feet as a learner, which is reversing God's order.

Man was formed first and is God's representative and head, and should maintain his rightful position as leader and teacher. Because Eve took the lead in transgressing and was deceived by Satan, manifesting that she was a poor leader, in God's government women are barred from taking the place of authority and teaching. They are to learn in silence and subjection. A woman, then, is never to take a public place as a recognized teacher of God's Word or to teach in the assembly or anywhere in mixed audiences where she takes a place of equality with or over men, for then she is usurping authority over man.

Woman's place is one of subjection and retirement in the assembly and not of leadership. Man is morally, spiritually, the mind of humanity, and woman is the heart. The heart is the chest hidden from view, while the head is outside and public. Those who take part publicly in the church take a place of leading in the assembly, whether in prayer, praise, or ministry and this place of leadership is not given to women.

IN THE CHURCH

1 Corinthians 14:34-38 gives us clear instructions as to the woman's place in the gathered assembly." Let your women keep silence in the churches; for it is not permitted unto them to speak, but they are commanded to be under obedience, as also saith the law. And if they will learn anything, let them ask their husbands at home: fore it is a shame for women to speak in the church. What? Came the Word of God out from you? Or came it unto you only? If any man thinks himself to be a prophet, or spiritual, let him acknowledge that the things that I write unto you are the commandments of the Lord. But if any man be ignorant, let him be ignorant."

Here is it plainly laid down that a woman is not to speak in the Church. The expression, "in the Church" or "in the churches", is used five times in this chapter and it always means the gatherings of Christians in assembly, the coming together of the whole Church. In such an assembly meeting women are not to speak at all, but to be in silence and under obedience.

In 1 Corinthians 11:15, the apostle speaks of a woman praying or prophesying. This passage permits such activity by a woman but does not indicate where it was to be exercised. The 14th chapter distinctly says such ministry of women is not permitted in the assembly, but that there she is to keep silent. It is quite evident, then that it is outside of the local assembly that a woman is to pray and prophesy.

Acts 21:28-9 speaks of Paul's company coming to the house of Philip the evangelist and that he had four daughters who prophesied-it would certainly seem from the context that they prophesied at home and not in the assembly; this was quite in order.

It is important to notice that this prohibition of women speaking in the Assembly is not just the word of the Apostle Paul-a bachelor-as some would speak of him, but that these things are "the commandments of the Lord" (1 Cor. 14:27). And if anyone would be spiritual and pleasing to the Lord, he or she must acknowledge that this is the statute of God. It is simply a matter of obedience to God's expressed will. To try to reason around this plain scripture and go on in self-will and disobedience shows that the heart is not willing to do God's will and that His Word is not respected.

The Corinthians, as also many today, may have thought themselves free to do as they pleased in this matter. The apostle, therefore, says "What! Came the Word of God out from you? Or came it unto you only?" (verse 36); that is to say, do you have authority from the Lord as to what you shall do in this matter? The Word of God has not come from you-.but to you. They were therefore to submit to the commandment of the Lord by the apostle.

It is sometimes said that the word "speak" in this passage means to chatter, gossip, or whisper during service and that this was what the apostle was prohibiting. But this is a very incorrect and misleading statement. Young's Concordance shows that it is the Greek word "Paleo" which is used here and in the whole chapter. it is translated "speak" throughout this chapter and 241 times in the New Testament. It means to talk or speak. Thus, in the same sense that the prophets are to speak two or three (v-29), the women are not to speak in the assembly. It is the same word in both cases.

Others would say that this prohibition of women speaking in the assembly applied only to Corinth where the women were ignorant, loud, and brazen. This statement is wrong. The beginning of this Corinthians epistle shows us that Paul addressed it, "Unto the church which is at Corinth...with all that in every place call upon the name of Christ Jesus our Lord" (chapter 1:2).

Surely this Is decisive. The instructions given in this epistle are not of mere local application but are also addressed to all professing Christians everywhere. And in the very passage under discussion, the apostle speaks of women keeping silent in the "churches". He does not say "in your church", but "in the churches."

WOMEN TO BE SILENT IN THE MEETINGS OF THE LOCAL ASSEMBLY

God has ordained that speaking in the meetings of the local assembly is to be entirely a male prerogative because the man represents Christ, as we have seen, while the woman represents the Church which is always silent and submissive when being taught by Christ through Holy Spirit-led brothers. The Instructions are too plain to be misunderstood. "Let the I women keep silent in the churches, for they are not permitted to speak, but let them subject themselves, just as the Law also says. And if they desire to learn anything, let them ask their husbands at home, for it is improper for a woman to speak in church" (1 Cor. 14:34-35).

The Holy Spirit foresaw how unpopular this prohibition would become and thus inspired Paul to write in 1 Corinthians 14:37, "if anyone thinks he is a prophet (one who speaks God's mind) or spiritual (one who really knows spiritual things), let him (or her) recognize that the things which I write to you are the Lord's commandments."

There is a major push today for women preachers and women elders in many of the Christian denominations. However, it is plainly unscriptural! People can argue about the culture and conditions in Corinth at the time of Paul's writing and that Paul was a bachelor who didn't understand women, or was a woman-hater (untrue). The fact remains that these instructions are the Lord's (not Paul's) commandments.

The woman is not to speak-not to preach, not to ask questions, not to pray audibly. She is to willingly put herself into subjection to this commandment of the Lord. These instructions apply to every local assembly following the Lord's way of gathering, for they were written not only to the local assembly at Corinth but also to "all who in every place call upon the name of our Lord Jesus Christ" (1 Cor. 1:2)

In II Timothy 4:2, Paul told Timothy (a man) to "preach the Word...reprove, rebuke, exhort with great patience and doctrine." Paul also told Timothy not to "neglect the spiritual gift that is in you" (1 Tim. 4:14).

Many do not realize that even if one prays publicly, that is leading the gathered assembly in prayer. It is not merely an individual praying. That one is the mouthpiece of the assembly in prayer or in praise. Therefore, for a woman to pray in an assembly prayer meeting or in a mixed meeting would be taking a place of leadership contrary to Scripture. 1 Timothy 2:8 the apostle says, "I will therefore that men pray everywhere." This unlimited liberty in prayer is not given to women.

In this respect, we can also learn from Hannah in 1 Samuel 1:9-17. The godly woman prayed in the house of the Lord when worshipers were assembled. Notice it says of her, "she spoke in her heart; only her lips moved, but her voice was not heard" (verse.13). To have audibly prayed in that mixed company was not proper, yet she could pray in her heart and hear and answered. So also today women can likewise pray and praise in their heart in the gathered assembly and join in on the "Amen" to public prayer and praise.

Then in 1 Timothy 2:8, as opposed to the women, Pau by inspiration said, "I want the men in every place to pray, lifting up holy hands without wrath and dissension." Public prayer under any circumstances (when men are present) is the man's responsibility. Of course, every privilege carries certain responsibilities. The men are to be in the right spiritual condition – free from wrath and dissension. It may be better to remain silent if our attitudes are wrong.

We have been from 1 Corinthians 14:35 that wives are to ask their husbands at home when questions are arising out of something taught in the meetings of the assembly. It is part of the (Christian) husband's job to answer those questions. This requires knowledge of the Word of God and the willingness to study and search out the answer. Such knowledge doesn't come by magic or by watching television all evening every evening or by heavy involvement in sports or other such "weights" (Heb. 12:1-2).

SHAME OF AN UNCOVERED HEAD

"But ever woman praying or prophesying with her head uncovered puts her own head to shame: for it is one and the same as a shave (woman). For if a woman is not covered, let her hair also be cut off, but if (it be) shameful to a woman to have her hair cut off or to be shaved, let her be covered."

When a woman's head was uncovered or shaven in the Old Testament, it was a mark of shame as seen in Numbers 5:18, where a wife was under suspicion by her husband, and in Deuteronomy 21:10-13 regarding a beautiful woman taken captive by an Israelite. So here in 1 Corinthians, chapter 11 the apostle says that if a woman prays or prophesies with her head uncovered, it is the same as if her head was shaven. And since having her hair cut off or shaven is a mark of shame, she should have her head covered. She must have no marks of shame upon her in the presence of the Lord. She is not to appear before God as one who I suspected of being unfaithful to her husband. The covering on her head would indicate that she owns him as her ha enjoys his fullest confidence.

In passing, it is well to notice from those verses in 1 Corinthians 11 that it is shameful for a woman to have her hair cut off, but "if a woman has long hair, it is a glory to her" (verse 15). These words of scripture should settle the question of short hair for any godly woman. Should a woman cut off any of her God-given glory and throw it away?

LONG HAIR NOT A COVERING

The KJV and most other translations say in 1 Corinthians 11:15, "for her hair is given her for a covering." From this, some teach that a woman's long hair is her head-covering and that no other covering is needed. But this phrase is incorrectly translated and does not share the meaning of the original scripture at all. An altogether different word in Greek is used here than the one correctly translated "covered" in verse 6. There, the word is "katakaluptespho" and means "to cover up, covering one's head. "Here in verse 15, the word is" "peribolaiou" and means "that which is thrown around" (Liddell and Scott Lexicon).

Thus, the JND Translation correctly renders this phrase "for the long hair is given (to her) instead of a veil." That is, long hair is given to a woman by nature as a veil cast around her. It is not the covering for her head which the apostle is insisting on in the foregoing verse-If man's glory is to be covered in the presence of God, as we have previously explained, then surely woman's long hair which is her personal glory, must be covered in His presence also.

Paul first sets forth the difference between man and woman and says that man should have his head uncovered and a woman should have hers covered. Then he further appeals to the sense of propriety and comeliness, based on the different constitutions of man and woman by nature, as another reason why she should have her head covered and appear differently than man before God. "Judge in yourselves: is it comely that a woman prays unto God uncovered? Doth not even nature itself teach you?" (v.13-14). Even in nature, God has given women long hair as a veil to conceal herself. That which is becoming to a woman, then, is to cover her head when she prays to God.

NO SUCH CUSTOM "If any man seems to be contentious, we have no such custom, neither the churches of God" (v.16): The apostle had declared the mind of God in this matter and if any were going to argue about it, he simply adds, "we, nor the churches of God have no such custom as you contend of. "It is often in little things like covering or uncovering one's head, that the state of heart is manifested, and a test is given as to whether one's will is subject to God and His Word whether it desires instead to go against the Word and according to the fashions and order of the day Customs may change, but the principles of God's Word in this and other matters abide.

COVERING HER HEAD

I briefly alluded to the matter of a woman having a covering on her head while praying or prophesying and when in the assembly. We will now consider this more in detail.

The apostle gives instructions as to this in 1 Corinthians 11:3-16. There we read, "But I wish you to know that Christ is the head of every man, but woman's head (is) the man, and Christ's head is God."

"Every man who has something on his head while praying or prophesying disgraces his head" (1 Cor. 11:4). We have seen that the man pictures and represents Christ When a man prays or preaches with a hat or other covering on his head, he is symbolically showing the weakness of submission, picturing a weakness in Christ. That is a disgrace to the Lord of glory who is man's Head, whom man represents in God's picture of Christ and His Church. Every man praying or prophesying, having (anything) on his head, puts his head to shame. But every woman praying or prophesying with her head uncovered puts her own head to shame; for it is one and the same as a shaved (woman). For if a woman be not covered, let her hair also be cut off. But if it be shameful to a woman to have her hair cut off or to be shaved, let her be covered. For man indeed ought not to have his head covered, being God's image and glory; but woman is man's glory. For also man was not created for the sake of the woman, but woman for the sake of the man. Therefore, ought the woman to have authority (i.e. a token of authority under which she stands) on her head, on account of the angels...judge for yourselves: is it comelier that a woman should pray to God uncovered?"

From these scriptures, we see that God has established a certain headship and order which He desires we should recognize and observe. it is not just a matter of custom for men to have their heads uncovered and women to have theirs covered in the presence of the Lord-There is a scriptural reason and significance to this order.

God is the head of Christ. Christ is man's head and man is woman's head. Since man is the image and glory of God and Christ is his head, it would be a dishonor and a shame to Christ his head, to have his own head covered when praying and prophesying (speaking publicly). Christ's glory is to be seen and not covered.

But the woman was created for man and of man, and she is the glory of man. Therefore, her head must be covered when she prays or prophesies, for man's glory must not be seen, especially in the gathered assembly. Christ's glory and not man's is to be displayed there.

Furthermore, verse 10 says that the woman ought to have authority on her head because of the angels. That is, she should have a covering on her head as a sign of the authority of man to whom she is subject. When a woman wears a covering on her head in the presence of the Lord, it is an acknowledgment that the man is her God-given head. A woman who comes into the presence of the Lord without a head covering shows thereby that she wants to be like the man and that she does not want to take the submissive place. She dishonors her head, though she may not be conscious of it. It may be done in ignorance, but this what it means.

The angels are spectators in the Assembly and they should see God's order observed there. They see order in all creation, and they ought not to see disorder among Christians. The seraphim cover themselves in the presence of the Lord (Isa. 6:1-3), and they look to see women doing the same in obedience to God's Word. God that "the principalities and powers in heavenly places" might learn "by the Church the manifold wisdom of God" (Eph. 3:10-11). This wisdom of God" is the mystery of Christ and the church, which is typified by husband and wife, one the head and the other subject to him (Eph. 5:22-32).

Covering one's head applies to unmarried women as well as to married women. Women in general and men in general are spoken of in these verses of 1

Corinthians 11. Numbers 30:3-5 teaches that a woman in her father's house in her youth must be subject to his authority. Her vows could only stand if her father allowed them. Likewise, a wife's vows were only valid if her husband allowed them. So a woman is to acknowledge the authority of her father or her husband or man in general when in the presence of the Lord. Her head-covering is a token of this acknowledgment.

IN THE HOME

Since the home naturally comes before the church in moral order and in the order of life's timeline, as it is the foundation of all society, it is proper that we first consider the special role that scripture gives the woman in this most blessed sphere. This will also help us to better see the divinely prescribed position given to women in the Church. Her role in the home and in the church are in harmony with each other, and if a woman learns to take her proper role in the home, she will most likely discern her proper role in the church.

The basic relationship of the home is that of husband and wife, and then, if children are given, there is that happy affinity of father and mother and children. In this delightful relationship of a wife, or a wife and a mother, a woman occupies a very important and influential place in the home. A home is not a real home without a godly wife or mother.

We have previously referred to the role which God gave to Eve as Adam's helpmeet. Brought to him by God, she took her place at his side as his wife and helpmeet of God's providing. She was created to be his partner and the companion of his bosom-one flesh with himself. Man having been created first, was the head and when the fall came, God definitely said that she was to be subject to her husband's rule. 'She was, however, not to be trampled upon by him, but to be at his side in equality with him, under his arm to be protected by him, and near his heart to be loved by him. This is woman's special place in the marriage relationship as ordained of God in creation.

But from The Fall to The Cross we hear nothing of woman's rightful place in creation. "The heathen had degraded her into being a man's slave. By the law she was protected from being trampled on under certain circumstances (Ex. 21: Lev. 18:18); yet, she never had under the Mosaic economy her proper place with man. But after the manifestation of the second man (Christ) and the accomplishment of His work of atonement, the original order of creation is again adverted to, and woman regains her true place with man" (C.E.S).

The proper role is outlined in Ephesians 5:22-23. Here husbands are told to love their wives as their own bodies and as Christ loved the church and gave Himself for it. And wives are exhorted to submit themselves unto their own husbands, as unto the Lord, for the husband is the head of the wife, even as Christ is the head of the church. Therefore, as the church is subject to Christ, so the wives are to be to their husbands in everything. While the husband is to see that he loves his wife even as himself, the wife is exhorted to see that she reverences her husband.

This is God's order for man and wife in the home in this dispensation of Grace. Though the wife is to be tenderly cared for and regarded in the highest love by the husband, she is to own him as the head of the home and to be subject to him and reverence him as her husband. She is to do this "as unto the Lord" (Eph. 5:22), recognizing the Lord behind her husband as the One from whom her husband's authority is derived. She is also to remember that, in her submission unto her husband, she is a reflection of the church's subjection unto Christ. A wondrous privilege indeed!

In 1 Timothy 5:14, the younger women are told to "marry, bear children, guide the house." Guiding and ordering the household is a woman's special work, but the husband is the responsible head-of the house. A woman who assumes the headship of the house, to the contempt of her husband, will surely be unhappy and wretched, and will certainly reap the bitter fruits of her own rebellion in the lawlessness of her children brought up in disorder. Though women today demand liberty and equal rights with men, and feminine submission is unpopular and cast aside to a great extent, it is still God's command and desire that wives be in subjection to their husbands as the head of the house. Without this, there can be no true home-life and joy and blessing.

Having seen the woman's position in the marriage relationship and in the home. We may now consider her service in this blessed sphere. Much of a woman's time is spent in the home doing the common-place duties of life, and a great service is thereby rendered unto God. Colossians 3:23-24 says, "Whatsoever ye do, do it heartily as to the Lord...for ye serve the Lord Christ," in caring for the needs of her husband and children, and in keeping up the home as a place of refreshment, cheer and shelter in a world of trouble, a woman fills a very important place indeed!

The mother is truly the center and the heart of the home. The attractions of home depend largely upon the attitude and spirit of the wife. A prudent wife who manages her household in a wise and thrifty economy, and graces the home with love and cheerfulness is a great blessing to her husband and children and to all who enter her home. A husband's success or ruin in life often depends upon his wife's conduct in the home. Many men largely owe their position today in life to the wisdom and sound judgment of their wives.

The practice of that true Christian virtue of hospitality is largely made possible in the home by the wife. This is a most valuable and needy service in the church and certainly brings a rich reward of present and future blessings. In this way, women have a real part in the work of Christ-opening their homes for the Lord's servants and for the Lord's people and for the unsaved too, that they might hear the gospel and be saved. Aquila and Priscilla inviting Apollos to their home and teaching him the way of God more perfectly is an example of such service (Acts 18:26).

One of the most valuable services of a mother in the home is the training of children. This is her special work since she spends more time with the children than the father and exercises a powerful influence over their lives for good or bad. Notice how often the mother's name is given in the books of Kings and Chronicles in connection with the various Kings of Israel. The Spirit of God thus points out to us what was probably the most important factor in the molding of the character of the men who ruled God's people the mother.

The foundations of character are laid in the home-training of children, and a mother's hand is the instrument that God delights to, use in laying them. The mother's most important and divinely-appointed work is at home with her children, and she should devote herself wholly to their care, training, and upbringing. If a mother neglects this momentous work at home, or leaves it to others, and seeks to do service for the Lord in other spheres, she leaves her work undone and will surely fall to rightly accomplish someone else's work to which she has not been called. The training and teaching which children receive from their mothers in their young years of tender sensibilities is most influential upon their whole life and will leave an impression upon their young, plastic and receptive minds and hearts which cannot be erased. How important, then, is the work of mothers in the homes. May it not be neglected.

Thus, we observe and must declare that it is in the home circle that woman finds her special sphere in which to serve and glorify God. it is here in the more private domain of her own that she shines the brightest and exerts the most influence for good. Domestic life, which is often despised and forsaken by women today, is the place she is best fitted to fill.

We do not mean that there is no service which woman can do, or that there is no work which she can perform in assembly life. We merely state that the home or domestic circle is preeminently the sphere of woman's service. And in this home sphere we see that her scriptural place is one of subjection and submission to her husband.

In the foregoing, we have mainly considered the position and service of married women in the home sphere. The unmarried will also find a real field of Christian service in the domestic circle. They too can serve in temporal things, care for children, the sick and the aged, or make coats and garments like Dorcas (Acts 9:39). "praying or prophesying disgraces her head, for she is one and the same with her whose head is shaved." (v.5). Since a woman doesn't audibly prophesy in the meetings of the church (as we will see later), you can see the general application of these verses.

As to prayer, when the woman says or even thinks her "amen" to the man's prayer or Word of praise or worship, she has also in effect prayed. Thus, a godly Christian woman would not want to play "brinkmanship" and try to insist that she only needed a head-covering when she was personally preaching or praying audibly. The idea is that, in the presence of the things of God, she shows her submissive spirit by being covered. She has her head and even her hair – her personal glory – covered in the presence of God and God's representative – the church – the man. If she refuses, she is like the bold woman of Corinth who paraded around in short hair. She would be one who manifestly refuses to accept her submissive place.

The chapter goes on, "if a woman does not cover her head, let her also have her hair cut off, but if it is disgraceful for a woman to have her hair cut off or her head shaved, let her cover her head" (v. 6). I don't know whether the early church ever acted in discipline in cutting off anyone's hair, nor are we told to do so. However, the principle is that if she is going to act like a man, boldly proclaiming a picture reserved for the one exercising headship, then she might as well look like the man by having her long hair cut off. It gives us the impression that God is serious about this matter: it is not optional. The assemblies of that time had no such custom as arguing about or questioning these instructions (v.16)

THE MAN'S HEADSHIP: THE WOMAN'S SUBMISSION

We have seen from 1 Corinthians 11:3 that the man is the head of the woman, and in Ephesians 5:23 that the husband is the head of the wife. The husband is directly responsible if Christ is to take that place of headship. Unfortunately, there are too many weak-kneed or irresponsible husbands who don't have the courage or intent to step up to their God-given responsibilities in this matter. This has brought havoc to unnumbered Christian homes and has often put the wife into a position she wasn't intended to occupy.

The husband is never told to force his wife into submission. Rather, wives are told to be subject to their husbands as their husbands are to the Lord. As the church is subject to Christ, so also the wives ought to be to their husbands in everything"

(Eph. 5:22-24). "You wives, be submissive to your own husbands so that even if they are disobedient to the Word, they may be won without a word by the behavior of their wives as they observe your chaste and respectful behavior." (1 Pet. 3:1-2) Peter then gives the example of Sarah, Abraham's wife, who "obeyed Abraham, calling him 'lord', and you have become her children if you do what is right" (3:6) "Let the wife see to it that she respects her husband" (Eph. 5:33).

A marriage that has the blessing of God has all parties fulfilling their respective roles. The constant bombardment of television, radio, magazine articles, and various "women's rights" movements is for the woman to take charge, to not play second fiddle to anyone.

Many women have proven they can do just that! They've proven themselves to be able business managers, mayors, lawyers, judges, engineers, congress-persons, etc. The godly woman does not take the submissive role in the home and assembly settings on the basis of inferiority but on the basis of the Word of God. She does it "as to the Lord" even if better educated and smarter than her husband. Being "one," they of course counsel together. The wife submits her will to God and to her husband because he is her head. She respects him for the role, picturing Christ, that God has given him.

Peter gives essentially the same instructions as Paul: they both were apostles and God-inspired their words as recorded in scripture. However, Peter adds another good reason for wives to submit. Their ungodly husbands who disobey (Greek "apeitheo" disobey: refuse to be persuaded), whether saved or not, can see a sermon every day as they carefully observe the godly behavior of their wives. God holds out a promise, although perhaps not an absolute one, that the husband can be and will be won (saved or restored) by a wife who does not compromise her Christian principles. She obeys her husband when it doesn't counteract obedience to Christ, her ultimate Head. She doesn't nag. She shows him cheerfulness, love, chaste behavior and reverence-She of course prays for him. He thinks, "why is my wife acting this way?

I don't deserve it. There must be something to this Christianity." God may work His mighty work of salvation in his heart and then what a wonderful home it will be. God may teach the wife patience through the trial, but we can lay hold of His promises in His own time if we uphold our end of the bargain.

CHURCH OF GOD IN CHRIST, INC.

GENERAL ASSEMBLY

Dr. Frank J. Ellis, Chairman

DOCTRINAL REVIEW COMMITTEE

Bishop George D. McKinney, Jr., Chairman

Report

"A VIEW OF MALE DOMINATION"

AND HEADSHIP IN SCRIPTURE AND THE

CONCEPTS OF MINISTRY ABOUT RULING

AND SERVING"

by

Dr. James A. Parson, Sr.

Baltimore, Maryland

160

A View of Male Domination and Headship in Scripture and the Concepts of Ministry About Ruling and Serving

To our most eminent. and erudite chairman, Bishop George D. McKinney, Dr. and distinguished and scholarly fellow-members of the Doctrinal Review Committee. It is both a high honor and favored privilege to me having been chosen by our illustrious international chairman of the General Assembly, Dr. Frank J. Ellis, to serve on this responsible and history-making committee of our great Holiness/Pentecostal Church.

I have been charged by Chairman McKinney to research and report on the topic: "A View of Male Domination and Headship in Scripture and the Concepts of Ministry About Ruling and Serving. There could be no better introduction to the topic than that given by John Piper and Wayne Grudem in the preface to their book entitled <u>Recovering Biblical Manhood and Womanhood</u>: <u>A Response to Evangelical Feminism</u>: "A controversy of major proportions has spread through the church. It began over 20 years ago in society at large. Since then, an avalanche of feminist literature has argued that there need be no difference between men's and women's roles-indeed, that to support gender-based role difference is unjust discrimination. Within evangelical Christianity, the counterpart to this movement has been the increasing tendency to oppose any unique leadership role for men in the family and in the church. 'Manhood' and 'womanhood' as such, are now often seen as irrelevant factors in determining fitness for leadership.

Many evangelical Christians have defended this position in writing... and many others, in articles, lectures, and classroom teaching although they have disagreed on details, their common theme has been the rejection of a unique leadership role for men in marriage and in the church.

Yet these authors differ from secular feminists because they do not reject the Bible's authority or truthfulness, but rather give new interpretations of the Bible to support their claims. We may call them 'evangelical feminists' because by a personal commitment to Jesus Christ and by profession of belief in the total truthfulness of Scripture, they still identify themselves very clearly with evangelicalism. Their arguments have been detailed, earnest, and persuasive to many Christians.

What has been the result? Great uncertainty among evangelicals. Men and women simply are not sure what their roles should be. Traditional positions have not been totally satisfactory, because they have not fully answered the recent evangelical feminist arguments. Moreover, most Christians will admit that selfishness, irresponsibility, passivity, and abuse have often contaminated 'traditional' Patterns of how men and women relate to each other.

But the vast majority of evangelicals have not endorsed the evangelical feminist position, sensing that it does not really reflect the pattern of Biblical truth. Within our churches, we have had long discussions and debates, and still the controversy shows signs of intensifying, not subsiding. Before the struggle ends, probably no Christian family and no evangelical church will remain untouched."

We join in concerted prayer with our chairman and fellow members of this committee that our great church of God in Christ, through the leading of the Holy Spirit, will engage this controversial issue with brotherly and sisterly love and ultimately "keep the unity of the Spirit in the bond of peace."

In the chapter "Male-Female Equality and Male Headship: Genesis 1-3" from the book Recovering Biblical Manhood and Womanhood, Raymond C. Ortlund, Jr. takes the position that as Genesis 1-3 goes, so goes the whole Biblical debate on manhood and womanhood. He believes that "One way or the other, all the additional Biblical texts on manhood and womanhood must be interpreted consistently with these chapters."

Ortlund contends that "both male-female equality and male headship, properly defined, were instituted by Ged at creation and remain permanent, beneficent aspects of human existence." He defines, male-female equality as follows: "Man and woman are equal in the sense that they bear God's image equally" and male headship: "In the partnership of two spiritually equal human beings, man and woman, the man bears the primary responsibility to lead the partnership in a God-glorifying direction." Ortlund states that the antithesis to male headship is male domination. He defines male domination as the "assertion of the man's will ever the woman's will, heedless of her spiritual equality, her rights, and her value." Ortlund cautions his readers to keep this distinction between male headship and male domination in mind throughout the essay to avoid the misunderstanding of his viewpoint.

Ortlund points out that evangelical feminism argues that God created man and woman as equals in a sense that excludes male headship and that male headship/domination (no distinction in feminism) was imposed upon Eve as a penalty for her part in the fall. In this view, says Ortlund, "it follows, that a woman's redemption in Christ releases her from the punishment of male headship."

In light of the evangelical feminist position, Ortlund sets out to answer two questions: (1) "What did God intend for our manhood and womanhood at the creation?" and (2) "What did God decree as our punishment at the fall?" He says that the first two chapters of Genesis answer the first question and the third chapter answers the second question.

Ortlund responds to the first question, initially on the basis of Genesis 1:26-28 (RSV).

(Verse 26) Then God said, "let us make man in our image, after our likeness: and let them have dominion over the fish of the sea, and over the birds of the air, and over the cattle, and over all the earth, and over every creeping thing that creeps upon the earth."

(Verse 27) So God created man in his own image in the image of God he created him: male and female he created then.

(Verse 28) And God blessed them, and God said to them, "Be fruitful and multiply, and fill the earth and subdue it; and have dominion over the fish of the Sea and over the birds of the air and over every living thing that moves upon the earth."

Ortlund says "verse 26 teaches the glory of man in three ways. First, God says 'Let us make man...' In verse 24 God had said, 'Let the earth bring forth living creatures."

By the sheer power of His spoken will, God had caused the living creatures to emerge from the earth. In the creation of man, however, God Himself acted directly and personally.

Second, man was created to bear the image or likeness of God. To image God is to mirror His holiness. Other interpreters construe the image of God in a more general sense ... But however one interprets the imago Dei, God shared it with man alone. Man is unique, finding his identity upward in God and not downward in the animals.

The third indication of man's greatness in verse 26 is his special calling under God: '... and let them have dominion ...' Man stands between God above and the animals below as God's ruling representative. Man is the crown of creation.

In verse 27, God fulfills His Purpose as declared in verse 26 ...

So God created man in his own image, in the image of God he created him; male and female he created then.

Finally, in verse 28, God pronounces His benediction on man. In verse 22, God spoke His blessing out over the mass of the lower creatures. But here in verse 28, we read, 'God blessed them and said to them, 'with man alone, (male and female alike without distinction), God shares an I-Thou relationship.'

In His benediction, the Creator also authorizes male and female together to carry out their mission to rule the lower creation."

At this point, Ortlund admits that "Most evangelical feminist would. heartily agree with this interpretation of the text." But he then proceeds to challenge two points of feminist interpretation.

First, he cites the comments of Gilbert Bilezikian in his book Beyond Sex Roles: "In commenting on verse 26, Gilbert Bilezikian notes that God refers to 'them' both male and female, as 'man.' He writes: the designation 'man' is a generic term for 'human beings' and ... encompasses both male and female. This fact is made especially clear in Genesis 5:2 where the word man designates both male and female: "He created them male and female; at the time they were created, he blessed them and called them 'man'. (NIV)"

Ortlund says this striking fact demands explanation: "After all, if any of us modern people were to create a world, placing at its apex our highest creature in the dual modality of man and woman, would we use the name of only one sex as a generic term for both? I expect not. Our modern prejudices would detect a whiff of 'discrimination'! a mile away. But God cuts right across the grain of our peculiar sensitivities when He names the human race, both man and woman, 'man'.

Why would God do such a thing? Why would Moses carefully record the fact? Surely God was wise and purposeful in the decision as He is in every other. Surely His referring to the race as 'man' tells us something about ourselves."

Ortlund continues: "How may we understand the logic of God's decision to describe the human race as 'man'? Let me suggest that it makes sense against the backdrop of male hardship. Moses does not explicitly teach male headship in chapter 1 but, for that matter, neither does he explicitly teach male-female equality. What Moses does provide is a series of more or less obvious hints as to his doctrine of manhood and womanhood.

The burden of Genesis 1:26-28 is male-female equality ... But God's naming the race 'man' whispers male headship, which Moses will bring forward boldly in chapter two.

God did not name the human race 'woman'. If 'woman' had been the more appropriate and illuminating designation, no doubt God would have used it. He does not even devise a neutral term like 'persons'. He called us 'man' which anticipates the male headship brought out clearly in chapter two

Ortlund responds to the first question, secondly, on the basis of Genesis 2:18-25. He points out that there is a paradox in the creation account. "While Genesis 1 teaches the equality of the sexes as God's image-bearers and vice-rulers on the earth, Genesis 2 adds another, complex dimension to Biblical manhood and womanhood. The paradox is this: God created male and female in His image equally, but He also made the male the head and the female the helper. That is, God calls the man, with the council and help of the woman to see that the male-female partner-ship serves the purposes of God, not the sinful urges of either member of the partnership.

What will now emerge clearly from Genesis 2 is that male-female equality does not constitute an undifferentiated sameness. Male and female are equal as God's image-bearers. They are spiritually equal, which is quite sufficient a basis for mutual respect between the sexes. But the very fact that God created human beings in the dual modality of male and female cautions us against an unqualified equation of the two sexes.

God has no intention of blurring sexual distinctness in the interest of equality in an unqualified sense. In fact, there are many areas of life in which God has no intention of leveling out the distinctions between us. I have to conclude that God is not interested in unlimited equality among us. And because God is also wise, I further conclude that unlimited equality must be a false idea."

Ortlund goes on to explain how Genesis 2 teaches the paradoxical truths of male-female equality and male headship. He says: "The crucial verses are 18-25 but we should first establish the context. God created the man first (2:7) and stationed him in the Garden of Eden to develop it and to guard it (2:15). God laid a dual command on the man. First, the man was commanded to partake freely and joyfully of the trees God had provided (2:16). Second, the man was commanded not to eat of one tree, lest he die (2:17). Here we see both God's abundant generosity and man's moral responsibility to live within the large, but not unrestricted, circle of his God-ordained existence. For the men to step outside that circle, to attempt an autonomous existence, free from God, would be his ruin.

That is the scene as we come to verse 18.

The Lord God said, 'It is not good for the man to be alone.

I will make a helper suitable for him.'

In the conspicuous phrase, 'a helper suitable for him!' (2:18,20), we encounter the paradox of manhood and womanhood.

On the one hand, the woman alone; out of all the creatures, was 'suitable for him'. She alone was Adam's equal.

On the other side of the paradox, the woman is the man's helper. The man was not created to help the woman, but the reverse…

So, was Eve Adam's equal? Yes and no. She was his spiritual equal and, unlike the animals, 'suitable for him'. But she was not his ¢qual in that she was his 'helper'. God did not create man and woman in an undifferentiated way, and their mere maleness and femaleness identify their respective roles. a man, just by virtue of his manhood, is called to lead for God. A woman, just by virtue of her womanhood, is called to help for God.

The paradox of Genesis 2 is also seen in the fact that the woman was made from the man (her equality) and for the man (her inequality). God did not make Adam and Eve from the ground at the same time and for one another without distinction. Neither did God make the woman first, and then the man from the woman for the woman. He could have created them in either of these ways so easily, but He didn't. Why? Because, presumably, that would have obscured the very nature of manhood and womanhood that he intended to make clear.

Another indication of the paradox is that Adam welcomes Eve as his equal ('bone of my bones and flesh of my flesh'), yet he also names her (she shall be called Woman'). God charged the man with naming the creatures and gave him the freedom to exercise his own judgment in each case. In doing so, Adam brought the earthly creation under his dominion.

Still another signal of the Paradox is detected in verse 24. Because the woman alone is the man's very flesh, their reunion in marriage is a 'one flesh' relationship. Adam could not have joined himself to a lesser creature without degrading himself. But it is the man who leaves his parents to found a new household with his new wife at his side. His wife does not leave her family to initiate the new household; this is the responsibility of the head."

Ortlund next proceeds to answer the second question, "What did God decree as our punishment at the fall?" on the basis of Genesis, chapter 3. He says, "Those who deny the creation of male headship in Genesis 1-2 often argue that, in Genesis 3, God imposed male headship/domination (no distinction is allowed) upon woman after the fall. As the corollary to this interpretation, they go on to argue that redemption in Christ reverses this decree and reinstates the woman to 'full equality' with the man. We have seen, however, that God built male headship (not male domination) into the glorious, pre-fall order of creation."

He then goes on to summarize the doctrine of manhood and womanhood as taught in Genesis 3, emphasizing especially verses 16-19:

"Genesis 3 is one of the crucial chapters of Holy Scripture. If it were suddenly removed from the Bible, the Bible would no longer make sense. Life would no longer make sense. If we all started out in Edenic bliss, why is life so painful now? Genesis 3 explains why. And if something has gone terribly wrong, do we have any hope of restoration? Genesis 3 gives us hope."

Coming to Genesis 3:6b, Ortlund says, "After his careful, detailed description of Eve's deception, Moses describes the actual act of Adam and Eve's sin very simply as a matter of fact, without a hint of shock: '2. she took some and ate it. She also gave some to her husband, who was with her, and he ate it' (3:6b).

Mack well what the text says and what it does not say. The text does not say, 'she took some and ate it. Her husband, who was with her, also took some and ate it.' What actually happened is full of meaning. Eve usurped Adam's headship and lead the way into sin. And Adam, who (it seems) had stood by passively, allowing the deception to progress without decisive intervention-Adam, for his part, abandoned his post as the head. Eve was deceived: Adam forsook his responsibility. Both were wrong and together they pulled the human race down into sin and death.

But if Adam and Eve fell into sin together, why does Paul blame Adam for our fall in Romans 5:12-21? Why doesn't Paul blame both Adam and Eve? Why does Genesis 3:7 say that it was only after Adam joined in the rebellion that the eyes of both of them were opened to their condition? Why does God call out to Adam, 'Where, are you?' (Genesis 3:9) Why doesn't God summon both Adam and Eve to account together? Because, as the God-appointed head, Adam bore the primary responsibility to lead their partnership in a God-glorifying direction.

In Genesis 3 verse 16 God decrees a just settlement with the woman:

I will greatly increase your pains in childbearing; with pain, you will give birth to children.

Your desire will be for your husband, and he will rule over you.

God's decree is two-fold. First, as a mother, the woman will suffer in relation to her children. She will still be able to bear children. This is God's mercy providing the means by which He will carry out His death sentence on the Serpent. But now the woman will suffer in childbirth. This is God's severity for her sin. The new element in her experience, then, is not childbirth but the pain of childbirth.

Second, as a wife, the woman will suffer in relation to her husband. The exact content of her marital suffering could be defined in either of two ways. Either she will suffer conflict with her husband, or she will suffer domination by him.

However, Genesis 3:16 should be interpreted, "nothing can change the fact that God created male headship as one aspect of our pre-fall perfection. Therefore, while many women today need release from male domination, the liberating alternative is not female rivalry or anatomy but male headship wedded to female help. Christian redemption does not redefine creation; it restores creation so that wives learn godly submission and husbands learn godly headship."

In his essay, "The Meaning of Authority in the Local Church" from "Recovering Biblical Manhood and Womanhood", Paige Patterson sheds important light on the nature of ordination in the New Testament. Patterson points out that in the KJV, the word "ordain" is the English translation of more than twenty Hebrew and Greek terms. He says, "Most of these words also are translated at times by numerous other English words. The translators of the NIV have simplified the matter by almost uniformly translating the various Greek terms with the word <u>appoint</u>. Titus is instructed by Paul to 'appoint elders in every town' on the island of Crete (Titus 1:5). In Mark 3:14, it is said that Jesus 'appointed twelve', whereas in 1 Timothy 2:7 Paul confesses that he was 'appointed a herald and an apostle.'"

He concludes that "Such translations may reflect a conviction on the part of the NIV translators that 'ordination' as practiced in most communions today has little in common with New Testament practice." He cites A. H. strong who wrote, "The word 'ordain' has come to have a technical signification not found in the New Testament. There it means simply to choose, appoint, set apart."

Patterson goes on to say that examination of the salient "ordination" texts (Mark 3:14; acts 14:23; I Timothy 2:7; Titus 1:5) appears to sustain the judgment of Strong and the NIV translators. He concludes, "Of the four texts, three use common words, each of which has the sense of 'appoint', 'place', or 'establish'. Only Acts 14:23 uses a word (cheirotoneo) that can mean 'to stretch forth the hand', or 'elect' or 'appoint'.

Patterson admits that, "A possible connection suggesting formal ordination can be imagined by linking Acts 14:23 (Paul and Barnabas 'ordained them elders in every church') with I Timothy 4:14. Timothy is told not to neglect the gift that he had received through 'prophecy with the laying on of the hands of the presbytery.' But he says finally that "Even. If there is an emerging pattern in Acts 14:23, I Timothy 4:14, and 5:22, the induction rites of the early church were probably simple in comparison to present practice. No concrete evidence can be generated to suggest that the ecclesiastical officers of the primitive church were inaugurated in any particular fashion or ceremony."

I have done research in numerous books on the subject of "Ministry Associated With Ruling and Serving" and the viewpoint which I consider to be closest harmonized with scripture is that set forth by Alex W. Ness in <u>The Holy Spirit, Volume Two</u>, Chapter Five, "Women's Ministry in the Church." Ness says, "Women, as well as men, are members of the Body of Christ citing Galatians 3:26-28 and 1 Corinthians 12:13. Ina redemptive, positional standing we are all made one in Christ. That does not mean that we are one in structure. We must look at chapters eleven through fourteen of 1 Corinthians to get the picture He then cites 1 Corinthians 11:3.

To deny that the husband is the head of the wife is paramount to denying God is the head of Christ and that Christ is the head of the man. This is the first principle that must be established.

Several things come to the surface out of the scripture 1 Corinthians 11:5: It is permissible for a woman to pray or prophesy in an assembly providing she is covered. What then is her covering? The question comes to light that it is not what but Who is her covering. We saw that her covering is her husband (verse 3). When is her husband her covering? When she is in subjection to her husband (1 Timothy 2:11); when she does not usurp authority over the man (verse 12) but will learn at "home in silence."

It is to be further noted that the exhortations, whether they be in 1 Timothy 2 or 1 Corinthians 11 or 1 Corinthians 14, all speak of a woman's relationship with her husband. For a woman to teach her husband is tantamount to the Church teaching Christ.

The letter to the Ephesians, chapter 3, verse 23 brings this truth into clear focus.

With this context in view, we can readily understand submission and any ministry that assumes a place of authority over a man. Teaching by a woman can only be justified when it is in the context of Priscilla and Aquila. I can accept the teaching of a woman on two basis: (1) That she has the full blessing and approval of a husband with whom she is living in structural harmony. (2) If for some legitimate reason her husband is not with her and that she comes into submission to the pastor [or bishop] where she is ministering. If the aforesaid conditions are met, then she has covering and as a result, has a ministry.

But where does that put a woman who has no husband? If she is single, she comes under the Supervision of her father. If she is a widow, she has either her father or father-in-law or pastor and bishop."

WOMEN IN MINISTRY

CHURCH OF GOD IN CHRIST, INC.

GENERAL ASSEMBLY

DR. FRANK J. ELLIS, CHAIRMAN

DOCTRINAL REVIEW COMMITTEE

BISHOP G. D. MCKINNEY, JR., CHAIRMAN

REPORT

"EXPLORING THE QUESTION OF ORDINATION
OF WOMEN AND THE CHARACTER OF MALE
HEADSHIP"

BY

PASTOR R. J. HOSTON

BETHESDA C.O.G.I.C.

ROCHESTER, NEW YORK

The Character And The Desired Ends Of A Wholistic Ministry

When we think of the Ministry, we sometimes refer to the parting words of the eminent apostle Paul to his faithful student Timothy. (II Timothy 4:2 Preach the word; be instant in season, out of season; reprove, rebuke exhort with all longsuffering and doctrine.) The emphasis is usually placed on preaching, reproving, and exhorting from the Lord's word. However, linguistic delivery is a small part of ministry. Ministry is really wholistic in nature. It is the attempt to heal the total man. That is to bring healing spiritually, emotionally, physically, and psychologically.

Wholistic ministry is so important until the Lord Jesus Christ first had to establish a ministry before He could establish his church. Therefore, the Church is really built upon the Ministry that Christ established. This Ministry had to have two things. First, it had to have a vision, a desired end or what it hoped to accomplish in its constituents. Secondly, it had to have a character or a way to define how those who are engaged in it should act. While the Lord was in His earthly ministry, He gave us the character of the ministry and its desired ends. First, the desired ends of the Ministry is seen in the response that Jesus gave to Peter at Caesarea Philippi in Matthew 16:18: "and I say also unto thee, that thou art Peter, and upon this rock I will build my church; and the gates of hell shall not prevail against it." Let us note that in this Scripture the Greek word PETRUS from which we get the name Peter, means a piece of a rock or stone. The Greek word rock, however, is translated from the Greek word PETRA. PETRA is in the feminine form meaning a huge rock. Therefore, when Jesus said "upon this rock I will build my Church," the rock he was obviously referring to was himself. The Church, then, was to be built upon the huge rock which was himself. When we understand the relationship of the two rocks (observe how Peter, who was the stone, confessed through the revelation of the Father that Jesus the Huge rock was the Christ, the Son of God.) we can begin to see in this response what Jesus was trying to show, aside from the fact that He was establishing the Church, that in order for man to know his sonship, the Father would have to reveal it. He was also trying to show the end which he wanted this ministry to accomplish. That is, in all that we do, whether it be male or female ministering the Word, food or clothing distribution, abuse counseling, etc., the end is to make dead stones alive by bringing them unto a full revelation of Jesus the Christ for the purpose of confessing Jesus Christ as God's Son and Savior of the World. (1 Peter 2:5).

Now the way or the character in which this Ministry should accomplish its ends can of the flesh (Gen 9:4). Therefore the Eucharist is showing us how Christ gave His body and shed His blood because He loves us, and for the purpose of birthing many sons into the Kingdom. Just as Jesus gave of Himself unto death, we are to adopt ™ 'that same commitment to ministry. This is the ministry of servanthood. We are the broken pieces of the unleavened bread distributed among falling humanity. We are the extension of Calvary in the service of divine love for the Master. Our paradigm or rule of faith is crouched in the inerrancy of God's Word, our Joy is the successful accomplishment of the birth of a son or daughter into the Kingdom, our accomplishment is when we see one go from the gutter most to the uttermost. This is wholistic ministry.

DEFINING THE SCOPE OF THE MINISTRY

When it comes to women in ministry it is important to explore the following questions: Is the ministry of servanthood and reconciliation gender specific? Do we have a scriptural basis for God calling women into the ministry in the 21st century? As we engage ourselves in attempting to answer these questions, I think that first we must understand and define the scope of the Ministry itself, The Lord-has developed a gifted Ministry with great diversity. Note the following scripture: "Now there are diversities of gifts, but the same spirit and there are differences of administrations, but the same Lord and there are diversities, of operations, but it is the same God which worketh all in "1 Corinthians 12:4-6. Gifts come from the Greek word CHRISMA, which means a gift given by grace. They are spiritual endowments or enablements by the Holy Spirit that are made available in the Christian community for profit and edification. These gifts are wisdom, knowledge, prophecy, healings, etc. These gifts are of the Holy Ghost and are made available to anyone in the body of Christ. These are gifts that you don't work for, or have to fast and pray for.

Secondly, there are administrations of ministries. This comes from the Greek word KYBERNESIS, and it signifies a steersman or one who holds the ship on course as directed by the captain. This presents to us the idea of headship or authority given to an individual. There are gifted individuals that have been developed by Christ and given to the Church. Note that there is a difference between the gift of prophecy and the individual prophet. Note also the wording of the scripture: "Now; there are diversities of gifts, but the same SPIRIT and there are differences of administrations, but the same LORD." The gifts are given by the Spirit while the administrations or the enablement for one to govern is given by the Lord. Finally, there is the operation, workings, or the effects that God accomplishes through the gifts and Ministries. Therefore, the scope of Ministry is delineated in the books of Romans and Corinthians.

IS THERE A PLACE FOR WOMEN IN WHOLISTIC MINISTRY?

When we look at it in the light of the scope of Ministry, we now have to ask ourselves the question: Can God call women, develop them for Ministry and give them to the Church for the purpose of administering or taking authority in His Church? That is, can women pastor, evangelize, be apostles, teach and govern in the Church? Now, if God is committed to His word and as the older folks use to say, God is no shorter than His Word, we will have to answer this question in the light of 1 Timothy 2:12. "But I suffer not a woman to teach, nor to usurp authority over the man, but to be in silence." There are three Greek words from which authority is translated.

1) EXOUSIA-means delegated power.

2) DUNAMIS-means power of a potentate or high officer.

3) AUTHENTEO (OW-THEN-TEH'-O)-This means to exercise authority on one's own account. To have dominion or to domineer over. This is exercising authority without the authority to do it. AUTHENTEO is the word that was used in the above scripture. In fact, it is the only time that this word is used in scripture.

This scripture seriously questions the idea that God would scriptorily call women for the administrative Ministry of pastoring, teaching and apostleship, etc. Therefore, if God scriptorily would not call women to administrative ministry, then we should not ordain them for it.

IN SEARCH OF AN ANSWER

Over the past several months, I have had the opportunity to talk with a New Testament scholar from Colgate Divinity School, professors from Elim Bible Institute, and read books and articles of several authors that have done research and biblical exegetical work on the subject of the ordination of women. Their exegetical work centered around Genesis 1-3, the creation Story; 1 Cor 14:34,37, women keeping silent in the Church, 1 Cor. 11:2-16, women's submission to the covering of male authority and head; 1 Tim 2:8-15 and Acts 2:17, women pastoring and preaching to men; and Gal 3:28, the equality of men and women in the Body of Christ.

My reason for talking with these different scholars on the subject and reading different authors, is my quest to hear and understand the pulse of the Body of Christ. In my quest, I found that there is more than one pulse. To say the least, there is a multifarious flutter that reverberates through the Christian Community that at times, can be confusing.

Pluralistic Pulse

The Pluralist pulse strongly believes that there is no spiritual, mental, social, or physical distinction that would make the woman unfit for ministry. This perception founds its scriptorial base on the belief that all believers are priests and in Acts 2:17: "And it shall come to pass in the fast days, saith God I will pour out my Spirit upon all flesh: and your sons and your daughters shall prophesy." There are several other points that this perception is based upon. First, the word headship (Greek kephale) in the scripture could not only mean authority or rule but the source or the sum of things. Therefore, when the scripture in 1 Cor. 11:2-16, where the word head is used, it can not only mean man having the authority over the women but man being the source or the place from which woman came. Thus, the fact that woman came from man does mean that man should hold a position of superiority over woman.

Secondly, biblical history indicates that women have held authoritative positions. Miriam was called a leader (Micah 6:3-4); Deborah the Judge, lead the Children of Israel to victory in battle (Judges 4:4-6); the declaration of Peter on the day of Pentecost regarding the enablement of both sons and daughters to prophesy (Acts 2:17-18); Phoebe was a deacon (Romans 16:1); Junia was acknowledged by Paul as a faithful apostle (Romans 16:7); the placement of Priscilla's name before Aquila indicates her position of influence and prominence over her husband (Romans 16:3).

Thirdly, the ordination of women is not based on the conferring to a rank or authority, but to a place of servanthood. it is believed that authority is not in a person but corporately with Christ being the chief head or authority and the Word of God being the rule or authority of our faith. Although the Elders are charged to feed the flock of God and govern the Church, they are not to dominate but serve. Jesus set the precedent when He said in Mark 10:44: "And whosoever of you will be the Chieftest, shall be servant of all,"

Fourthly, the scriptures that appear to be in conflict with what Biblical history reveals about women, the priesthood, and the oneness of all believers in the Body of Christ, are harmonized by the fact that these scriptures give women an inferior status (1 Tim. 2:12, 1 Cor 14:34), are stated in the context of the Old Testament or Law. The authoritative teaching of Jesus in the New Testament supersedes that of the Law. In conclusion, this pluralistic view which believes in the equality and priesthood of all believers strongly advocates for the Ordination of women.

The Egalitarian Pulse

The Egalitarian pulse is rooted in the scripture, Gal 3:28: "There is neither Jew nor Greek, there is neither male nor female: for ye are all one in Christ Jesus." From this scripture, they draw the equality of men and women. Thus men and women should subdue their geological niche as co-rulers. The Egalitarian pulse also draws upon furthers evidence from the bible in that God called women to leadership positions in the church and blessed their work. The elect lady that John addressed in the book was claimed to be a pastor, Priscilla, Theda who was mentioned by many of the church fathers. This view is like the pluristic view, and believes strongly in the ordination of women and that women should not be restricted in any area of Ministry.

TOWARDS A FUNCTIONAL ANSWER

When I looked at these various views on women in the Ministry and the hermanutial and exegetical investigation of the same scripture, I tried to understand how they came to different conclusions. I think it depends largely on one's approach to the Bible. If one has problems (as the Feminists, Pluralists, and Egalitarians do) with the Bible being written in a patriarchal or male-dominated society, one would question the nomenclature of the Bible, the message of God is identified with male gender, the terms like subordination of women to men and the headship of man. Therefore, if one believes that the Bible is culturally biased to men, it is easy to selectively remove those scriptures instead of rightly dividing those scriptures that are believed to be culturally biased to men.

There is a story about a young man that got his first pastoral charge after finishing seminary. With great excitement and Holy Ghost fire he stood erectly with authority and power behind the sacred desk and announced his first Sunday morning subject. "We preach Christ and Him crucified." After service, the deacons came to him told him that the subject sounded too violent and bloody. They ask him if he could change his message next Sunday. So the following Sunday he complied and preached "We preach Christ." After service, the deacons came to him again and ask if he could broaden his ministry and preach something other than Christ. So the next Sunday he complied and preached, "We preach." The deacons came to him again after service and said that the subject he preached was too dogmatic and harsh. So the next Sunday the young pastor announced his subject and it was "WE". This is a sad commentary on where we may be going as a church body. This is when WE can decide on the changing of eternal biblical truths. WE may be able to decide what days and times of the week that we will have service, however, WE cannot change the gender of God and call God she, the headship of man, and the fact that he was created first. Eternal truths will have to be rightly divided and not selectively removed. My approach to this study has been crouched in two facts.

First, God's Word is without human error or opinion. II Peter 1:20-21 says "Knowing this first, that no prophecy of scripture is of any private interpretation for the prophecy came not in old time by the will of man: but holy men of God spoke as they were moved by the Holy Ghost."

Secondly, God's word is the paradigm of rule for life. 2 Tim 3:16 says "All scripture is given by inspiration of God and is profitable for doctrine, for reproof, for correction, for instruction in righteousness." In my study, I came to the following resolve:

THE CREATION STORY

1. Man and Woman were both created in the image of God (Gen 1:26-28), The fact that they were both created in the image of God gives us the liberty to declare their equality.

2. The woman was created for man as a helper. The fact that she was suitable or adequate for him denotes her equality with him. (Gen 2:20-23; I Tim 2:13).

3. Notice Gen 2:24: "Therefore shall a man leave his father and his mother, and shall cleave unto his wife: and they shall be one flesh." Just because the scripture here says "one flesh" I don't think one can declare this equality. Their oneness relates more to their interdependence upon and need for each other rather than their equality.

4. What we are seeing here is that there may be an ontological equality between man and woman; however, there is also a functional relationship that existed before the fall. This relationship was a harmonious, interdependent one where each complimented the other. Man was head and his headship was not one of dominance but love and servanthood.

THE FALL

1. I Timothy 2:14 says "And Adam was not deceived, but the woman being deceived was in the transgression." The word deceived here means to be thoroughly beguiled or deluded. Adam was said not to be deceived. This

may indicate that Eve may not have had the same depth of understanding of God's Word as Adam.

2. As a result of this transgression, the harmonious relationship changed. Genesis 3:16 says Unto the woman He said, I will greatly multiply thy sorrow and thy conception; in sorrow thou shalt bring forth children and thy desire shall be to thy husband, and he shall rule over thee." The desire she had for her husband was the same intimacy they had before the fall.

However, the husband's ruling or authority took on a character of dominance and intimidation instead of love and servanthood. As a result because of Adam's changed character, he could not give her what she had received before the fall.

THE RESTORATION

Although women had held positions of leadership from the fall to the birth of Jesus, in the life and times of Jesus women had stopped being active in temple worship. They had been relegated to an inferior or subservient position. Tradition has it that the Torah would be better burned than given to a woman. The structure of the temple even emphasized the male-female class distinction. There was a restrictive area for the woman. Jesus brought a new day in his treatment of women. He conversed with the woman at the well in public which was forbidden, He allowed Mary to sit at His feet while he gave instructions. This went against the prevailing thought of the day. It was believed that women were incapable of learning. Finally, the death, burial, and resurrection of Jesus liberated women. The gender wall that was in the temple and was a reflection of society was broken down in the life and death of our Lord and Savior, Jesus Christ.

THE MESSAGE DEFINED AND CONTINUED

The 12 men continued that message after the ascension of Christ. Acts 2:17 says "And it shall come to pass in the last days saith God, I will pour out of my spirit upon all flesh: and your sons and your daughters shall prophesy..." Note the daughter Phache, the Deacon, the elect lady (2 John 1:1), Euodia and Syntyche who were a part of the Spiritual leadership at Philippi, the 4 Virgins at the house of Phillip that prophesied, Priscilla and Lydia.

Ephesians 2:14 says "For He is our peace, who hath made both one, and hath one, and hath broken down the middle wall of partition between us." The breaking down of that wall gave both men and women access to the throne of Grace.

Galatians 3:28 says "There is neither Jew nor Greek, there is neither bond nor free, there is neither male nor female: for ye are all one in Christ Jesus." Again, this scripture doesn't assert our equality, but our oneness.

CONCLUSIONS

In the light of the liberation of women, does it mean that women can preach, be ordained, and assume leadership roles in the church?

1. I believe that women are equal with men in terms of being in the image of God, and in their dominance over the creation. However, there is a punitive relationship between male and female that makes man the head. This headship was given to him before 'the fall', and it mirrors the same functional relationship of the Father and the Son. Even though they are both God, the Son submitted to the will of the Father, (Philippians 2:6-7). Thus, just as the oneness of the Body of Christ and its functional relationship is defined in 1 Cor 12:14: "For the body is not one member, but many," the functional relationship of male-female relationships is defined in 1 Cor 11:3-11 Christ is the head of the man and man is the head of the woman.

2. The headship is crouched in the character of servanthood, (Ephesians 5:22-25). As Christ loved & gave (served) Himself for the Church, we are to love and give (serve) our wives.

3. Although we are one, sons and daughters can prophesy, and all believers are priests. We cannot forget that the Bible places values on gender roles and the physical and emotional characteristics that are unique both to men and women. This uniqueness needs to be ministered to. The Bible recognizes these differences by commanding the aged women to teach the young women. As a church, we must also commit to the values that the Bible places on gender roles, motherhood & fatherhood, vocational homemaking, work ethics, personal responsibility, and male headship.

4. We cannot forget that 'the fall' introduced distortion in the male-female relationship. In Gen 3:16 God declared that the relationship would be characterized by the man ruling and the woman desiring. The ruling of man became dominance and the desire of woman was changed into

usurpation, subtle control, and addictive abuse (i.e. the battered woman syndrome.). Since 'the fall' there has been a tremendous wounding in male-female relationships. In fact, that relationship in the 20th Century can be characterized by two porcupines trying to hug each other. However, we cannot as a Church be influenced by those theological positions and social movements that were birthed through inner hurt and wounds that developed after the fall of mankind.

It is Vue that men have declared their independence from God, and as a result, women are declaring their independence from men. It is true that men have abdicated their headship role in the home. However, we must be careful of the social feminist movement and the egalitarian Christology that exists among us with some advocating the re-imaging of God and addressing God as she. We must also be careful of the Egalitarian and pluralist Christology which uses the serptorical idea of the oneness in Christ and the priesthood of all believers to assert the equality of males and females. This Theology leads to the distortion of gender roles, and in fact, an androgynous male-female relationship. This ignores the oneness between the sexes. It is under this pretense that I reject the ordination of women. I believe that under that pretense one has allowed this wounding to yield a distorted view of God's plan for male-female relationships.

5. I do believe that male-female relationships in the home and church should be a harmonious working relationship (that relationship was delineated earlier). This is because of the need we have for each other. There are things that men can do that women can't and vice-versa. I do agree that in Ministry, the Bible does not restrict us from ordaining women. Certainly, the women that I have sighted here from the Bible had a calling from God. Ordination is simply confirming what God has already done. Therefore, it would not be unscriptural to ordain women.

In my own Pastoral Ministry, my wife has a tremendous anointing in her life, and she fulfills a vital part in this Ministry that we share. However, in the ordination of women, I believe that it is scriptural (note the discussion in this paper) to ordain women with a male covering. That is, women may operate in the gifts of the Spirit, prophesy, pray, preach, evangelize, etc., and, in institutional type Ministry, or on a pastoral staff with the sr. pastor as a male covering (note Priscilla & Aquila). I do not believe they can become Bishops, presiding Bishops, General Board Members, or hold a position of authority like that without a male covering.

The keyword here is Head. The Greek word that is used here is said "Needless to say they were all equally convincing in their Biblical exegetical, and/or social or cultural reasoning for having or not having women in the Ministry." In my research, it was interesting to me how well learned Biblical scholars can arrive at different conclusions on a scholarly exegetical investigation of the same scripture. For example, the traditionalist Robert E. Culver takes the scriptures in verse16, and draws the conclusions that women should not be ordained, keep silent in the Church, man is the head, covering or authority of women, and that there are definitely ontological God-given gender roles. Susan Fah who is not a traditionalist but believes in male leadership co is the head the word head is translated from the Greek word *kephale* in 1 Corinthians 11:3; "But I would have you know that---the head of every man is Christ: and the head of the woman is the man, and the head of Christ is God." The traditionalists Robert D. Culver and Susan Foh interprets the word HEAD as being authority while the feminist and egalitarian Alvera Mickelsen interprets it as being the source. The egalitarian or what I also call the androgynous perception where there is no male/female distinction or gender roles would reject the idea of head as an authority because of the traditionalist.

BIBLIOGRAPHY

Edited by Bonnidell and Tobert Clouse: Women in Ministry four Views, Downers Grove, Illinois 60515, InterVarsity Press, 1989

Mary Stewart Van Leeuwen: Gender & Grace, Downers Grove, Illinois 60515, InterVarsity Press, 1990

Pa61 K. Jewett, The Ordination of Women, Grand Rapids, Michigan 49503, Wm. B. Ee'rdmans Publishing Co., 1980

Vinson Synan: Women in Ministry, A History of Women's Roles in the Pentecostal and Charismatic Movement, Ministries Today January/Feb issue 1993

Recovering Biblical Manhood and Womanhood

James H. Cone: Black Theology: Documentary History, 1966-1979 pp389-397, Maryknoll, New York 10545, Orbis Books.

March 16, 1995

Office
5825 Imperial Avenue
P.O. Box 740039
San Diego, CA 92174
TEL: (619) 262-2671
FAX: (619) 262-8958

Ms. Michele Jacques
2200 High Point Trail
Atlanta, GA 30331

Dear Ms. Jacques:

Greetings in the precious name of our Lord and Savior, Jesus Christ!
During our telephone conference call on last Thursday, the consensus that the
committee as a whole would meet in Memphis on Monday, April 3, 1995. Dean
Haney will notify the committee regarding the exact location of our 4:00 p.m.
meeting.

Please bring to that meeting a one-page summary of your deeply held beliefs
whether for maintaining the present Church of God in Christ position on Women
ordained or the approval of the ordination of women.

Let us covenant and agree to pray daily for guidance as we prepare our final
report. If you have any further questions, please feel free to contact my office at
(619) 262-2671.

Yours in Christ,

George D. McKinney

Bishop George D. McKinney, Ph.D.
Jurisdictional Prelate
GDM/tf
Enclosure

"Except the Lord build the house, they labour in vain that build it . . . "--Ps. 127:1

March 16, 1995

Office
5825 Imperial Avenue
P.O. Box 740039
San Diego, CA 92174
TEL: (619) 262-2671
FAX: (619) 262-8958

Bishop P.A. Brooks
30945 Wendbrook Lane
Birmingham, MI 480010

Dear Bishop Brooks:

Greetings in the precious name of our Lord and Savior, Jesus Christ!
During our telephone conference call on last Thursday, the consensus that the committee as a whole would meet in Memphis on Monday, April 3, 1995. Dean Haney will notify the committee regarding the exact location of our 4:00 p.m. meeting.
Please bring to that meeting a one-page summary of your deeply held beliefs whether for maintaining the present Church of God In Christ position on Women ordained or the approval of the ordination of women.
Let us covenant and agree to pray daily for guidance as we **prepare** our final report. If you have any further **questions,** please feel free to contact my office at (619) 262-2671.

Yours in Christ,

George D. McKinney

Bishop George McKinney, Ph.D.
Jurisdictional Prelate

GDM/tf
Enclosure

"Except the Lord build the house, they labor in vain that build it . . . "--Ps. 127:1

Our Findings Socially

1. The Justice Issue.

a. Do women do the same job as men without ordination?

(1) What added responsibilities will ordination increase?

(2) Other than Bishop or Superintendent what is she not already doing without ordination?

(3) Will women be able to do more with ordination?

"Ordination" as we understand it in the traditional church is not the understanding of the early church where there was no clergy-laity distinction. The only distinction was those of gifts. Since males and females alike were gifted for ministry, everyone was allowed to use their gifts. Proper and Public authorization of one to guard and guide the affairs of a religious body of believers is ordination in the traditional church. It is a process duly performed and accepted by the church at large for its select members in the ministry,

We see women in the New Testament functioning formally and informally in the ministry, with the same. title as their brethren, in which they have been called by Jesus Christ and empowered and gifted by the Holy Ghost to accomplish what God pleases. Some Examples are Phoebe, a servant of 'Jesus Christ (Romans 16:1), and Paul a Servant of Jesus Christ (Romans-1:1). Priscilla and Aquilla. Tryphena and Tryphosa, Persia. Julia and Paul are mentioned as Laborers together with God. (Romans 16; 1 Corinthian 3:9).

Being a grass root indoctrinated member of the Grand Ole Church of God in Christ. it becomes a very confusing issue when I take a long unbiased look at the context of the New Testament in the light of its Biblical execution of ministry and then compare it to our traditional methodology. Something is wrong in our justice system for our discriminating attitudes and prejudice toward women.

The ordination of women seems to lend credibility, authority, and acceptance to women in the ministry, disallowing the fact that these things in a natural are already in place through the calling of God and the unction of the Holy Ghost. What then does "ordination" offer the woman? In an abbreviated natural sense, we could consider it to give eligibility:

a. to Pastor, and be protector and overseer of the flock of God

b. to have a strong open administrative position of authority, that is now closed to women.

c. to bill a Council of Advice rather than a counselor.

d. to have committed support of the Church.

e. to have authority to Preach (calling it such, since there seems to be no, distinction in the Scripture when done by either sex)

f. to have authority to ordain, perform marriage ceremonies, to perform all church sacraments.

With these thoughts in mind, is it really the responsibility of the church to accept or affirm Christ's call or the Holy Ghost's gifts that are bestowed upon another? To accept and understand New Testament theology is to abandon sexist ways and practices. We must be careful that we do not create a mocking world and weakened church as we reject or compromise the Gospel of Jesus Christ's redemption that makes us all one in Christ. We must also be careful lest perhaps we are found fighting against God (Acts 5:39).

Geographical location plays a major role in answering the question, what the women are not already doing without ordination. In many of our southern communities, our churches employ what is known as a Circuit Pastor. This servant of God can only visit his appointed congregation periodically, usually once per month. Since he is often committed to more than one congregation. If this Circuit Servant is not fortunate enough to have a male assistant in his congregation the women of the church have to keep the doors open and keep the church functioning and maintained until that Pastor makes his periodic visitation.

Yet her responsibilities are grossly limited because the absence of ordination disqualifies her to perform certain church ordinances. These are some of the duties she is not permitted to perform in the absence of the Pastor: After she has decorated the church and prepared the reception meal, she cannot perform a wedding ceremony. She can bake the bread, buy the wine, prepare the sacrament table but cannot serve Sacrament. She can bring the basin, towels, and water but cannot order the Foot Washing ceremony. Other responsibilities she is forbidden to do without the dignity of duly authorized ordination are: accept a position in Chaplaincy as a livelihood in correctional facilities, hospitals, or industrial sites and also serving on certain Judicial Boards, etc.

The women of the church have travailed and brought forth children. These children have been taken and given to another. The women that have birthed the children are left with aching breasts, full of milk, with no children to feed. Her children have been snatched by the authorities and placed in the care of foster parents. Some of these foster parents have never birthed children, often insensitive, and have no natural feeling of parenthood. Many times the children are abused, drifting from place to place, rebelling, disrespecting authority, having a false sense of security. with displaced loyalty and inability to bond. Women have no voice in their children's spiritual well-being because she is not ordained by man.

But thanks be unto God. who always leads us in triumphal procession Ln Christ and through us spreads everywhere the fragrance of the knowledge of him. For we are to God the aroma of Christ among those who are being saved and those who are perishing.

To the one, we are the smell of death, to the other the fragrance of life. And who is equal to such a task? Unlike so many, we do not peddle the word of God for profit.   On the contrary, in Christ, we speak before God with sincerity, like men sent from God. (2 Corinthians 2:14-17 NIV)

2106 West Poplar St, Antonio, Texas • 78207
Phone and Fax (210) 732-6804 (210) 684-9527
Elder J. W. Denny

March 15, 1995

To My Brothers in Christ

My Dear Sirs.

I stand with and for the doctrine of The Church of God in Christ, as revealed by the Founding fathers and for the enforcement of Articles 9 and 18 of the 1926-Constitution, namely, "Power and Restrictions; of the General Assembly" which limits the General Assembly "from tampering with or changing the Doctrine of the same church."

The matter that is in review is a matter that should be reviewed and, settled by the Judicial Branch of our church government immediately.

Yours in Christ,

Elder. J.W. Denny

Introduction

"We confidently expect that theology or doctrine will find-its deserved place in religious thought and education. Whatever has been saved, in recent years, derogatory to this branch of study, has been ill-timed in view of the world's great need of sober and satisfying truth. The truth about God and destiny and the way to eternal life can never be unimportant to an immortal being. If men think at all these are things that must press for consideration. They are age-long and race-old questions and can be forgotten only when the race has sunk into idiocy or lost the image of God.

" 'As a man thinketh in his heart to is he.' All a man's life turns on what he thinks; and most of all on what he thinks of God."—David S. Clarke.

I. The Nature of Doctrine

Christian doctrine (the word "doctrine" means literally "teaching" or "instruction") may be defined as the fundamental truths of the Bible arranged in systematic form. This study is also commonly called theology, which means literally "a treatise or reasoned discourse about God." (The two terms will be used interchangeably in this section.) Theology or doctrine may be described as the science which deals with our knowledge of God and His relations to man. It treats of a thing in so far as they are treated to God and divine purposes.

Why do we describe theology or doctrine as a "science?" Science is the systematic and logical arrangement of certified facts. Theology is called a science because it consists of facts relating to God and Divine things, presented in an orderly and logical manner.

What is the connection between theology: and religion? Religion comes from a Latin; word meaning "to bind" religion represents those activities that bind man to "God in a certain relationship. Theology is knowledge about God. Thus, religion is practice while theology is knowledge. Religion and theology should go together in the balanced experience, but in practice they are sometimes separated so that one may be a theologian without being truly religious and on the other hand one may be truly religious without possessing a systematic knowledge of doctrinal truth. "If ye know these things, happy are ye if ye do them," is God's message to the theologian. "Study to show thyself approved unto God, a workman that needeth not to be ashamed, rightly dividing the word of truth." (2 Tim. 2:15), is God's message for the spiritual man.

What is the difference between a doctrine and a dogma? A doctrine is God's revelation of a truth as found in the Scriptures; dogma is man's statement of that truth as set forth in a creed.

II. The Value of Doctrine

I. Doctrinal knowledge supplies the need for an authoritative and systematic statement of truth.

There is a tendency in some quarters not only to minimize the value of doctrine but to dismiss it as outgrown and useless. However, as long as men think about the problems of existence they will feel the need for an authoritative and systematically arranged answer to these problems. Doctrine will always be necessary as long as men ask, "Where did I come from, what am I, and whither am I going?"

It is often said, "It does not matter what a man believes so long as he does right." This is one way of dismissing doctrine as having no importance in relation to life. But every person has a theology whether he knows it or not; man's actions are influenced by what he believes. For example, there would be a wide difference between the conduct of a ship's crew who knew that they were headed for a definite destination, and a crew who realized that they were drifting aimlessly without a definite course or destination.

Human life is a journey from time to eternity, and it matters much whether one believes that it is an aimless, meaningless journey, or one planned by man's Maker, and directed to a heavenly destiny.

2. Doctrinal knowledge is essential to the full development of Christian character.

Strong beliefs make for strong character; clear-cut beliefs make for clear-cut convictions. Of course, a person's doctrinal belief is not his religion any more than the backbone is the man's personality. But as a good backbone is an essential part of a man's body, so a definite system of belief is an essential part of a man's religion. It has been well said that "a than does not need to wear his backbone in front of him, but he must have a backbone and a straight one or he will be a flexible if not a humpbacked Christians.

A French Unitarian preacher once made the statement: "Purity of heart and life is more important than the correctness of opinion." To which another French preacher answered: "Healing is more important than the remedy, but without the remedy, there would be no healing." Certainly, it is more important to live the Christian life than to merely know Christian doctrine, but there would be no Christian experience if there were no Christian doctrine.

3. Doctrinal knowledge is a safeguard against error, Matt. 22:29; Gal. 1:6-91 2-Timothy, 4:2-4.

It is often said that the stars came before the science of astronomy, and that flowers existed before botany, and that life existed before biology, and that God existed before theology.

That is true. But men in their ignorance conceived superstitious notions about the stars, and the result was the false science of astrology. Men conceived false ideas about the plants, attributing virtues which they did; not possess, and the result was witchcraft. Man in his blindness formed wrong conceptions of God, and the result was paganism with, its superstitions and corruption.

But astronomy came with true principles about heavenly bodies and so exposed the errors of astrology; botany came with the truth about plants and so, banished the errors of' witchcraft. In like manner, Bible doctrine exposes false notions about God and His Ways.:

"Let no man think error in doctrine a slight practical evil," declared D. C. Hodge, the noted theologian. "No road to perdition has ever been more thronged than that of false doctrine. Error is a shield. over the conscience, and a bandage over the eyes."

4. Doctrinal knowledge is a necessary part of the Christian teacher's equipment.

When a consignment of goods reaches a store the ca are unpacked and placed in their proper compartments and receptacles, so that they may be handled in an orderly manner. This is a rather homely illustration of one purpose of systematic study. The Bible indeed follows. a central theme. But the variou4 truths relating to its great theme are scattered throughout the various books. In order, therefore, to gain a comprehensive view of each doctrine, and impart it to others, one must gather the references relating to it and place them in compartments (topics), and in smaller receptacles (subtopics).

III. The Classification of Doctrine

Theology includes many departments.

I. Exegetical theology (exegetical comes from a Greek word. meaning to "draw out" the truth) seeks to ascertain the true meaning of the Scriptures. Knowledge of the original languages in which the Scriptures were written is involved in this department of theology.

2. Historical theology traces the history of the development of doctrinal interpretation. It involves the study of church history.

3. Dogmatic theology is the study of fundamentals of the faith as set forth in church creeds.

4. Biblical theology traces the progress of truth through the several books of the bible and describes the manner in which each writer presents the important doctrines.

For example, in studying the doctrine of the atonement according to this method one would study how the subject was dealt with in the various sections of the Bible the Acts, Epistles, and Revelation. Or one could find out what Christ, Paul, Peter, James or John said about the subject. Or one could ascertain what each book or section of the Scriptures taught concerning such doctrines as God, Christ, atonement, salvation. and others.

5. Systematic theology. In this branch of study, the Biblical teachings concerning God and man are arranged in topics, according to a definite system; for example, scriptures relating to the nature and work of Christ are classified under the heading, Doctrine Christ.

The material contained in this book is a combination of Biblical and systematic theology. It is Biblical in that the truths are taken from the Scriptures and the study is guided by the question: What do the Scriptures say (exposition), and what do the

Scriptures mean (interpretation)? It is systematic in that the material is arranged according to a definite order.

A SYSTEM OF DOCITLINE

According to what order shall the 'topics be arranged? No hard and fast lines may be laid down. There are many arrangements, each having its value. We shall try to follow an order based on God's redemptive dealings with man:

1. The Doctrine of the Scriptures. From what source shall we derive inerrant truth about God? Nature indeed reveals His existence, power, and wisdom, but it tells of no way of, pardon, provides no escape from sin and its consequences, supplies no incentive to holiness and contains no revelation of the future. We leave God's first book of Nature-and go to God's other Book in the Bible where we find God's revelation concerning these matters.

On what grounds do we accept the Biblical view as being the right one? The answer to this question leads to the study of the nature, inspiration, accuracy and reliability of the Scriptures.

CLOSING STATEMENT

WOMEN IN MINISTRY

God's plan for the proper relations of men and women, and of women to the Church.

IN THE BEGINNING

To learn the mind of God by studying his Word requires humility, willingness to learn, and an open mind, as well as the guidance of the Holy Spirit. The computer age has produced the saying "garbage in, garbage out," because although the computer is totally accurate and incorruptible, our skill and the accuracy of the data we input will affect the quality of our results. Similarly, when studying God's word, we bring to it our own prejudices, the ideas that our secular culture has been imparting to us since birth, what various churches have taught us to expect to find, and the needs and desires of our own egos. It is arrogance to believe that we are capable of overcoming all our limitations so as to be able to correctly perceive God's clear message unaffected by any input from the self.

The idea that women are supposed to be subordinate to men and must be kept in their place is so current in both church and secular society that it can be very difficult to notice when the Bible tells us something different. The story of the creation of Adam and Eve, the only place in the Bible where men and women can be seen in their pure, unfallen state, is highly instructive in this regard. First, of course, God specifies that he created both men and women in His image, and gave them both dominion over all living things. Dominion is not a male prerogative. (Gen. 1:27-28)

Genesis ch.2 has been used to prove that Adam was intended to be primary over Eve in three ways: he was made first, giving primacy; she was made from him, making her subordinate; and she was made as his helper, an obviously inferior position. However, if we let Scripture interpret Scripture, not by the cut-and-paste method of bringing in bits from all over the Bible that seems to prove what we want to find, but looking at the close context, we find something very different.

First, the idea that the order of creation establishes primacy. Well, according to Genesis I, God created the animals first, so if Adam is superior to Eve, the animals by the same argument are superior to Adam. But this is mere human cleverness. A worthier argument can be found by seeking the mind of God as He revealed Himself in history. Hebrew culture, like many others, gave primacy to the eldest son, but they also o faithfully recorded that when God acted in their history, He regularly chose the last over the first. Jacob took his brother's birthright and became Israel. Joseph was placed over all his brothers and saved Israel in the time of famine. David was chosen over his older brothers and anointed king over Israel. In the Maznif cat, fresh from her encounter with the Holy Spirit, Mary exulted in the proud being brought down and the humble exalted. Jesus said that the last shall be first and the first last, and Peter pointed out that the stone builders had rejected became the cornerstone. Over and over, God chose the last, the weak, the ones disregarded by human society and elevated and anointed them. Being born first is no argument for being primary with God.

Second, the idea that Eve being derived from Adam makes her automatically subordinate. But Adam's reaction to Eve, when he was in the unfallen state, closer to the mind of God than any other man has ever been, teaches us differently. God and Adam had been looking among the animals and finding that none of them was a suitable companion for him. When God introduced Eve, Adam's reaction was not, "She was made from me so I get to be the boss," but "This, at last, is bone of my bones and flesh of my flesh, someone like me." He responded not with hierarchy but with kinship, likeness, identity. Now since God obviously knew what He was going to do, and had no need to check out the animals first, He was using it to teach Adam (and us) how to respond to another human being. This passage is anti-sexist and anti-racist as well. It teaches us to look past all the possible divisions and alienating factors of rich or poor, old or young, Black or white, male or female, and see simply another human being, one like us, related to us as no other living thing is.

Third, does the fact that Eve was to be Adam's helper place her in a subordinate position? God established that Eve should be a help meet for Adam, or in less archaic language, a suitable helper. (There is no such word as "helpmate.") Now it seems obvious to many people that a helper is automatically in an inferior position, but this is absolutely something we bring to the text, not present in it. A doctor would be very surprised to hear that by rendering help, he becomes inferior to his patient, still more the state which gives ai to its welfare clients! In fact, the Hebrew word translated as "meet" literally means "alongside him" or "corresponding to him," (Anchor Bible, Genesis, p.17) which clearly has connotations of equality. Even more definitive is the fact that the Hebrew word for help, "ezer," appears 21 times in the Old Testament. Sixteen of those times God is the helper, as in Psalm 121. The remaining uses refer to an equal helper, like a military ally, for example, but never is the "ezer" an inferior or subordinate.

The story of the creation of Adam and Eve thus contains no implications of hierarchy or status between them, but on the contrary, repeatedly emphasizes equality and balance. The first time the subordination of women is mentioned is when God is describing the conditions which will be obtained as a result of the Fall, when He tells the woman that her husband will rule over her. (Gen.3:16) Paul says in Galatians that we have been set free. Why then would we want to return to bondage? **And in what other area of our Christian lives do we so determinedly enforce the conditions of fallenness?** Three hundred years ago, a woman was burned alive for using a painkilling herb during her labor and childbirth. She was held to be in rebellion against God. As recently as the last century, when anesthetics were becoming commonplace, there were frequent objections raised against relieving the pain of childbirth for women.

Yet this was when the Industrial Revolution was well established, and there was no outcry against the fact that men were being excused by machines and laborsaving devices from earning their bread in the sweat of their brow!

When we bring attitudes like this to our Bible reading, it is not surprising that we notice the passages which put women down, but not those which show them favorably. Deborah is very seldom mentioned, but she was not only a Judge, appointed by God to the highest office in Israel but became by His appointment a war leader as well. We remember Martha because she was scolded by Jesus for wanting her sister's help in the kitchen, but do we realize that she was the only other person besides Peter to make the Great Confession: You are the Christ. Also, her faith was so great that she told Jesus ahead of time that she knew He could raise Lazarus from the dead. We remember that Martha was scolded, but we can't seem to grasp that the issue was whether Mary was to be forced to do "women's work." Since Jesus supported Mary as being, correct in her choice to join His teaching session with the other disciples, how can we account for all the conservative Christians who are insisting that women belong in the home, and are to be severely restricted in the capacity in which they may serve the church? Jesus told Martha that Mary had chosen the better part. This implies that Martha had also chosen her role, which she was free to do, but she had no right to impose her choice on anyone else. How different a picture of the will of God is given by this passage than what is practiced today! Mary was commended for choosing to take the same role as the male disciples. What would Jesus say to us?

When Jewish men were basing their pride on being "sons of Abraham," Jesus corrected their desire to elevate themselves by telling them God could make sons of Abraham out of the rocks. When they didn't get the message, He became highly confrontational by referring to a woman as a "daughter of Abraham. No one else in the Bible or in other writings ever elevated women to equality in this way. Mary of Magdala is traditionally supposed to have been a reformed whore, frequently identified with the woman taken in adultery, none of which has any Biblical justification, but her extensive role in ministry in the early church, described in extra-biblical writings, has been completely forgotten.

PAUL AND THE SUBMISSION OF WIVES

Paul, who has most unfairly had the label of woman-hater applied to him, actually put into practice the attitude of Jesus toward women. He clearly treated his female associates as co-workers, not inferiors. This is obscured by incorrect translation. Paul uses the same word (diakonos) to describe Phoebe that h uses for his male confederates. But in this case, and only in this case, it has been translated as servant rather than deacon. Paul several times used female imagery in reference to himself, describing himself as a nursemaid to children. And so much is made of how he told wives to submit to their husbands, but how seldom do we hear about the totally radical way in which he mandated complete sexual equality in marriage, by saying that just as the wife's body belongs to the husband, so does the husband's body belong to the wife. This is not a description of a dominant/submissive relationship.

So what did Paul mean when he talked about wives submitting to their husbands, and how is it to be reconciled with the passage mentioned above? This is worth considering because many people seem to think t at the submission of wives to their husbands is a special case of the submission of women to men in general. However, this is precisely not what Paul is saying. According to Ephesians 5:21-22, the submission of each wife to her husband is a special application of the mutual submission of all Christians to one another. Most translations partially obscure this by making v.22 a separate sentence and many editions even present it as beginning a new paragraph. But the original Greek is worded in this way: submit yourselves to one another in the fear of Christ, wives to your own husbands as to the Lord. The idea of wives submitting to their own husbands is a dependent clause on the command for all Christians to submit to each other; the verb is not even repeated. So we must remember that any attitude and behavior expected of wives in relation to their husbands is expected of all Christians to each other, men as well as women.

The Southern Baptist Church has recently issued a directive that wives should "submit graciously to their husbands' servant leadership" which is most unscriptural. The corresponding command to husbands in v.25 is not for husbands to lead their wives, but to love them, self-sacrificially and nurturingly, as Christ loved (not led) the Church. Jesus was very specific on this point. He didn't call for servant-leaders; he told anyone who wished to lead to instead be a servant. He didn't lead the church; he died for it.

The mutual submission required of all Christians includes an attitude of agape love, of true courtesy, of a willingness to keep one's own ego out of the way and focus on the good of the other. An excellent example is the principle of giving up one's own freedom to avoid causing a weaker brother to fall (1

Cor. 8). Furthermore, husbands are told to love their wives in a way that ought to be every woman's dream. Why, then, did Paul think it at all necessary to make any point of wives submitting to their husbands? Because of a problem common not to all women, but to all of fallen humanity. We have seen tragic examples of how a child with an abusive parent will ignore and take for granted the steady, reliable love of the other parent while striving desperately for the love of the abuser. And it is typical of men to refuse to value a woman who is lovingly always there for them and go off to pursue the one who "plays hard to get." It is an unfortunate trait of fallen human nature to value what is difficult or impossible to obtain and scorn what is readily available, of however much inherent worth. In the social order of Paul's time, it was the norm for husbands to be harshly domineering. A man could divorce his wife on a whim. Wives did not need to be told to submit; they were forced to. But when Paul tells husbands to love their wives in a Christlike way, he is changing the whole equation. With a flaw not common just to women, but to all fallen human creatures, it would be easy for a wife to try to take advantage of her newly loving husband, or to retaliate for his past treatment of her. Paul wanted to guard against this possibility, so he reminded wives that the attitude which they and all Christians were to have toward each other applied also in the home.

Let me state these two propositions again for complete clarity: a wife submitting to her husband is a special case of a general principle. That principle is not that all women are in any sense subject to all men. Rather it is that all Christians are to have an attitude of loving submission to each other.

Wives are instructed to submit to their husbands: the corresponding command to husbands is to love their wives, not to lead them. A marriage so constituted is a marriage of mutual submission, love, respect, and equality. And it accords beautifully with Paul's description of good marital relations in 1 Cor. 7:3-5.

So far, I have not dealt with Ephesians 5:24, which states that the husband is the head of the wife. This certainly sounds like leadership. A theological debate is raging in certain quarters over the meaning of the word "head" in the Greek language. First of all, we must be consciously aware that although we would prefer to believe that we take the Bible literally, we cannot in this case. A woman's head is at the top of her body; her husband cannot be her literal head. He is only her head metaphorically speaking, and we need to correctly understand the metaphor. And the metaphorical meaning of "head" is different in the language in which Ephesians was written than in English, the language in which we read it now. In both Hebrew and English, the metaphorical use of the word "head" has connotations of authority and leadership, as the head of a corporation is the boss, the CEO. Yet there is convincing evidence that in Greek the head is a metaphor for the source, like the head of a river. This would certainly accord well with the kind of love a husband is to have for his wife. He is to be the source of good for her, as Christ is the source and wellspring of life for the church.

In the Hebrew of the Old Testament, "head" has the same metaphorical connotations of authority, supremacy, and leadership which it has in English. However, when the earliest translators, to whom these were living languages spoken daily, translated the Old Testament into Greek, they did not replace the Hebrew word for head with the Greek word for head. Why? Because although the word could be explicitly translated, it no longer conveyed the same metaphorical meaning. The Hebrew implications of authority and supremacy would have been lost in the translation to the Greek metaphor "head." Instead, the translators chose the Greek word "archon" (a word connoting high political status, a position of leadership) to replace the Hebrew word for head. There would have been no reason for this change if the metaphorical use were the same in Greek.

Therefore, when the New Testament writers, who wrote in Greek, spoke of the husband as the head of the wife, or of Christ as the head of the church, they simply were not discussing authority and leadership, but an outpouring of love and life.

PAUL AND THE DIFFICULT PASSAGES

It is now time to embark on an exploration which many find questionable, or even flagrantly wrong. We are going to look at Scriptures which are frequently used to keep women out of the pastorate and consider alternative readings and meanings for them. If this seems like a dangerous or unnecessary undertaking, please consider the following. I once read a tract which accused a certain group of people of being rebellious, of flouting God's will, of going against the plain sense of Scripture in order to fit it to their modern humanistic philosophy, of attempting to destroy the social order which God had established, etc. Every word of that tract could have been used to condemn us and the endeavor on which we are here engaged, and in fact, all these things have frequently been said against any woman who wants equality and full participation in the Church. The fascinating thing is that this tract was written 150 years ago by a person of the pro-slavery position, against the abolitionists. Those who believed with all their hearts that slavery was offensive to God and a great sin against the people enslaved were seen as being in rebellion against God and destructive of morality and good social order. After all, the system of slavery was a very precious institution to those who benefited from it, and they had a great deal invested in reading the Bible in such a way as to justify it and oppressing those who disagreed with them.

Jesus understood that when God moves; when a new idea is in the very center of God's will, it may seem as rough and harsh as the new wine which no one wants, because they prefer the ways they know. People are attached to the way they have always done things, and find it easy to believe that what seems familiar and right to them must be God's will. But as Jesus warned the Pharisees, "for the sake of your tradition, you have made void the word of God." (Matt.15:6) So let us carefully and prayerfully examine these troublesome Scriptures.

The letters of Paul contain a broad spectrum from the loftiest theology to advice about individual quarrels and a request to bring along the cloak which he forgot. For a full understanding, we need to be sure how he meant his words to be understood. Sometimes he expressed a principle which he intended should be normative for all people at all times. Sometimes he wrote prescriptively, giving advice for a particular situation. And sometimes he wrote in a corrective mode, to change something. amiss. A difficulty often arises when the corrective statements, which are likely to be the most simplistic and easily accessible, are received by us as if he intended them to be normative for all time, while the big picture is ignored. For example, in Galatians 3:28, Paul makes a sweepingly inclusive statement which must be precious to all of us: There is neither Jew nor Gentile, there is neither slave nor free, there is neither male nor female: for ye are all one in Christ Jesus. At one stroke Paul made away with the tradition by which Jewish men made themselves an elite: each day as their first prayer they thanked God that they were not a Gentile, a slave, or a woman. But Paul said, there is no elite in Christ, we are all one. This to me, is a clear example of a normative statement, an overarching principle, against which other scriptures may be tested for understanding.

Now let us look at 1 Cor. 11:1-16. In verse 5, Paul takes it for granted that women will be praying and prophesying; he just wants to make sure that their heads are covered. Prophecy is speaking the word of the Lord in the congregation: in our modern terms, preaching. We should hope always that we prophesy when we preach. So much is clear. But there are such difficulties and contradictions in this passage! The format of this entire section of 1 Corinthians is that there are questions about problems in the church, and people have brought these to Paul by letter and in person; one by one he answers them. He begins here by commending them for doing as he taught, but then he goes into a confusing and self-contradictory explanation of why women must cover their heads when praying and prophesying. There are as many different explanations of v.10 "For this cause ought the woman to have power on her head because of the angels" as there commentators who have attempted it. Because I believe that a passage such as this must harmonize with the normative statement in Galatians, I am not satisfied with any explanation I have heard. I belie re that when Paul commended them in the first verse for keeping his teachings, he was thanking them for living out the principle which says they are all one. When they met for church, they met as brothers and sisters, one in Jesus, the women with uncovered heads, speaking freely as they might do in the family of God as in their family at home. But, says

Paul, although you have been faithful to what I taught you, this must change. He knows the principle, but the church is coming into disrepute. By both Jewish and Greek custom women who have uncovered heads have no morals. People who did not understand about the family of God must have been saying, "Have you seen? That church is full of whores!" But Paul had a principle which was dear to him, and he had not the temperament to easily make concessions to worldly customs; I think his ability to be single-minded about this is reflected in his prose. He says that women must cover their heads, then that their hair is given them for a covering. He says woman came from man, nevertheless, in the Lord neither is without the other, for all things are of God. He asks, "does not nature teach that long hair is shameful in a man?" No, Paul, it does not. Consider the mane of the male lion, and the more elaborate plumage of male birds. And if long hair in a woman is her glory, given her for a covering, what about Black women who frequently are unable to grow long hair (by the same nature you appeal to.) God made them as they are, and found His creation to be very good. Finally, Paul throws up his hands and says, "Judge for yourselves."

Well, if we may judge for ourselves, let us reason together, as God asks. Let us look at nature, as I have done above, and consider whether this is not one of the corrective passages, in which the application of the unchanging principle may change with the situation or the custom. The unchanging principle is that Christians are to give nonbelievers no grounds for casting aspersions on them. The application at that time was for women to cover their heads; an equivalent application in our society might well be to give women an equal place, for lack of which the church is brought into disrepute. And if we do not believe that some things in the Bible may change with the times, we had better take the braids off the women, make sure all the men kiss each other with the holy kiss of fellowship, and never let an unmarried man be ordained as a deacon.

We recognize that the application of God's Word may change with changing circumstances, as Paul discovered. At first, when he believed the end would come soon, he advised people not to marry. He also advised slaves to seek not to be free, but to honor their masters. However, society has now, with the benefit of hundreds

208

of years of practice in Christianity, evolved to the point that slavery is no longer an institution respected or practiced. And just as our society has evolved enough to recognize that enslaving others is a wrong that should not be and is not allowed, our attitude toward women has evolved as well. The women of New Testament times had been kept in seclusion, not educated, refused all participation in public life, and in general had a long way to go before equality was practical. And there were some astonishingly negative attitudes to be overcome in the men:

> The woman herself alone is not the image of God whereas the man alone is the image of God as fully and completely as when the woman is joined to him. (Augustine)

> As regards the individual nature, woman is defective and misbegotten, for the active force in the male seed tends to the production of a perfect likeness in the masculine sex, while the production of women comes from a defect in the active force or from some material indisposition, or even from some external influence, such as a south wind. (Acquinas)

> God's sentence hangs still over all your sex and His punishment weighs down upon you. You are the devil's gateway, you are she who first violated the forbidden tree and broke the law of God. It was you who coaxed your way around him whom the devil had not the force to attack. With what ease you shattered that image of God, man! Because of the death you merited, the Son of God had to die. (Tertullian)

We have had many years of increasingly normal and natural communication between the sexes, and the pace of change has recently picked up. After all, 150 years ago, women were still being told that if they went to college, their wombs would shrivel up! And if any of us has a sneaking suspicion that the Old Boys quoted above knew what they were talking about, it will perhaps help us in humility to remember that there are also Old Boys around who are quite sure that there was a time when Black people knew their place better than they do now.

I honestly do not wish to give offence in my drawing of parallels between the way the oppression of Black people was thought to be mandated by God's word, and the way the oppression of women is still so held by many. But why is it that good Christian men who have struggled for their place as equal participants with all colors in church and society are still convinced that it is appropriate to keep their sisters from an equal standing with themselves? Stokely Charmichael, who might be called an apostle of the civil rights movement, was asked what was the place of women in the civil rights movement? He infamously answered, "The place for women in the civil rights movement is prone." Surely this is so ungodly that we cannot afford to have any vestige or taint or similarity to this attitude in any of our decision-making or practice in the Church. Do we deserve freedom unless we ardently desire to extend it to our Sisters?

One of the most troublesome passages we will encounter in our search is found in I Timothy 2:11-15. This contains the bare statement "I suffer not a woman to teach nor to usurp authority over the man." For many people that settles the whole matter. But then Paul goes on to say that Adam was not deceived. Why is this significant? Is a person who sins knowingly after having been personally instructed by God somehow more fit to exercise authority over others than someone who was misled? Particularly when God instructed Adam not to eat of the tree before Eve was even created, so as far as we know, she received her instruction at second hand from her husband, which would have far less force than a command direct from God. And how in the world can Paul say that women will be saved by childbearing? That is indeed salvation by works! It seems so certain that Paul cannot have meant that, that some have tried to stretch the grammar to say that women will be saved by the bearing of the Child, i.e. Jesus. But then, why mention it? Are men not saved the same way? Or do women need more salvation than men do?

With so many inexplicable difficulties in the passage, one would think a person would have to be foolhardy to dare use it at the normative level, as a directive for all time. Yet this is often done. However recent archeological research, coming providentially, I believe, at this time, offers one single, simple explanation for the whole passage. There was a gnostic heresy current at the time, which undoubtedly was highly attractive to women who had been so much oppressed all their lives and were now tasting freedom as Christians. In a highly condensed version, it went like this: Spirit is good and matter is bad. Therefore, Jehovah, who caused the spirit to be imprisoned in matter, is a bad God. The serpent, who brought knowledge to mankind, was the good god. Adam either did not exist or was only at the level of a beast, until Eve bravely took the initiative and did a good thing by receiving that knowledge from the serpent and passing it on to Adam. She was Adam's superior. However, since imprisoning spirit in matter is an evil thing, women sin by having children. If she wants to be saved, a woman must become like a man and not have children. Revolting, isn't it?

Yet if we consider that Paul was not making normative pronouncements, but was correcting the gnostic heresy which was attracting so many women, the passage makes perfectly good sense. (A note on the phrase "To usurp authority": the Greek word is "authentein" which appears nowhere else in the Bible. We must go to extra-biblical sources to find its meaning. The word which is always translated as authority is "exousia."

One document shows that "authentein" has connotations of referring to the initiator, the one responsible. The question was: of two persons whose actions contributed to a death, which one was the "autthentos" the one whose fault it was? In using this word with its associations of violence, Paul shows his contempt for the heresy he was opposing. I am sure the gnostics would have chosen a word with more hero connotations to describe Eve's initiative.)

Paul frequently writes as if he were sending a telegram, using as few words as possible. Well, if we had to make parchment, or pay for it, we would also be more sparing of words. But let me offer an expanded version of the passage, which in light of the heresy he was combating, makes a sensible unity of it all and resolves the conflicts. "Let the women learn in silence with all subjection, sitting at the feet of the teacher as the men do. I am not presently permitting (a wording more justified by the Greek verb tense than most translations read) women to teach, for they are teaching that woman was the initiator over man. This s not true; Adam was first formed, then Eve, and Eve did not do a good thing by listening to the serpent, she was deceived, where Adam was not. And women should not refrain from childbearing, because it is not true that she loses her salvation that way.

Women can indeed be saved in bearing children. The important thing is to continue to practice the Christian virtues of faith and charity and holiness with sobriety, and not go running off after heresies." Seen this way, the difficulties are resolved by realizing that Paul is dealing with the contemporary problems caused by a particularly rampant and attractive heresy. He wanted the women to have time to learn how to learn, which their society had never afforded them. There is no reason to suppose that he would have continued the proscription past the end of the problem.

PAUL AND HIS FEMALE CO-WORKERS IN MINISTRY

Perhaps the primary justification for all the careful word studies on these and similar passages which would seem to exclude women from the ministry, is that it clearly was the practice of the time to have women serving in equal positions to the men. In Romans 16:7, Paul speaks of Andronicus and Junia, who are of note among the apostles. Here, as in many other cases, the translators have through the years obscured Junia's role, by turning her into a man. It is clear that the early church writers spoke of her as a woman, but recently translators have begun to spell her name as Junias, and the RSV even inserts a word not in the Greek, to read "Andronicus and Junias, who were men of note among the apostles."

Paul referred to Phoebe as a "diakonos" of the church at Cenchreae. But although the KJV translates the word "diakonos" as "minister" the other 21 times it appears in the New Testament, when it is applied to Phoebe, it is rendered as "servant." The Living Bible does even worse. The diakonos Timothy is a minister, but as the diakonos Phoebe is a "dear Christian woman!" **Surely it is sinful to so tamper with God's Word to suit our prejudices.**

In Romans 16:2 Paul called Phoebe a "prostatis" which the KJV renders as succourer, but when applied to a man it is commonly translated as leader or guardian. The verb formed from the same root, "proistemi" was applied to bishops and deacons when Paul told them to "rule" their households. That same passage in the KJV reads "If any man desires the office of Bishop," but this is not justified by the Greek, which uses the indefinite pronoun "tis" so that the correct reading would be "if any **one** desire the office of bishop."

The commentators have added their bit to these efforts of the translators to obscure the important and equal place which women held in the ministry during Biblical times. When John wrote to the Elect Lady, he used the feminine form of the word for master or lord. That word, "kyrios," is the same word which is famously used to refer to Christ himself as Lord of all. Being elect, she was chosen. She was the woman chosen as master over that church, an idea which some seem to find so intolerable that they have suggested that the use of the word of authority and power was "playful" in this case, or that she was a metaphor for a congregation.

When we see so many people so determined to change the meaning of God's Word, we surely have a great and mandatory calling to restore truth and clarity, and in the process, restore our Sisters to the place which God has for them.

THE ORDINATION OF WOMEN: GENDER OR POTENTIAL?

David W.M. Cassidy M.Div.

The ordination of women is a subject that is being discussed by many denominations both Catholic and Protestant. While many organizations have settled this issue a long time ago, denominations such as the Church of God in Christ (C.O.G.I.C.), still remain opposed to the ordination of women as a matter of ecclesiastical or denominational polity. The purpose of this paper is to discuss the ordination of women within the Church of God in Christ. It is an issue that is continually surfacing in the church but, to my knowledge has not been addressed before the General Assembly of the Church, nor has there been a Board of Elders appointed for the purposes of forming a new or more comprehensible policy on the issue other than that which appears in the official manual. This paper will focus particularly on a statement found on page 146 of the C.O.G.I.C. Official Manual (1973 edition), 'Women In Ministry', which says;

> Women may teach the Gospel to others (Phil.4:3; Titus 2:3-5; Joel 2:28), have charge of a church in the absence of a pastor, if the pastor so wishes (Romans 16:1-5) without adopting the title of Elder, Reverend, Bishop, or pastor. Paul styled the women who labored with him as servants or helpers, not Elders, Bishops or Pastors. Therefore, the Church of God in Christ cannot accept the following scriptures as a mandate to ordain women preachers: Joel 2:28; Gal. 3:28-29; Matt. 28:9:11.

We will be examining those terms that this section of the manual states are "for men only" titles, and thereby, men only positions. Upon a closer (exegetical) look at those words we will see that Paul did not style women in ministry any different than he did men. Such sexually biased-styling is often the androcentric rendering of male translators and interpreters of text.

The question remains to be answered; are individual words alone enough to insist that only men have a right to ordination? All individual words appear in a particular context, and that context impinges upon the literal meaning of individual words. In such contexts, definitions of individual words must be derived or understood from the context and hot just the "literal" definition of the individual word. Anyone who seeks to derive meaning from scripture must confront the issue of context along with grammar and syntax. Do words in context have gender-specific connotations? Are these same words, translated in a gender-specific manner, actually used in the [Greek] text in an inclusive or generic way? Do words, or more appropriately, must words, carry different meanings when associated with women in the Bible than they do when they are associated with men in the biblical text?

This project is not meant to be a "close" reading of the Greek texts involved but a look "topically" at words that have been used to support a particular theological and doctrinal position. This paper is written with the lay-person in mind as most ministers within the Church of God in Christ have no formal theological training in the biblical fang ages, historical, critical methodology, or biblical hermeneutics (Afrocentric or Womanist), or biblical-historical theology. It is my hope that this brief discussion will raise some difficult hermeneutical, and textual questions that will inform our theology concerning ordaining women to the ministry. It will hopefully argue that the question of worn n in ministry is not just a "woman" issue, but an issue that will address the "male-ist" assumptions about the priority of men over women with God. This paper will finally argue that qualification for ministry is far more important than the sex of the one d ministry.

Those C.O.G.I.C. Women

There is no question that the Women's Department is the largest, most successful, and most financial department within C.O.G.I.C. Inc. According to the Official Manual (1973 edition), there are National Supervisors of Women, Jurisdictional Supervisors; Missionaries, both State, district and local; Evangelist, and they supervise at least five other auxiliaries:

a. The Prayer and Bible Band

b. The Young Women's Christian Council

c. Purity Class

d. Sunshine Band

e. Any other auxiliary, national, state or local necessary for the operation of their work.

It can also be said without question, that women are the majority members of the Church of God in Christ, and are largely responsible for the bulk of the ministry that is done through local, state and national assemblies; through social, missionary, and evangelistic efforts. All one has to do is to attend C.O.G.I.C. services throughout the week and see who is in attendance. If anything, in most of our churches, the men who are in charge are mere figureheads. The financial backbone within the church is probably 90% female.

If we have permitted women to be so extensively involved in the ministry of the C.O.G.I.C. (the church could never survive without them), and have witnessed their "God-ordained" effectiveness, how can we "mere" Elders/men deny them ordination and full participation as ecclesiastical equals?

The concern about women in ministry, especially where ordination is concerned, often becomes a question of gender roles and equality. George W. Knight, a writer for Christianity Today (February 20, 1981, p.16), suggests that the New Testament considers men and women equal in the sight of Christ, yet, women are not to lead and teach either the church corporate, or men in the church. How can one be equal in "sight" yet unequal everywhere else? The scriptures that he (and so many others) use on behalf of such arguments are often Pauline; 1 Timothy 2:11-14; 1 Corinthians 14:35ff. Others make use of the narrative in Genesis chapter three to support their argument against the ordination of women. This text in Genesis is often used to prove that women have been subordinated to men, a punishment that is a direct result of Eve's sin.

However, there is a verse in the first creation account in Genesis (verses.1:26-28) which reads: "Then God said, let us create man (humankind) in our image and likeness to rule." Three times in this short periscope the word "image" is used. Without going into an in-depth analysis of the literary and rhetorical devices of repetition practiced by the ancient Hebrew writers, suffice it to say, being created in the image of God from a theological standpoint was and is of great significance and importance. An image is "a physical likeness or representation of a person, photographed, sculptured, or otherwise produced; reflecting a likeness; form; appearance; counterpart copy; semblance; etc."

It is very interesting that the second account of creation in Genesis (2:7) Go is forming (Heb. Yatsar, yaw-tsar) humankind from the dust of the ground. Using art stir terminology we could say that God sculpted people and would not in any way do damage to the Hebrew yatsar, which means to mold into form; espe. as a potter; fashion frame. However, God is not only making a sculpture but transferring the very divine image and likeness into it. What continues to be problematic about interpreting this text is that there are those who will ascribe such a literalness to chapter two, that these are often the only verses referred to and the only verses in Genesis which allows those who would so interpret them to define the image of God only as male. This is done in complete indifference to chapter 1:27, 28 where "God created humans in God's own image, both male and female"; And in verse 5:1,2; ". . . and at the time they were created God blessed them and called them "Adam" (Hebrew word - adomah) "man."

The term Adam with only a few exceptions in the Bible is used in a generic sense, that is, it means "human-kind." The attempt of the writer is to portray the creation of the human species and not one individual with a proper name "Adam." The sense of these two chapters is that male and female were created simultaneously not separately as some have supposed. Nor did God create the female superior to the male but called them both, "Adam."

As Dr. Na'im Akbar, a clinical psychologists, concludes;

There are considerable problems in making the Deity "male" as opposed to "female:' If God is just a male, then it means that there are 50% of human possibilities that God is not. This means that you have cut off God's possibilities and limited your concept. You have introduced an unnatural psychology into those who are women, who would see themselves less favored because God is of a different gender.

What Dr. Akbar has touched on underscores this paper; and that is how our image of and the way we read/interpret the Bible has been used against women and have become frustrating and limiting to the female (and male) psyche, if not to our continuity as a church community, our socio-political development, and our spiritual wholeness. Such a non-critical approach to biblical exegesis leads to a social structure within the Church of graded subjugation by those who so male-centeredly interpret the Bible. This male-centeredness (sexism) is especially responsible for the oppression of women in the ministry in the C.O.G.I.C. and is passed on to society at large.

"ORDINATION"

Let us look at a few of the biblical verses used to exclude women from ordination. First of all, let me say that there are no scriptures that explicitly state, "women are not to be ordained under any circumstances." Had there been such a text there would be considerable evidence to support an argument for not ordaining women. The word cheirontoneo[2] often translated "ordain" or used to refer to some activity which may indicate a process that we now call "ordination," is somewhat obscured by the way it is used within certain translations of the Bible, especially the King James Version.

One particular passage of Scripture (Acts 14:23) translates the word cheirontoneo, "ordained" (KJV), while in other translations (NASV, RSV, NIV) the word is consistently translated "appointed." The process, as the word indicates, involves "an election or selection to a particular task or office by raising hands, in this particular instance by the presbutos (Apostles), but in other instances "chosen" by the congregation (2 Cor. 8 19). Even though the word <u>ceirontatheis</u> is translated "appointed" by better translations, even when this word is used in reference to men, the word in and by itself carries no gender limiting connotations and therefore, does not by itself exclude women when it is used. According to <u>Vine's Expository Dictionary of Old and New Testament Words</u> (1981), the words often translated "ordained" (but in reality is; appoint, prepare, to set, to become, decide, judge, separate) has no representative word in Greek from which we have derived as a definition; "a sacred 'God-given' mandate, act, or process for investing with the office of minister/confer holy orders upon, priest or rabbi of either sex. The idea or practice that we currently call "ordination" is actually post biblical in character and only remotely related to the Bible. In that, "ordination" within the Bible is primarily an act of God's calling and appointment/ordination (Mark 3:13; Luke 10:1ff; Acts 13:2, 4; cf. 6:3; 20:28; 1 Cor. 1:1; 2 Cor. 1:1; Gal.1:1; Eph 1:1; Col.1:1; John 15:16). God calls, the person answers, the church confirms on the basis of the candidate being "full of the Spirit and wisdom" the only prerequisite. They were not first ordained and then because of ordination, became full of the Spirit and wisdom." Therefore, the calling aspect is up to God.

"ELDER"

When one refers to women ministers in the Church of God in Christ, one is constrained to use the term "missionary" as a ministerial designation. Women are not allowed to use the term "Elder, Bishop, Pastor, nor Reverend" because it is believed that these terms refer only to "male" ministers. However, when one examines the Greek word that is translated elder, <u>presbuteros</u>[3] it is a word that is not exclusively used in connection with "male" ministers. The word "Elder", often found as <u>presbuteroi</u>,[4] the nominative/vocative, masculine plural form (Acts 2:17, 1Pet.5:5) carries a double meaning, which can be translated, the "older people" but at the same time 'Elders" in terms of ministers. The concept of being old, however, is the dominant theme, not maleness. If the term <u>presbyteros</u> is used in connection with men as 'male' ministers, then the feminine counterpart, <u>presbutera</u> "older women" (1 Tim.5:2) should be similarly associated with "women," or as a. designate for "female" ministers. If the <u>presbutero</u> (dative, singular, masculine) in

220

1 Timothy 5:1, is a male minister, then also we must conclude that the women who are also referred to as presbuteras[5] (accusative plural, feminine, vs.2), are female ministers. The only other choice is "older men and older women who are not "ministers" but who are doing ministry (which still makes them ministers).

The accusative use of <u>presbuteras</u> implies that a question has been asked or anticipates the question; what about women? For the accusative answers questions, like to what extent? "In what direction?; "To what purpose?" In verse 14, the term there is presbuteroi. The two prominent translations of verse 14 are; "The elders who direct affairs of the Church" (NIV); "The elders who rule well," (NASV, RSV, UV). This text indicates that there were elders who "rule" in ways other than in the area of "preaching and teaching (doctrine)." Those who labored in preaching and teaching are "especially" worthy of double honor, while those who just "rule" are not. The term here then does supply evidence for a gender-specific androcentric rendering of the '<u>presbuteroi</u>' reference to men only. More than likely, as indicated by the contexts from which it is an extension, does however include female elders who also "rule well." Even if this ruling is in the "teaching of the younger women," which (by age alone) makes them elders; or a part of the group of "older people" who rule. Thus, there is the strong possibility of female elders who are appointed by special groups (Apostles) and others by their congregations to "rule", even if that position was limited by custom to a certain segment of ministry.

"DEACON"

Another word that is used in connection with ministry is diakonos. This word, translated most often as servant, is a designation for those who are servants of the Gospel, or God's helper in the Gospel. This <u>diakonon</u>[6], (masculine, accusative, 1st. person singular masculine or feminine designation) 6 is used in Romans 16:1 in connection with Phoebe, a woman. Phoebe, contrary to the designation as "deaconess" in the <u>Official Manual</u>, is referred to as a deacon in the biblical text. Not only as deacon, but she is described by Paul as a "Great help to many," <u>prostatis</u> pollon[7]. The word <u>prostatis</u> (probably where we get the word prosthesis), is derived from the verb <u>proistemi</u>, which indicates one who is at the head (of), rule, direct, to set over, appoint with authority; and is used when referring to officials and administrators of the Church.[8] It is translated elsewhere eight times as "a ruler of many" (Rom. 1:28; 1 Thes. 5:12; 1Tim. 3:4-5; 12; 5:17). Yet, when the same word is used in its feminine form the translators used "great help." This is glaring evidence of translator bias or feminine-stereotyping (if she is a woman she can lot be as important as a man). However, prostatis (feminine) means one who stands in front or before; a leader; a protector, champion or "patron." In Hellenistic religious associations, this was a position of great influence.[9] In one sense prostatis, if compared to poimaino,[10] which when translated is used figuratively of activity protects, rule, governs, fosters; in the sense of lead', 'guide', 'rule' a herd or flock; is used to describe those who lead Christian churches, then Phoebe is in fact a shepherd. While Phoebe is not described by Paul as a poimainenos (shepherd), clearly this was her activity.

Phoebe was much more than a mere helper, she was a first-rate diakonon (quite possibly an Elder), a minister of such significant standing within the church at Cenchr ae, that Paul refers to her by name, contrary to Jewish custom. In the same manner, Priscan (Gk. or, Priscilla, vs.3) is named in the majority of cases throughout the New Testament before her husband, indicating (according to Bauer's Greek Lexicon, s.v. "Priscan") that she was a more important person than her husband (Ro:16:3; 1 Cor.16:19, 2 Tim.4 19). They are described by Paul as "fellow-workers" (sunergous), those who helped him in spreading the Gospel. When Paul refers to himself and Apollo (1 Cor. 3:5-9) he uses sunergous along with diakonos, which means that they both have equal status in ministry, in other words, co-workers. Priscan was therefore considered by Paul to be the more prominent of the two in the spreading of the Gospel, therefore, Paul places her respectfully, "as her service has won her the right to be", mentioned before her husband.

In the ministry of the gospel, the quality of service, and not gender, should determine one's status. In Romans 15:31, Paul refers to his own service to the church as diakonia. In Romans 13:5, he refers to himself and Apollos as diakonoi (pl), "ministers" of the gospel (see also 2 Cor. 6:4).

"SIMILARLY THE WOMEN…"

In the case of I Tim. 3:8, 11ff, gunaikas, translated wives (KJV, NIV), is better translated "women" (RSV), because of the absence of the definite article. Gunaikas[11] is an accusative plural, not in its genitive plural form gunaikown which would have shown the woman in relationship to a man, which would suggest husband and wife. The phrase "their wives" does not appear in the Greek text. This text indicates, however, that those attributes or qualities that are being demanded of male deacons are also to be expected of female deacons. Thus, the use of the word osautos translated "similarly," is used to conn et the preceding texts with that which follows, the required qualifications for the women. Here, equality is suggested by the fact that women are believed to be capable of possessing the same qualities as their male counterparts in ministry.

Contrary to popular opinion, the word deacon is not to be used exclusively with the idea of waiting on tables or menial tasks. The word deacon is frequently used in the New Testament to designate those who minister (at least 18 times in the KJV alone) in the doctrine and preaching of the word (Acts 20:24; 2Cor 4:1; 6:3; 11:8; 1 Tim. 1:12, R.V., etc.). Also (as mentioned earlier), Paul so designates himself as a diakonon, in a figurative way and in reference to his Apostolic ministry. Ephesians 4:12, is a clear example of ergon diakonias. "work of the ministry," in the sense of what is done and not "who" is doing it. Therefore, the term deacon is not a term that is exclusive to the "servant/attendant" form of "male" only ministry but is the essence of all ministry by either male or female. The ideal of servant-hood rather than a slave/master (doulos) relationship is the foundational consciousness from which all who desire to be diakonal tou euanggelion, 'ministers of the gospel', are to approach ministry.

We must not fail to mention that where the word deacon is used in referent to a male or a female it is always used in its masculine form, that means its intention is not gender-focused. Therefore, within the biblical texts there is no such separate designation (technically) as "deaconess," or a female or male deacon. Gender is not the issue, nor important where a deacon is concerned, ministry is.

Contrary to the Official Manual's definition (141), diakonos does not denote the service or ministration of a bondservant (doulos, 141). According to Vines Expository dictionary (72), "diakonos" views a servant in relationship to his work, diakonia; while doulos (an adjective that indicates involuntary servitude), views a servant in relationship to the master, despotes." Therefore, a deacon is not a type of, nor an indication of a second-class subservient minister, but a fellow worker in the Gospel. It would appear that when Paul has referred to women as deacons he is accepting and acknowledging their ability to fully function in that capacity as an equal "fellow-worker" in ministry.

"MISSIONARY"

I cannot conclude this brief study without examining the use of the term missionary as a "ministerial designation" for women in the Church of God in Christ. First of all, there is no word 'missionary' in the Greek texts of the New Testament. The word that comes nearest to describing a "missionary" (in the sense of being, doing, or having a mission) is Aimstolos (one sent forth. Vines p.63), and their sending, apostellein (to send out or off). Such a word (used over 79 times in the N.T.) was used by Paul of Andronicus and Junius (Gk. Junia) in 1 Corinthians 8:23. Junia, from a lexical point of view (see Bauer, p.380), was a woman's name. There is nothing in the texts nor is there much historical evidence to suggest that these two were husband and wife. The objection to Junia being seen as a woman is based upon the fact that Paul calls her an apostle (see I.D.B. S.v. "Junia"). The problem with translators is that they often decide sex on the basis of titles and titles on the basis of sex. It is this sexual textual bias in translations that keeps worn and oppressed in church and society, and a major reason women are denied ordination. Paul says that Andronicus and Junia were outstanding "among" the apostles. They had both been imprisoned with Paul. This is also letting us know that they were not his converts, but had been Christians when he met them. Whoever in biblical texts is referred to as an apostle, "marks the bearer of the title, among other qualifications, as a missionary of a Gospel. (See the Interpreter's Dictionary of the Gospel, verses "Apostle").

There is no scriptural basis for the use of the word 'missionary' as a wholesale descriptive of women who are involved in ministry. The correct description of one (male/female) who is a missionary, or on a mission having been sent by the Lord (from a literal biblical interpretation) is Apostle. Men in the C.O.G.I.C., as far as I know, are never called missionaries.

The church has "sexualized" this term against any and all evidence of Scripture. To be biblical, we, therefore, must call women "missionaries" by their biblical title, "apostle." The way the church has used this word is not in any way biblical. It has been us make second class ministers of women without regard to their actual call, function, or quality of service. It serves no other purpose than to carry over the degradation and diminution of women on the basis of gender into the area of ministry. it is a purely sexist use of the word missionary, and defeats the purposes of Christ by denying a part of the body to function properly as God has intended. Furthermore, it fosters attitudes that devalue women and denies them opportunities for leadership and full participation in the ministry of the Gospel and the mission of the Church of God in Christ.

CONCLUSION

This paper has tried to show that many of the issues surrounding the ordination of women, if it were left up to certain words alone to decide, would not be a question of gender but of qualifications for ministry. When discussing the New Testament, practices that are indigenous to a particular specific (patriarchal) culture should not be considered apart from that culture. There are many practices of Palestinian Judaism that cannot be transferred as permanent fixtures into a Hellenistic, Gentile, nor post-biblical Christian context. For example, Jesus did not practice the strict culturally conditioned Sabbath keeping of the Palestinian Scribes and Pharisees. Contrary to their practices he ate without the washing of hands, he also healed a blind man on the sabbath, and refused to stone a woman "according to the law." Stoning no matter how biblical an act it is not transferable to modern Christianity or into our present social context.

To assume that the Bible's task is to do away with all other languages, cultural and social structures, and replace them with a Palestinian androcentric language, patriarchal social structures, and Palestinian cultural expressions is to miss the point of the purpose of a Bible. That purpose simply is, to inform about the workings of God among humankind, for the purpose of producing and maintaining faith in the ultimate. The purpose of the Bible is not to reinforce one culture against another. Nor was the Bible written (or inspired) for the empowerment of one sex over another. There is no text within the Bible, to my knowledge, that says; faith comes by hearing ordained men and leaves by hearing ordained women. But faith comes by hearing the Word of God. Again, the sex of the voice is not the issue, but the character of the inspired words spoken by the voice. Sex, to my knowledge, has never made anyone "genetically" a better minister of the Gospel. On the contrary, one may conclude by a preponderance of evidence, by mere numbers alone, that women are far more willing to hear (and obey) the Word of God than are men. Women give more, attend more, recruit more, and do more in this church and dare I say in any church anywhere.

Ordination is not a perfecting process. Many have been ordained whose ministries at the least indicate inadequate preparation with little or no potential for successful ministry, and at the worst indicate no call of God at all. Many who have been refused ordination, for whatever reason, have gone on and produced successful ministries on the personal revelation that they were in fact called by God. The single most important purpose of ordination is that a group of examiners has determined that one is qualified, mature, and responsible enough to do ministry. It is a statement of a group of witnesses who have determined that a call of God is in evidence in this person's actions and activity, and that they support and stand with God and this individual.

Women have proven over and over again to be as capable of excellence in ministry as any man this church has ever produced. It is time we show it openly a d in our denominational polity by "ordaining" those who have proven to be called by God and qualified for the task of ministry as we would ordain any male, qualified for the task of ministry. Gender is a poor judge of genius. Let us select, appoint, or ordain on the presence of potential and not merely on the presence of a penis.

---

1. Nairn Akbar, Chains and Images of Psychological Slavery. (New Jersey: New Mind Productions, 1984) 41.
2. A Greek English Lexicon of the New Testament, 2nd. ed., s.v. "Cherontineo" Walter Bauer. (Chicago: University of Chicago Press, 1979)
3. Ibid., s.v. "presbuteros."
4. The Analytical Greek Lexicon, 5th. ed., s.v. "presbuteroi," (Michigan: Zondervan Publishing House, 1977).
5. Ibid., s.v. "presbuteras."
6. Ibid., s.v."diakonon."
7. Kurt Atland, Bruce M. Metzger, The Greek New Testament, 3rd.ed., (West Germany: United Bible Societies 1983).
8. Analytical lexicon, s.v. "proistemi."
9. Ramsay MacMullen, Roman Social Relations. (New Haven: Yale university Press, 1974)74.
10. Ibid., s.v. "Poimaino."
11. -Bauer, Analytical Greek Lexicon, s.v."gunaikas.'

SUPPORTING DOCUMENTS TO MOVE TOWARD CHANGE

To: Bishop George D. McKinney, Jr.

From:

Judge Henry G. Watkins

San Diego, California

Regarding: Ordination of Women within the Church of God in Christ

There is neither Jew nor Greek,

There is neither bond nor free

There is neither male nor female

For ye are all one in Christ Jesus

Galatians 3:28

LEGAL ANALYSIS:

Whether C.O.G.I.C.'s Constitution And Promulgated Policies Preclude The Ordination Of Women

BACKGROUND

The Church of God in Christ (COGIC), Official Manual (1973), is the primary authority on the rules of the Church. The Church's Constitution is set forth in Part 1 of the Manual, and is the basic legal document prescribing rules and policies of the Church and its constituent parts. The Preface to the Manual states that it "shall establish guidelines for the conduct of both the ministry and laity of the Church of God in Christ, International." [Underlining added]. The Foreword by Presiding Bishop J. Patterson, states that the Manual, which replaced the earlier 1952 version of the Manual, was a response to the Church's tremendous expansion and changes. Bishop Patterson states that the Manual is "an earnest attempt to transcribe in contemporary terms the doctrine and discipline of our Church. He continues, "Hopefully it will exhort men to consult their hearts instead of their heads."

THE COGIC CONSTITUTION

The Constitution in prescribing the powers and authority of Jurisdictional Bishops, provides that: "A Jurisdictional Bishop shall have the right to appoint and ordain Elders." Art, IV, Sec, A.2. There is no restriction on the Jurisdictional Bishop's appointment or ordination power. The Constitution clearly defers to the Jurisdictional Bishop's God-led vision and insight.

The general procedure for a licensed Minister of a local Church to obtain ordination is for the candidate, upon the recommendation of his Pastor, to go before the Ordination Committee of the Ecclesiastical Jurisdiction of which his Church is an affiliate. The candidate must satisfy the following requirements: 1) moral fitness, 2) spiritual fitness, 3) attested loyalty to the Church, and 4) complete any prescribed course of study. Art. III, Sec. D.14. These are the only requirements. Thus, there is no requirement of male gender.

Jurisdictional Bishops are not limited in their ordination powers to those candidates referred to them by their Ordination Board. Thus, Jurisdictional Bishops may exercise their ordination powers without regard to the Ordination Board. However, as a practical matter, Jurisdictional Bishops are so busy with other matters that they will usually rely upon the Ordination Board to refer appropriate candidates for ordination.

There is no restriction in COGIC's Constitution against ordaining women. Each Jurisdictional Bishop is empowered to appoint and ordain Elders of his choosing. Accordingly, a Jurisdictional Bishop has the right to ordain women.[1]

Despite some beliefs to the contrary, there is nowhere stated or implied in the Manual that women may not be ordained. The Manual does, however, state that "nowhere can we find a mandate to ordain women to be an Elder, Bishop or Pastor." Pages 159-60. The word mandate means an authoritative command or instruction. The Manual does not state that women are barred from ordination Therefore, a particular Jurisdictional Bishop may, if he perceived to be so led by God, decline to ordain women because such ordination is not mandated. But, each Jurisdictional Bishop is authorized to ordain women if he "consults [his] heart instead of [his] head," [2], and believes that God leads him to this course. This is because all the Manual states is that its authors do not believe the ordination of women to be mandated. But one may freely choose to do a thing that he is not mandated or required to do.

Indeed, the Manual impliedly supports the ordination of women. In explaining the word Prophet, the Manual notes that the authors of the Old Testament books are viewed as "oral Prophets", while the authors of the New Testament books are viewed as "literary Prophets." A Prophet is defined as "the mouthpiece of God. He receives God's messages and is compelled to transmit it to the people."[3] This definition includes Ruth and Esther as Prophets or mouthpieces of God. And the scripture informs that a Prophet is a preacher.[4]

The Church of God in Christ has ordained women for more than 10 years. Women have been ordained to work as chaplains in the military, and at prisons and hospitals. Although these ordinations have been for working outside the Church of God in Christ, there is no legal basis under COGIC's Constitution or policies to circumscribe the duties of one ordained in the Church. The ordination papers issued for such women do not purport to bar them from acting as ordained elders in the Church. Instead, man's customs and traditions have resisted the legitimate role of ordained women within the Church.

Ordination ultimately comes from God's anointing. There can be no argument that God's chosen are empowered to act on His behalf outside the Church, but that they are somehow stripped of His anointing at the doorsteps of the very COGIC Churches that ordained them.

Also, women have acted as Pastors in COGIC Churches for years. But they have been labeled Administrators and Evangelists, and such. These women have headed Churches, given Communion, christened babies, admitted members to their congregations, and otherwise done things Pastors do. That they are called by another name does not alter the fact of what they are, for a rose by another name is as sweet. A man is known by his works, not by his title. A tree that bears figs may be called an orange tree, but it will be known by its fruit, and what it is called does not change what it is--a fig tree. One may ask if women serve as Pastors and Elders why then is it necessary to give them the title if titles are not important? While it is true that titles do not define who we are, those who use titles to ignore reality are hypocrites. Hypocrisy is defined as "the practice of professing beliefs, feelings, or virtues that one does not hold; insincerity."

The American Heritage Dictionary.[5] In short, a hypocrite says one thing and does another. It is hypocritical to ordain women for work outside the Church, but not for work within it; it is hypocritical to have women serve as Pastors but profess the belief that they are something else. The Bible warns that we should not be hypocrites. Matt. 23:13-29; Matt. 24:51. Further, the scripture speaks of hypocrites as those who lay aside the commandment of God to hold the tradition of men. Mark 7:8.

The Church has de facto[6] and in part de jure[7] recognized women as serving in the roles of women Pastors and Elders. It is time to Honor god and close the gap between word and deed. This is no more than to embrace truth, and the truth shall surely set us free.

In the final analysis, the Jurisdictional Bishop, as the rest of us must rely upon his own message from God. Where a Bishop chooses to ordain women in response to God's prompting the Church must stand behind him, for if each member of a congregation chose his own personal view over that of his Pastor there would be no need of a Church. Thus, just as congregants must honor and respect Pastor's vision so must the Church officials honor and respect the vision of those senior to them, for it is written: "And how shall they hear without a preacher? And how shall they preach, except they be sent?" Romans 10:14-15. Preachers receive their authority from God and are respected for their closer walk with Him. They have been blessed to be able to hear God's words and see His signs more clearly than the rest of us who see God's signs as through a glass, darkly.[8] Thus, the Church's tradition of respecting the vision of the preacher is greater than man's tradition of excluding women from the ministry.

While not strictly a legal argument, some have suggested that the ordination of women may not be a desirable policy because it will somehow undermine the Women's Department. This is an emotional response to change which seeks to cling to old traditions, traditions, but it lacks logic. No one has ever argued, for example, that moving from the Deacon Board to the ministry undermines the Deacon Board. One moves to the ministry in response to God's calling, and even if the Women's Department initially lost some of its members who were called to the ministry, God's will surely supersedes our own.

Further, the assumption that most women will pursueth ministry finds no support in experience. Many women have stated that they have no interest in becoming evangelists or in seeking ordination. Also, some women have left COGIC in the past because they could not obtain ordination from their Bishop. Some of these have gone on to be ordained in other Churches. Thus, the ordination of women may well have the effect of retaining women in COGIC and drawing other spirit-filled women to our ranks. This would strengthen the ranks of the Women's Department rather than diminish it.

The Manual recounts that though "the drastic changes initiated by this God-sent man [Bishop Patterson] provoked undue criticism" it was the general consensus that "God had given him the reign and vision for the Church."[9]

The Manual also states that the Church believes in "the Freedom in the Holy Ghost. This is the freedom to follow the dictates of God's Spirit, to be as Christ-like and as creative as possible."[10] The Church of God in Christ has strongly counseled men of God to rely on their hearts instead of their heads, to seek and pursue God's will as revealed to them, and to make changes consistent with scripture, to accommodate the changing needs of the Church. Bishop Patterson's last sermon in November of 1989, was prophetic in many ways and supports moving away from tradition for tradition's sake to closer approach the will of God. He pointed out that in COGIC it used to be viewed as wrong to wear neckties, eyeglasses, or to get dental care. He applauded the Church's departure from these unsupported traditions to more legitimate needs. This Prophet's words have pointed the way for the 1990s and beyond.

---

1. Some may contend that because the Constitution employs the male pronouns, "he" and "his" in referring to the ordination of ministers this shows that only men may be ordained. But such a contention would be in error because the Manual, as the Bible, uses the masculine pronoun to include male as well as female. See for example Art. V111, Sec. 2 (a), which refers to "any member of a local Church .. of which he is a member." Also, the Manual in explaining "The Doctrine of Man" refers clearly to "the human race" in its use of the term "all men." Pages 58-61. [It should be noted that due to various printings of the 1973 Manual the page numbers in each printing may not exactly correspond to other printings]. The section of the Manual explaining "Church Membership" addresses the obligation of absent members to hold in escrow or send tithes and offerings to the Church until "his" return. Page 95. Finally, the section addressing "Admission to the Church" states that a candidate for Church membership may be received as a member after showing the sincerity of "his" faith. All these examples unequivocally relate to men and women alike despite the use of the male pronoun or the word "man." Page 96.

2. Manual's Foreword by Bishop J.C. Patterson.

3. Page 149, of Part V, on "The Christian Ministry"

4. I have not here sought to present an exegesis of scripture for I defer to the superior insight of men of God.

5. One kind of hypocrite is he who honors God with his lips but whose heart is far from Him. Mark 7:6.

6. That is, establishing a practice in fact while not expressly and openly sanctioning it.

7. A de jure practice is one openly declared and sanctioned. The ordination of women to serve as elders outside the Church is a de jure recognition of the ordination of women.

8. See 1 Cor. 13:11-1

9. XXXV11, of the Manual in the section entitled "The Story of Our Church, The "Church of God in Christ."

10. Id at page XXXIX

LEGAL ANALYSIS AND JUSTICE

By Reverend Hazel Dawson

DO WOMEN DO THE SAME JOB AS MEN WITHOUT ORDINATION?

Firstly, we shall classify the "job" that Jesus told as should be done. Secondly, the "job description" and thirdly qualification." Then we will determine whether women qualify and if they have met the criteria for eligibility.

THE JOB

The job that Jesus commanded to be done is contained in what we call the "great commission" in Mark 16:15 "and he said, unto them, Go ye into all the world, and preach the gospel to every creature."

THE JOB DESCRIPTION

Proclaiming the gospel, bring glad tidings to every creature.

JOB TITLE = PREACHER, a public instructor.

THE JOB QUALIFICATIONS

Acts 1:4 And being assembled together with them, commanded that they should not depart from Jerusalem, but wait for the promise of the father which saith he ye have heard of me. (Verse 5) For John truly baptized with water but ye shall be baptized with the Holy Ghost not many days hence. (Verse 8) But ye shall receive power after that the Holy Ghost is come upon you: and ye. shall be witnesses unto me both in-Jerusalem and in Judaea, and in Samaria and unto the uttermost part of the earth.

HAVE WOMEN MET THE CRITERIA FOR ELIGIBILITY?

Acts 1:13 "And when they were come in they went up into an upper room, where abode both Peter, and James, and John, and Andrew, Phillip and Thomas Bartholomew, and Matthew, James the son of Alphaeus, and Simon Zelotes and Judas the brother of James.

(Verse 14) These all continued with one accord in prayer and supplication with the women and Mary the mother of Jesus and with his brethren.

Acts 2:4 And they are all filled with the Holy Ghost and began to speak with other tongues as the Spirit gave them utterance.

Acts 2:16 But this is that which was spoken by the prophet Joel;

(Verse. 17) And it shall come to pass in the last days, saith God, I will pour out of my Spirit upon all flesh: and your sons and your daughters shall prophesy, and your young men shall see visions, and your old men shall dream dreams.

(Verse.18) And on my servants and on my handmaidens I will pour out in those days of my Spirit; and they shall prophesy:

Having established what the job is the qualifications, and that women have indeed qualified and that they are eligible another question surfaces.

Is ordination what causes one to qualify for the job?

I venture to say that it is not.

Because man lacks omniscience he must rely on tools with which he identifies, proves, and classifies those who declare that they have been "called" (or want to apply for the job).

Ordination then is merely manes seal of approval, validation, and certification of the work that God has called one to do.

WHAT DO MEN MEASURE IN OTHER MEN IN ORDER TO DETERMINE THE AUTHENTICITY OF GOD'S CALL TO PREACH THE GOSPEL?

1. THEIR TESTIMONY-Do they have a testimony of repentance, salvation and baptism?

2. THEIR WORK-What is their involvement in the church and the field. How skillful are they in scriptural interpretation and dissemination?

3. THEIR LIFE-Is their Christian walk exemplary of a born-again believer?

4. STABILITY-Are they over-night wonders? Are they a novice or are they seasoned in the word and have they, by reason of use (experience) had their senses exercised to discern between good and evil?

When we look at what is reportedly measured, in a man's life before ordination, we can safely say that there are women who apply meet the measure.

Having addressed the question of whether women, who are not ordained, fulfill the description, meet the requirement, and perform the same job as men; we shall move on.

A. WHAT ADDED RESPONSIBILITY WILL ORDINATION INCREASE?

1. Will it cause us to start proclaiming the gospel? In all respect, we know that women have been on the front line, spreading the word for the Church of God in Christ. We have not given them the authority or title as men nor credited her with the success of the church, but we know that she has served and preached and led as some tenaciously declare) with much clarity, power, and conviction as most men and more than some. The proportion of their successful accomplishments to that of men in some areas is lower only because of restricted opportunities to serve in those highly visible areas.

2. If women are ordained will that cause them to start feeding the hungry, clothing the naked, sheltering the homeless and visiting those in prison? No, they do these things already. Of course, the Church has never had a problem with women heading the street feeding programs or going into the prisons, heading the hospitality group, or doing any work relevant to missions. Which is the real work of the church? We have no problem with a parishioner calling for women to anoint them with oil and pray the prayer of faith especially if they need someone at two o'clock in the morning.

B. OTHER THAN BISHOP OR SUPERINTENDENT, WHAT IS SHE NOT ALREADY DOING WITHOUT ORDINATION?

She is not performing those duties that are notably "center stage." Those duties that are highly ceremonial and that have, caused many men to suffer from illusions of grandeur, illusions of omnipotence, and omniscience, those ceremonial events that have caused man to have a superiority complex and a God complex. And for fear that they will lose their deitific positions, they relentlessly refuse to allow a woman to join their 3-C CLUB. "Called, Chosen and Chauvinistic".

I firmly believe that women, once ordained, will allow men to keep all the glory they have reserve unto themselves and they will be content to just do the work and fulfill the greats, commission.

This brings us to the question…

C. WILL WOMEN BE ABLE TO DO MORE WITH ORDINATION?

There are many ceremonial rituals that women are not able to perform without ordination such as:

> Matrimonial
> Burial
> Baptismal
> The Lord's supper

Not only are they restricted from performing these ceremonial rituals, the men of the state do not recognize their authority in performing these ceremonies if they are not church ordained.

Beyond these ceremonies, the refusal to ordain women has prohibited women from serving as faithful and serious capabilities.

Without ordination women do not have the freedom as ordained men to minister in jails, hospitals or the armed services.

This is most serious because the great commission was to go into all the world and preach the Gospel to every creature.

Who is man that he can restrict a woman from having access to every creature?

Prophesy = To speak or sing by inspiration

Prophetess = A female foreteller or an inspired woman.

Hypocrisy in the Attitudes and Practices of
The Church of God in Christ Regarding
the Ordaining and Ministry of Women

Jesus condemned the hypocrites of his day because they put on an appearance of Godliness and Scriptural correctness while in fact pursuing their own agenda rather than being concerned to do God's will. And it is doubtful that they were able to admit to themselves that their condition was one of false righteousness. I was mare likely an example of the "way that seemeth right to a man but the end of that way is death." We are all imperfect human beings, so we are certain to have among our attitudes and practices some which we may honestly believe to express God's will, which may seem right to us, but which further our own agenda of self-interest rather than God's plan for our lives and our church.

The Church of God in Christ, like every other Christian church, has a hierarchy, a power structure, which is established and carried out by men, and has developed traditional practices some of which cannot be justified either by logic or by a responsible reading of God's word. I refer in particular to the general refusal to ordain women while making an exception for women serving as chaplains, and allowing women who go overseas as missionaries to perform all the functions which are here reserved for ordained ministers. So in all honesty, it would seem that the church hierarchy does not have a problem with women who perform pastoral functions, provided they do it in a location where they are in no danger of occupying a pulpit whose prestige, power, and salary must belong to a man.

During the height of missionary fervor in the 19th century, it was common practice for churches who refused to ordain women to the pulpit on the grounds that Paul had forbidden women to preach, teach, and take authority over men to nevertheless send these "weaker vessels" to do these very things in primitive countries under conditions of hardship and danger, while only men could perform such functions in the relative safety and comfort of a church pulpit at home. Thus, the male hierarchies of many denominations safeguarded salaried positions of their brothers. Even worse, I suspect while church hierarchies were offended by the notion that a woman might have the temerity to want to teach "our" men, it was thought quite proper for her to teach the "primitive benighted heathen" who were almost always people of color! Surely C.O.G.I.C. cannot allow itself to continue an unquestioning following of customs which are rooted in assumptions which can fairly be described not only as ungodly but also 'as positively vile.

This brings us to the question of how Scripture is selectively used to support the present refusal to ordain women to the pulpit. It is surely hypocritical to ignore major themes of Biblical thought in favor of isolated proof texts, or to make passages which are confusing, and questionable as to translation, of more importance than the clearest, broadest, and most normative statements. One of the most plainly expressed positions Jesus ever took, both in word and in deed, was that the one faro would be the leader must be the servant. So the woman who cleans the church bathroom may be more important in God's eyes than the man who occupies the pulpit! Conversely, in order to follow Jesus's requirement here, the one in the pulpit must see himself and be seen as a servant rather than as one in a high position of authority. Therefore, a woman could not possibly "usurp authority" by occupying that place. The church seems to have chosen to ignore the words and example of Jesus who thought it worthwhile not only to state the principle but to live it by washing his disciples' feet, in favor of a passage in a minor epistle in which both the context and the translation are far from clear. Is not this because it "seemeth right" specifically to men, that they should just naturally keep power and control over women?

The hypocrisy in the above example lies in ignoring broad Scriptural principles in favor of passages which may well have been corrective of a specific problem, never intended for general use beyond that situation. An equally pervasive problem is the tendency to read Scripture according to a predetermined agenda. Although God requires all Christians not to be respecters of persons, to take the lowest place until invited up higher, and to esteem others more highly than oneself, men seem chauvinistically determined to read Scripture so as to prove their own primacy and superiority. Even if we honestly believe that the phrase "husband of one wife" was intended to exclude women rather than polygamists from the ministry, has C.O.G.I.C. ever applied the same passage to insist that unmarried men, childless men, and those whose children are not all living orderly lives, are excluded just as definitely as women are?

As people who have known what it is to be oppressed, and as Christians, Black men have an obligation not to be oppressors in their turn.

In the Black church, men are in the minority, but they nevertheless claim the leadership role, keeping women in positions of hard work and even responsibility, but without allowing the leadership accompanying authority, credit, and visibility. We know that when the Bible speaks of slavery it was an accommodation to the culture of that day, but not an expression of God's will and intention for all time, and in time God showed His people a more excellent way of equality and respect for all people as His creations. Can any man dare to stand before God and receive the benefits of this progress, this enlightenment for himself while denying it to his sisters?

The Old and New Testament clearly reveal that God is a God of Righteousness and Justice, (Micah 6:8). The Church of God in Christ and every bible assembly agree that the Church is obligated to conduct its affairs under the Biblical Standard of justice and righteousness. The Church's commitment to righteousness requires that all its doctrines, teachings, and practices promote and encourage its adherents to develop a right relationship with God and man. With regards to the ordaining of women in Biblical mandate to "do justly," (Micah 6:8), has urgent implications.

The Church's authority to ordain, to "loose and bind", to forgive sins, etc. is "delegated" authority from the Lord of the Church. Such awesome delegated authority must not be exercised arbitrarily, or irreverently, since the Church is accountable to the God of Justice.

All power and authority rest with God, including the power and authority to call and ordain workers for the ministry. Therefore, the question is raised, does gender-based ordination wrongfully deny the Church's blessing and affirmation to women who are called? Is there a parallel between the Church's practice of gender-based ordination and historical practices of race-based ordination, education-based ordination?

Report To The

Doctrinal Review Commission

Bishop George McKinney, Chairman

From

Bishop William James, Sr.

Committee Member

presented

November 11, 1993

"WHO CALLS PEOPLE TO THE MINISTRY AND HOW A PERSON IS CALLED"

"And it shall come to pass in the last days, saith God, I will pour out of my Spirit upon all flesh: and your sons and you daughters shall prophesy, and your young men shall see visions, and your old men shall dream dreams:

"And on my servants and on my handmaidens, I will pour out in those days of my Spirit; and they shall prophesy." (Acts 2:17,18)

The subject of a woman's place in the church will, undoubtedly, be argued as long as the church is in existence. Personally, I believe a study of "The Ministry of Women" is very relevant and very important to our generation. Many churches are re-evaluating their stand concerning women and are not only allowing them places of leadership in their government, but also are ordaining women to the ministry.

What does the Bible say and teach?

I am quite aware that this is a very controversial subject in many church quarters and, therefore, is avoided if at all possible. But WE DO HAVE THE WORD OF GOD to turn to for instruction. Let us approach the Word of God carefully, without prejudice and with truth and sincerity, and see what the Bible has to say about our subject.

In the Old Testament, at least three women are called prophetesses of the Lord. This means they spoke God's word and acted as His mouthpiece. MIRIAM, the sister of Moses, by inspiration of the Holy Spirit and by the appointment of God, exercised the prophetic office and a place of public leadership among the ancient people of God. DEBORAH was a prophetess and judge in Israel. All Israel (MEN AND WOMEN) came to be judged of this woman who, though she exercised her proper office as wife and mother, was the prophetess of God's people. She was their leader in warfare and the inspirer of Barak, the man of God who shared the authority with her. Then there was a woman who was the contemporary of Isaiah, named HULDAH. She was a prophetess who exercised in the days of the nation's grief with a remarkable and tremendous ministry.

Other Old Testament women are well known to you--Jael, the contemporary of Deborah, whom God raised up in the place of a man that she might put the erring and cowardly man to shame; Hannah, the mother of Samuel; Abigail, who saved from bloodguilt, David, the man after God's own heart; Ruth, the Moabitess, Queen Esther, who was brought into the Kingdom for a special purpose in the economy of God.

King James Version of Psalm 68:11 says: "The Lord gave the word (or the command); great is the host that publishes it." But the American Standard Version reads: "The Lord giveth the Word; THE WOMEN THAT PUBLISH THE TIDINGS ARE A GREAT HOST," which is according to the original text.

The women I have mentioned acted in their God-appointed places. THEY WERE NOT USURPING ANY MAN'S AUTHORITY. THEY WERE PERSONALLY CALLED OF GOD TO RENDER THIS PARTICULAR SERVICE IN THEIR DAY.

The capstone of this matter of the ministry of women in the Old Testament is the prophecy of Joel. Joel prophesied the events which would precede and herald the day of the Lord. He wrote: "Your sons and YOUR DAUGHTERS shall prophesy; your old men shall dream dreams and your young men shall see visions; even upon the menservants and the MAIDSERVANTS in those days I will pour out my Spirit."

In other words, Joel said the day would come when there would be equality of spiritual ministry among sons and daughters, men and women, menservants and maidservants. It would be in the day when the Lord pours out of His Spirit.

"For ye are all the children of God by faith in Christ Jesus. "For as many of you that have been baptized into Christ have put on Christ.

"There is neither Jew nor Greek, there is neither bond nor free, there is neither MALE NOR FEMALE: FOR YE ARE ALL ONE IN CHRIS JESUS.

'And if ye be Christ's, then are ye Abraham's seed, and heirs according to the promise." (Gal. 3:26-29) the ministry of women in the New Covenant Local Church.

Jesus Christ and suffered on Calvary's cross. He died on that cross to bear away our sins, according to the scriptures. He was b tied and rose again the third day, according to the Scriptures. After His resurrection, He showed Himself alive and appeared to His disciples for forty days. at the end of these forty days, Jesus Christ said to them:

"Thus it is written, and thus it behooved Christ to suffer, and to rise form the dead the third day.

"And that repentance and remission of sins should be preached in his name among all nations, beginning at Jerusalem.

"And ye are witnesses of these things.

"And, behold, I send the promise of my Father upon you: but tar ye in the city of Jerusalem, until ye be endued with power from on high." (Luke 24:46-49)

These words of Jesus are what the church general calls the "Great Commission." It is the commission to the disciples of Jesus to preach the gospel and evangelize the world. Now, to whom does this commission apply? Only to the eleven Apostles of Jesus Christ? Oh, no! It is quite evident from the Scriptures that this commission was given to a great host of believers. 120 of them accepted the opportunity.

The Bible record is very clear that those who were to be commissioned to preach and teach the gospel and evangelize the world were to "tarry (wait) in the City of Jerusalem until they received the promise of the Father (the outpouring of the Holy Spirit)."

Now comes the question: "Who, of those who heard the Great Commission, actually went to Jerusalem to receive the Holy Spirit?"

The first chapter of Acts gives us the answer. In verse 13 the names of the eleven apostles of Jesus Christ are mentioned. Then, in verse 14, I read: "These (the eleven) all continued with one accord in prayer and supplication, WITH THE WOMEN, and Mary the mother of Jesus, and with his brethren."

So, we see there was a company of people—apostles and men and women – waiting for the outpouring of the Holy Spirit on the Day of Pentecost. When the Day of Pentecost was "fully come, they were all in one accord and one place."

The like "gift of the Holy Spirit" was now received by Jew and Gentile, male and female, and, eventually would be given to both bond and free. Now, if this great gift of the Holy Spirit was given so freely to all, (and this great gift is also known as the "baptism of the Holy Spirit"), then the "lesser" gifts of the Holy Spirit are also meant for Jew and Gentile, bond and free, male and female. These lesser gifts mentioned in 1 Corinthians 12, are these: the word of wisdom, the word of knowledge, the discerning of spirits, faith, working of miracles, healing, prophecy, tongues, and the interpretation of tongues.

Again I repeat: "IF THE GREAT GIFT OF THE HOLY SPIRIT IS FOR MEN AND WOMEN ALIKE...SO ARE THE LESSER GIFTS OF PREACHING AND TEACHING."

For just a moment, let us turn our attention to some of the more prominent women mentioned in the New Testament.

The first preachers of the resurrection were women. Jesus told Mary Magdalene and the women, "Go and tell my disciples and Peter that I have risen from the dead and that I am going to Galilee and there they shall meet me." In Acts, Philip, the deacon (later the evangelist) went to Samaria ministering the Word of God. Surely one minister was enough in a family. But Philip had four virgin daughters who also prophesied. Five people in Philip's family had a New Testament ministry--the father and his four daughters.

"He that prophesieth speaketh unto men to EDIFICATION, AND EXHORTATION, AND COMFORT." (1Cor. 1.4:3)

What, exactly, do these words mean in our English language? Let's go to the Dictionary. First of all, notice that to prophesy is to speak publicly, where one can be heard by others. "He that prophesieth SPEAKETH UNTO MEN."

EDIFY means: "To instruct and improve; to profit morally or spiritually."

EXHORT means: "To incite by words or advice; to advise or warn earnestly."

COMFORT means: "To impart strength and hope to; now, usually, to relieve of mental distress; console." (Webster's Collegiate Dictionary)

Now, since sons and daughters are to prophesy, and prophecy is a quickened utterance for the edification, exhortation, and comfort of men, then it must be done in the church by both men and women.

When we read in 1 Timothy 2:11, 12, that the women are to keep silent, it means that they are not to bicker, argue, strive for preeminence or cause any sort of confusion in the church.

This certainly does not mean they are not to pray, prophesy, or be used in the manifestation of the gifts of the Holy Spirit.

Women should and must learn in quietness. They must not be busybodies or know-it-alls in the house of God. THEY MUST NOT USURP (to seize and hold in possession by force or without right)

AUTHORITY OVER THEIR HUSBANDS

"Let the woman learn in silence (quietness) with all subjection.

"But I suffer not a woman to teach, nor to usurp authority over the man, but to be in silence (quietness)." (I Tim. 2:11, 12)

These Scriptures do not forbid a woman to teach; the restriction lies in teaching, exercising, and usurping authority over the man. What does this mean?

Paul did not say, "I permit no woman to teach." He did say, "I permit no woman to teach and usurp authority over the man." In other words, if God has provided in the church a man who has been gifted and called by the Spirit of God to do the teaching, a man sufficient and able to exercise authority, he is the one to do it. But, IF THERE ARE NO MEN WHO ARE GIFTED OF GOD TO TEACH, SHE IS NOT USURPING AUTHORITY WHEN SHE TEACHES. SHE HAS THE RIGHT TO TEACH. She is performing the will of God.

With the birth of the church on the Day of Pentecost a new day arrived with liberation for the woman. Jesus Christ came into the world and died on the Cross of Calvary when He destroyed the enmity that existed between male and female, bond and free, Jew and Greek. And, on the Day of Pentecost, woman was visited with God's highest gift, THE GIFT OF THE HOLY SPIRIT.

Through the work of Jesus Christ on the cross and His ascension into heaven, a new body was formed here on earth by the Holy Spirit. This body is called "The Church," and it is made up of male and female, bond and free, Jew and Greek. In this body, both man and woman share the same spirit, are all partakers alike in the heavenly gift, and are given "gifts and graces according to the measure of the gift of Christ." But, with all the goodness and grace of God bestowed upon woman, she yet has ONE RESTRICTION: SHE IS NOT TO USURP THE POSITION OF A MAN.

The meaning of usurp is this: "USURP, ARROGATE." To usurp implies forcible seizure, as of power, without right; ARROGATE is to assume unduly or with presumption."

In other words, a woman may minister in the place the Lord has placed her, but she is to be careful that it be her particular place. She must forcibly seize a place that belongs to the man.

What about ordination? A woman need not lobby to be ordained as a minister because she sees herself capable of expounding the Scriptures as any man. Nor is ordination per se essential for feminine fulfillment. However, there may be special circumstances when a woman may recognize the need for formal ordination, such as the foreign fields where few men can enter the gospel ministry.

Or perhaps a woman called to the prison ministry may find herself required by government authorities to have full ministerial credentials. Ordination for her would simply show that others recognize her enabling ministry in jails.

ORDINATION OF WOMEN IN MINISTRY

From a "Called" Woman's View

Colonel Diane James

INTRODUCTION

The Church of God in Christ's official manual states "The Church of God in Christ recognizes that there are thousands of talented, filled, dedicated and well informed devout women capable of ting affairs of a Church, both administratively and spiritually

It concludes the apology with these words "The Church of God in Christ can not accept the following scriptures as a mandate to ordain women preachers: Joel 2:28; Gal 3:28-29; Matt 28:9-11.

The purpose of this paper is to defend the founding father's position on FEMALE ORDINATION. The writer of this paper will attempt to convey to the readers that the church's doctrine on Ordination (the established vehicle whereby male believers are given authorization to conduct the spiritual and administrative affairs of the church) is rooted in beliefs, history, and traditions. The writer must admit from the outset that this research is spiritual, view is personal and scope, limited.

BELIEFS

The major factor that precluded the female from Church of God in Christ ordination, was belief. I am of the opinion that belief dictates one's behavior. Case in point; a medical writer revealed recently that it is believed that bee stings help relieve multiple sclerosis symptoms.

The writer stated that a woman had already been stung ten times by bees, but she still sat calmly next to seven white boxes of hives, for more. In other words, the woman suffering from the debilitating disease needed a cure and believed through her data collection that bee stings would cure her. Consequently, she allowed herself to be stung repeatedly, in the hopes of better health. Her belief dictated her behavior.

The dictionary defines belief as a state or habit of mind in which trust or confidence is placed in some person or thing. Sara Little, in her book, To Set One's Heart, says that for a belief to be of any significance, it must be a component in a belief system. She went on to say that a belief system is a set of related ideas (learned and shared) that has some permanence, and to which individuals and/or groups exhibit some commitment. When ideas get shared and repeated time and time again, they soon become a belief, consequently it gets sustained, reformed, and embodied by the faith community.

It is essential that individuals in the faith community, know what he/she believes and that his/her belief be based on the Word of God. I believe "For as by one man's disobedience many were made sinners." Romans 5:12 says "as by one man sin entered into the world, and death by sin; and so death passed upon all men, for that all have sinned. In other words, I have come to grip with the fact that sin was passed down through Adam and Eve. I believe that we were all born into Adam's life of sin, but I also believe that "by the obedience of one, shall many be made righteous." The scriptures to follow will validate my belief. "And almost all things are by the law purged with blood, and without shedding of blood is no remission" (Hebrews 9:22). "But God commendeth his love towards us, in that, while we were yet sinners Christ died for us" (Romans 5:8). "Who His own self bare our sins in His own body on the tree, that we, being dead to sins, should live unto righteousness: by whose stripes ye are healed" (I Peter 2:24). "I am crucified with Christ: nevertheless I live; yet not I but Christ liveth in me and the life which I now live in the flesh I live by the faith of the Son of God the Son of God, who loved me and gave himself for me" (Galatians 2:20)

In other words, I am now in Christ Jesus, just as I was in Adam. I believe that all of us had to be born again, through the act of salvation. I believe that I now share in Jesus Christ's life. I believe that men and women alike are as the Scripture said, "have been reconciled to God by the death of His Son on the cross" (Romans 5:10).

For by the obedience of one, shall many be made righteous. We have been "buried with Him by Baptism into death; that like, as Christ was raised up from the dead by the glory of the Father, even so, we also should walk in the newness of life. My friends, when we accepted Jesus as Savior, we were given a new spirit, a new relationship to God, a new morality, a new standard to live by, one that the Holy Spirit enables and commands us to follow.

What we fail to realize is that the battleground between God and Satan is the human mind. Satan has convinced many of God's people that (1) something is wrong with women (2) Figure out what it is and fix it (3) what people say and how they treat women, tell women who they are and what they are worth. We have been adopted into the Royal Family. I honestly believe that two things happened at the cross for women and men. First, God dealt with our sins and secondly, God dealt with our flesh. However, many of us have not yet realized that the problem was dealt with at the cross. It was a flesh problem. The sins of the flesh, originating with Adam up until the hour of repentance, were forgiven at the cross. We died to those sins, our flesh was crucified. We no longer look at things the same way, understand things the same way, act the same way, our old minds were transformed into new minds, like unto Christ's mind, old things were passed away, now all things have become new, sexuality is not even thought of or focus on as anything of importance. This belief can be understood by reading Romans 6-11. Jesus Christ exchanged His life for our life. We must all learn to live the new life. Galatians 2:20 reads "I am crucified with Christ; nevertheless I live; yet not I, but Christ liveth in me; and the life which I now live in the flesh I live by the faith of the Son of God, who loved me and gave himself for me." In other words, the rules have changed. We live by the rules of the Believer's Life, Galatians 3:25-27; But after that faith is come, we are no longer under a schoolmaster. For ye are all the children of God by faith in Christ Jesus. For as many of you have been baptized into Christ have put on Christ.

To sum up belief, let me say that beliefs originate from numerous sources. Beliefs are thoughts, be they true or false; facts, (information that can be proven or tested for accuracy) or assumptions (the supposition that something is true). Most things are usually implicit and taken for granted such that they are not challenged even by fair thinking, right-minded individuals. The consequences of unexamined assumptions are institutionalized racism, sexism, ageism and other cultural bias.

Negative ideals imprison us and consequently, it is difficult, if not impossible to break out of perceptions. It gets cemented in place by what people say and re-say.

These saying and acts are often handed down from generation to generation, known as tradition.

TRADITION

Tradition is defined as (1) the handing down of information, belief, and customs by word of mouth or by example from one generation to another without written instruction. (2) Tradition is an inherited pattern of thought or action (as a religious practice or a social custom and (3) cultural continuity in social attitudes and instructions. Tradition was another factor that contributed to the founding father's position on Female Ordination.

Jesus entered the historical scene at a time when the culture was heavily, male dominated. Women were little better than possessions and had a few legal rights. They were seldom educated and were forbidden to be the Torah. They were not to be spoken to on the street, even by their own husbands. It was into this society Jesus came, speaking to women and interacting with them in ways that clearly indicated that he valued them as individuals for their personhood, not for their cultural roles.

The Bible tells us that Jesus announced that he had come to set us free.

What we must realize and try to understand that Jesus was doing away with the old order of role differentiation, separateness and inequality and setting new rules in motion. Rules that would order and command inclusiveness. Rules that would change their lifestyle and tradition. Jesus said to the disciples, "ye have heard that it hath been said, Thou shalt love thy neighbor, and hate thine enemy. But I say unto you, Love your enemies, bless them that curse you, do good to them that hate you, and pray for them which despitefully use you, and persecute you." (Matt 5:43-44).

In my opinion, the new order of Jesus's day was again recorded by St. Paul when he stated, "there is neither Jew nor Greek, there is neither slave nor free, there is neither male nor female; for you are all one in Christ Jesus" (Galatians 3:28). For me, the new order was to be the standard operating procedure for all Believers. We no longer have to separate the circumcised brothers from the non-circumcise nor separate the meat-eaters from the vegetarians, the Jews from the Gentiles, the Blacks from Whites, males from females, etc.

Even though cultural and societal rules were institutionalized and traditionalized, Jesus, not only told them the Good News, but demonstrated it through his teachings and lifestyle; his words and deeds. In the book of Luke chapter 8 verses 19, 20 and 21 reads "Then came to him his mother and his brethren, and could not come to him because of the crowd. And it was told him by certain, who said, Thy mother and thy brethren stand outside, desiring to see thee. And he answered, and said unto them. My mother and my brethren are those who hear the word of God, and do it." Jesus clearly demonstrated to his disciples a new relationship. Tradition says that your mother is the woman who birthed you and her children are your sisters and brothers, but the disciples were to see relatives in another light. God commands change (Eph. 4:17 through 25 which reads "This I say therefore, and in the vanity of their mind, Having the understanding darkened, being alienated from the life of God through the ignorance that is in them, — because of the blindness of their heart; Who being past feeling have given themselves over unto lasciviousness, to work at uncleanness with greediness. But ye have not so learned Christ; If so be that ye have heard him, and have been taught by him, as the truth is in Jesus: That ye put off concerning the former conversation the old man, which is corrupt according to the deceitful lusts; And be renewed in the spirit of your mind; And that ye put on the new man, which after God is created in righteousness and true holiness. Wherefore putting away lying, speak every man truth with his neighbor; for we are members one of another." The traditional views and lifestyles are to be done away with if not in keeping with God's way as demonstrated through Jesus Christ. The disciples saw that relationships as they knew it would change, tradition as they witnessed it will change and certainty beliefs as they once practiced will be altered. Jesus was demonstrating to his disciples that changes would have to take place in their life. First, they had to break old habits and second, it will take the power of Christ's life to replace them with totally new patterns. Jesus came to make a difference, to set all mankind free. Events throughout the scriptures let us know that Jesus broke with institutionalism and traditionalism. Whenever these events are believed, behaviors will change one closing remark on tradition. I believe that prior to our arrival ideas, beliefs, rules and patterns were sustained by the community, the community continued to perpetuate the traditions until we believe we have to live with it.

HISTORY

Obviously, I cannot cover history in its entirety, as it affected the backs, however, I will share my findings. The life of the black in the United States was born out of African enslavement. That is to say that the life of those blacks who accepted Jesus as their Lord and Saviour, were men and women, boys and girls who had experienced hard, cruel, inhuman treatment from slaveholders. It is reported that slaves were captured in the inter-tribal wars and were practically stripped of their social heritage. They were generally the young and vigorous males. These males were selected for the slave markets on the African Coasts. It was not until 1840 that the number of females equaled the number of males in the slave population of the United States.

The manner in which slaves were held for the slave ships that transported them to the new world was barbaric and dehumanizing. They were held in barracoons, a euphemistic term for concentration camps, and, packed spoon-fashion in the slave ships, where no regard was shown for sex, age differences, or family ties.

The enslavement of the black people destroyed the traditional African system of kinship and the family. There was no legal marriage and the relation of the husband and father to his wife and children was a temporary relationship dependent upon the will of the white masters and the exigencies of the plantation regime. When the slaves became curious about religion and wanted to gather for religious purposes, the slave masters set forth rules by which they were to adhere to. It was reported that the assembly of five or more slaves without the presence of a white man was prohibited. There was strong opposition to acquainting the blacks to the Bible, but situations dictated a change. Today is no different. It appears to me that history is repeating itself. The difference today is that it's not blacks that are prohibited to participate fully in God's Kingdom Building, it's the black Woman.

With much resistance, the slaves were introduced into the religious life of their white masters. However, they were prohibited to sit with whites. The galleries were reserved for the slaves. When the number of attending church increased, blacks were removed from the sea around the walls and ordered to sit in the gallery. Mistaking the section of the gallery which they were to occupy, members were almost dragged from their knees as they prayed. They left the church and together with other members, founded the Free African South.

The church, says E. Franklin Frazier in his book "The Negro Church in America," took root among the enslaved Blacks. He also stated that the key to understanding this 'invisible institution' may be found in the typical remark of an ex-slave who wrote: "Our preachers were usually plantation folks just like the rest of use Some man who had a little education and had been taught something about the Bible would be our preacher. The blacks had their code of religion, not nearly so complicated as the white man's religion, but more closely observed.

When we had our meetings of this kind, we held them in our own way and were not interfered with by the white folks."

One qualification which the black preacher needed among the slaves was to possess some knowledge of the Bible. This knowledge had to be combined with an ability to speak and communicate his special knowledge to the slaves." It is recorded that "the slaves were only authorized to preach, i.e, dramatize the stories of the Bible and the way of God to man, not provide religious instruction." Instruction in the Christian faith was reserved for the white ministers. Needless to say, this lifestyle influenced the belief and behavior of black males and females.

The Church of God in Christ was organized in 1895, thirty yea s after the thirteenth Amendment to the Constitution abolished slavery in the United States. Many of the members of the Church were slaves or children of slave parents. What we must remember is that slavery was an accepted practice in American culture. In fact, it was a part o the Constitution. That is to say that it was permissible to force the minority race of people to submit to the dominating influence. But my sisters and my brothers, we must remember what Paul said in Galatians 3:28 "there is neither Jew nor Greek, there is neither bond nor free, there is neither male nor female; for ye are all one in Christ Jesus."

SUMMARY

We must come to realize that "yesterday's Fad is today's norm. Fast food was a novelty in 1955. The food was considered edible, though not like home cooking by any stretch of the imagination. But 39 years later, we live in a world where fast food is the norm. Fast food doesn't stop at the local burger or chicken stand. Convenient foods flood our grocery shelves and freezers. Cooking for your family now involves opening bags of frozen veggies and simmering for 10 to 15 minutes before serving, rather than 2 or 3 hours of preparation time.

We as a church body must now recognize the fact that the time has come when we must re-visit the practice of our founding fathers and authorize the ordination of women to the ministry of the church. The doctrine must be changed. It is unjust and ungodly. We have come to understand that God is no respecter of persons. We have come to know that our ways are unlike God's way (Isaiah 55:8).

The church must come to understand that as human beings, we acquired and established set rules and regulations to live by. When new data comes into our mind that agrees with what we think, believe, etc, that data has an easy pathway to recognition. In fact, we then accept that data with clarity and understanding. However, on the other hand, when the new data does not match the expectation created by the pattern or rule s that has been established as true, it creates difficulties for the individual involved in the communication. In most instances, the data gets ignored, distorted, and often in extreme cases, persons are incapable of perceiving the unexpected data. The data is invisible. So then, what may be perfectly obvious to one person may be totally imperceptible with someone with a different set of rules or beliefs.

Our grandparents dealt with change at least as profound as what we are involved in right now. In 1890, radio was still considered magic, inconceivable, a voice traveling through the air without wires. The radio was not demonstrated until 1901. In 1890-1910, Henry Ford built the first automobile. The Wright Brothers proved people wrong when they about heavier than air flights. Electric lights had only begun ace kerosene lamps around this era.

We as human beings have demonstrated repeatedly the capacity to change. The constitution was a product of its thought of the 18th Century "Age of the Enlightenment." It derived its powers from the consent of its government; that men, have certain natural inalienable rights; that men are born equal and should be treated as equal before the law. At best, the law did not suit the backs need the law. At best, the law did not suit the black's needs.

It was through enlightenment that the Constitution was changed or amended_ Amendment XIII, Section I, dealt with racism. It reads "Neither slavery nor involuntary servitude, except as a punishment for crime whereof the party shall have been duly convicted, shall exist within the United States, or any state subject to their jurisdiction."

Amendment XIX dealt with sexism "The right of citizens of the United States to vote shall not be denied or abridged by the United States or by any State on account of sex." Amendment XXVI, Section dealt with ageism. "The right of citizens of the United States, who are 18 years of age or older, to vote shall not be denied or abridged by the United States or any State on account of age."

CONCLUSION

Excluding women from ordination is the culmination of a slowly developing process; beliefs, tradition, and history. Today, the male-centered view of society continues to exist. It is embodied in the institution of Western Society. Western Society that believed and practiced racism, any attitude, action or institutional structure systematically subordinates a person or group because of their color sexism, any attitude, action or institutional structure which systematically subordinates a person or group because of their sex.

We must move now to inclusiveness, that being a society and church, in particular, being uninhabited by differences and skillful in addressing issues confronting it and its people. The support for racism, sexism, and exclusiveness comes from fear. Perhaps fear of conflict, chaos, position or even death. What awaits us in an inclusive church is not death but new life and love. The gospel promises that "perfect love casts out all fear."

A minister who was born with cerebral palsy and called to preach. This minister admitted to his audience that he had a problem; he was disabled. He could not speak plain nor sing, however, God called him to preach. While preaching, on National television, in front of millions of viewers, he stopped and turned to his audience and asked them this question, "What's your problem? Silently, I responded in this way "The problem is, we as women have been pigeonhole into a nice, neat, little, cultural religious package. Negative ideals have imprisoned us and consequently, it is difficult, if not impossible to break out of the perceptions. It has gotten cemented in place by what people said and re-said. We must now break past these ingrained images because they are dangerous to us all. Isaiah 55:8-9 says, "For my thoughts are not your thoughts, neither are your ways my ways, said the Lord. For as the heavens are higher than the earth, so are my ways higher than your ways, and my thoughts than your thoughts."

The question now is, How does our shared faith in Jesus Christ (or God) help ease the difference between us or help ease memories of what has taken place in the past between us? We must live by the new mindset. We must continue to ask God for an understanding of spiritual truth and pray for that renewed mind. Paul tells us "if any man/woman is in Christ, he/she is a new creature; the old things are passed away, behold all things become new" (2 Corinthians 517). Through Jesus Christ, you will witness new things, acquire new ways, and new beliefs! Praise God! Same bodies, but new hearts, morality, thoughts, that will change or alter history and tradition.

The primary reason Paul wrote to the believers in Colossae was to inform them that through Jesus Christ they were free. False teachers had entered their fellowship and taught that while it was right to accept Jesus as the Messiah, one must also live under the regulation of the Mosaic law. The burden was great for the young church. The people were losing their joy and fallen into various forms of bondage or legalism.

Legalism is not freedom in Christ. We cannot attest to God's work of grace while living under the bondage of the law. I repeat, we cannot attest to God's work of grace while living under the bondage of the law, neither can women know of

God's work of grace while living under the bondage of the law. Completeness is found in Jesus, not by keeping certain rules or regulations. Paul writes "As ye have therefore received Christ Jesus the Lord,   so walk in him" (Colossians 2:6 through 15).

The truth of salvation is this; the moment we were saved, we were taken out of Adam's nature and placed into Christ's nature. Christ is now in us and we are in Him. We have a new nature in Christ, which is one of obedience to God, submission to God's love, loyalty, and devotion to Jesus Christ. Christ is our very life. There are no gender issues to contend with in Christ. In the book of Ephesian chapter one, two and three, we see the following:

IN CHRIST – WE ARE	IN CHRIST WE ARE
BLESSED	BEEN PREDESTINED UNTO THE ADOPTION OF SONS BY JESUS CHRIST TO HIMSELF ACCORDING TO THE GOOD PLEASURE OF HIS WILL.
SAVED THROUGH FAITH	REDEMPTION THROUGH HI BLOOD, THE FORGIVENESS OF SINS, ACCORDING TO THE RICHES OF HIS GRACE.
NO MORE A STRANGER AND SOJOURNER BUT A FELLOW CITIZEN WITH THE SAINTS THE HOUSEHOLD OF GOD.	BEEN BROUGHT NEAR THROUGH THE BLOOD OF JESUS CHRIST
REDEEMED THROUGH HIS BLOOD	BEEN SAVED BY GRACE
BUILT UPON THE FOUNDATION OF THE APOSTLES AND PROPHETS	OBTAINED AN INHERITANCE BEING PREDESTINED ACCORDING TO THE PURPOSE OF HIM WHO WORKETH ALL THINGS AFTER THE COUNSEL OF HIS OWN WILL
JESUS CHRIST HIMSELF BEING THE CHIEF CORNERSTONE.	BEEN MADE ALIVE WHO WERE DEAD IN TRESPASSING AND SINS

So you can see that I believe that our identity is in Christ; not in maleness, femaleness, whiteness, blackness, or the like. It is our faulty beliefs, tradition, and history that accounts for much of would begin to settle this controversy by asking the question that men are asking "Honestly Brothering. Which do you think is the greatest sin, racism, or sexism?"

In closing, let me make this statement to my brothers and my sisters in Christ, Jesus. I want you to remember that the problem didn't start with our Founding Fathers in Memphis, Tennessee, or with their fathers, under their slave masters' domination, it started in the garden of Eden with Adam. It was a flesh problem that was passed on from one generation to another, just as diseases are passed physically through genes, from one to another. Everything that God made was good and worthy (through repentance) to serve Him fully and completely. It was sin, the flesh, that marred God's plan, however through the Blood of Jesus Christ all have been provided a means by which we can be what God planned for us; sons and daughters. Yes, Satan something was wrong with women and men alike, but God fixed it through his son Jesus Christ. What we must do is believe it.

Biblical Authority for Ordained Ministry

A SUMMARY STATEMENT

Dr. Joseph D. Clemmons, Sr.

This essay seeks to explore the question of biblical authority for the ordained ministry. We propose to examine primarily the New Testament to determine if there are biblical grounds for either the exclusion or admission of women to the preaching and pastoral office.

We will look at the meaning and source of authority. We will examine the scriptures to see if there is an attitude or teachings of Jesus that may cast light on the subject. Further, we will look at four very difficult passages from the writings of the Apostle Paul, 1 Cor. 11:2-6; 14:33b-40; Gal.3:28 and 1Tim. 2:9-15, reviewing the findings and interpretations of others in the wider church and, hopefully, postulating some conclusions based on our own "decoding" of these texts for their, meaning, significance, and relevance for the task of this committee in particular and for the Church of God in Christ generally.

The above outlined format is not cast in stone. It is but a statement of an intended direction. While not anticipated, the nature of the research itself may require that we pursue alternate tracks to follow where the scriptures lead and to achieve the desired result.

This paper is presented as part of the response to the charge of the General Assembly to the Doctrinal Review Committee to investigate the question of WOMEN IN THE MINISTRY. To be sure any thorough investigation of the issue would include not only scripture but theology, history, and also tradition.

The scope of this paper will be limited primarily to the New Testament scripture. Exhaustive research of Old Testament scripture would not be very helpful to our purpose and would, indeed, make the topic voluminous and unwieldy. However, because the nature of the topic necessarily involves such questions as the triune nature of God, human sexuality, and the authority of scripture, some references must be made to the Old Testament.

This writer is starkly aware that when there are diverse opinions on an issue and varied interpretations of the same scripture, Christian scholars are tempted to see in the biblical text what they have brought to it rather than allowing the light of scripture to reveal itself to an open mind. It was William Sloane Coffin, the former Pastor of Riverside Church in New York City, in his "A Passion for The Possible" who said that Christians often use the suture much like a drunk uses a lamppost-as something to lean on for support rather than to provide illumination.

Care must therefore be taken that openness and objectivity be the guiding principles of honest investigation. Intellectual honesty is essential to the task. That there will be differences of opinion is a given. Thought is best sharpened on the anvil of controversy. A number of the Pauline epistles were his attempt to respond to a controversy that had arisen in the churches. Galatians being an example in point. It was written in response to Christians quarreling over the rite of circumcision.

Before turning to the question at hand, let it be strongly noted that God has no grandchildren. By that is meant, every generation must give fresh thinking and meaning to that "Faith once for all delivered to the saints." It must interpret the claims of faith in its generation in such a way that it has relevance to its life and work in this particular time and place where Christians debate, differ, disagree as well as pray.

We live in a social reality unparalleled in human history. We have come from an agricultural to an industrial to a service-oriented society and an age of information and knowledge made possible by electronics, computers, and communications technology. Our currency is no longer grain, spices, metals, and oil but-knowledge. This fact notwithstanding, there is an explosion of crime and violence such as the world had not sown.

In spite of the knowledge explosion, our children drop out of school at an alarmingly high rate and 135,000 of them take guns to school every day. They kill each other both within and outside the classroom in ever-increasing numbers. Values have plummeted to the basement of virtual non-existence. Aids is no the amber one killer of young men between the ages of 25 and 44 and now the third highest killer of women.

In every generation, a new bridge must be built between the ancient Word and the modern world, between a glorious Christ and an inglorious culture. While that task is essential, the church must not become victimized by the malady of paralysis by analysis. If the church is to be an agent of change developing as its product changed human lives, the sick made well, children who learn, young men and women who grow into half-respecting and God-honoring adults, it must spend more time doing ministry than it does debating who is to it.

Acts chapter 10 is instructive. It demonstrates that the Holy Spirit does not require a majority vote of a Council at Jerusalem before He falls on and speaks through the tongue of a gentile in Caesarea named Cornelius. The book of Acts and the scriptures generally are full of examples where the Holy Spirit took the lead the church said "Amen" to the Spirit's direction.

THE MEANING AND SOURCE OF AUTHORITY

When Jesus concluded his Sermon on the Mount, the record says, "...the crowds were astonished at his teaching, for he taught them as one who had authority, and not as their scribes" (Matt. 7:28-29). Again, one says Jesus was teaching in the temple, "...the chief priests and the elders of the people came unto him as he was teaching, and said, By what authority doest thou these things? Ad who gave thee this authority?"

These texts raise the question of the source of Jesus' authority for the ministry in which he is energized. these passages are cited here merely to demonstrate that the question of "By what authority?" is a valid one. It is either asked or assumed of all who minister. But before attempting to answer the question of the source of authority, it might be helpful to ask what is meant by "authority?"

Jackson W. Carroll in his book entitled, "As One With Authority", (1991) gives as good a definition as Any. "Authority is the right to exercise leadership in a particular group or institution based upon a combination of qualities, characteristics, or expertise that the leader has or that followers believe their leader has." Carroll goes on to say, "To exercise authority involves influencing, directing, coordinating, or otherwise guiding the bought and behavior of persons and groups in ways that they consider legitimate." With respect to the Christian tradition, it is the ordained clergy who through ordination is given the authority to proclaim the word, administer the sacraments, provide pastoral and general oversight, equip believers for the work of ministry, and provide those other tasks as above described.

Two things are to be noted about the definition. First, there is nothing in the definition about the person in authority "ruling" or "ruling over". Rather, to have authority is to have the right to lead in the manner described above. The term authority as used here is to be distinguished from the term power. The terms are sometimes contrasted. Often they are used synonymously. But power is the ability to control the behavior of another whether that individual does or does not give consent. The person with power may use force or other forms of coercion to accomplish his end. The person exercising the power may be using it legitimately, as in the case of a law enforcement officer. Or, the power may be used by an outlaw in which case there is an illegitimate use of power.

Authority, on the other hand, is the legitimate use of power. When members of a group or organization consent to the directives of a leader or mandates of a constitution, or to the teachings of scripture, they are saying, in fact, that that leader, constitution, or scripture has authority to guide and direct their lives. They submit voluntarily to that authority because it is commonly believed that the directives of the leader or scripture or constitution are consistent with the core values, beliefs, and mission of the group.

The issue of legitimacy hints at the SECOND thing to be noted about the definition of authority. Authority has a relational characteristic. It does not exist in and of itself. Authority does not exist apart from the receiving group's acknowledgment that the person exercising authority does in fact have the authority.

When he chief priests and elders asked Jesus, "By what authority doest thou these things? And who gave thee this authority?" (Matt. 21:23), they were acknowledging that there was indeed a large group who viewed his authority as legitimate even though it had not been sanctioned by the religious leaders of his day. Legitimacy and authority go together like hand and glove. Ordination is an institutionalized manner in which legitimacy is conferred.

The point to be made is that there is a relational character to authority. Authority emerges in social relationships that most often pattern themselves in roles, for example, parents and children, teacher and student, clergy and laity, professional and client, leader, and follower. The pattern of the role relationship can vary from highly asymmetrical authority relationships in which one of the role partners dominates the other because of unequal access to power," to "highly symmetrical authority relationships, where there is no domination but rather an equal sharing or balance of power on the part of the role partners" (Carroll, p.62). To this issue, Avery Dulles (1978, 168) speaks: "a historical study of the development of the Christian ministry would probably show that the Church in every age has adjusted its structures and offices so as to operate more effectively in the social environment in which it finds itself."

LIFELINE MINISTRIES

1805 South Hidden Hills Parkway,
Stone Mountain, GA 30088

AN APOLOGETIC FOR WOMEN IN
MINISTRY

Prepared by
Dr. Thomas Alvin Body, Sr.
Committee Member

For
Dr. George D. McKinney
Chairman of Doctrine & Reviews Committee
General Assembly Church of God in Christ

November 16, 2994

PREFACE

I have often sat at a typewriter and wrote articles for newspapers, magazines, or reports. But the most difficult time I've ever had sitting at a typewriter (computer) is now. The most probable reason is, that this writing is about change. Change to anyone, including theologians, is a very difficult task.

I call this paper an Apologetic because I am attempting to defend or make a defense (apologia) for "**Women in Ministry**." I say defend because there are very serious and studious members of our denomination (Church of God in Christ), who are diametrically opposed to "**Women preaching and/or pastoring**."

This paper has come from a long study of women's work in the Church and the Word of God. In these studies, I saw women who were Leaders, working in some form of ministry or another; (1) Winning, Nurturing, Sustaining, and Building up members in the Church (Body of Christ). (2) Working as administrators of large churches; (3) Pastoring some of the most successful churches in the "Church World;" (4) Being the greatest fund-raiser in the Local Assembly; and finally, these women provide a host of other ministries to and for the Body of Christ, that are far too numerous to account for in the limited space of the present work.

One of the persons I knew who served in the church in this capacity was my own mother. She was a "**Missionary**"[1] 'in the Church of God in Christ for 40 years. I saw her in the role of a "**dedicated Missionary**." The work she did, along with others in the same office, included; teaching messages in series in local congregations, praying at the altar until the sinners, who responded to her message, "came through" or got saved. She cooked, served food, worked on the Sewing Circle, worked as President of the Hospitality department of the State, thereby fulfilling, what was given to her by her superiors, and what she felt was the duty of a "**Missionary**."

The duties and/or responsibilities of the Missionaries, as I saw it, included; raising an annual report, starting prayer bands in the jurisdiction or anywhere else she was permitted to do so, "carrying the Gospel" to sinners wherever they were and bringing them into the fellowship of the saints. I saw Churches started by those women who were called "**Missionaries**." Their "**Speaking**" abilities were "Par Excellence" and some far exceeded those abilities of some of the men I've heated "**Preaching**." They had a pure interpretation of scripture and a very convincing appeal to the lost. As a result of such ministry, I have seen literally hundreds of souls come to Christ and some of the strongest disciples produced for Christ in the church. These *"Handmaidens"* (Acts 2:18) have been instrumental in the lives of Pastors, Superintendents, and Bishops throughout the Church.

1.This word Missionary is discussed in full in the chapter "How we make Women Missionaries/Teachers and not Preachers/Pastors."

As I look at the History of the Christian Church as a whole, and the Bible in the proper context we must give into women of the text which precludes and I hope that the following pages will do one thing for the reader.

A DEFENSE FOR WOMEN WHO PREACH

To write a defense for Women in Ministry, adequately, would be to compile a complete history of Judaism, its rights of women in official capacities, a history of their ministry for and with the Church from the time of Christ and the Apostles through the days of the Church Fathers. Moreover, it would take more than a single volume to deal with all the varieties of interpretations .given to various texts about women in the Holy Writ and to describe the measures that have been taken against them. This study does not pretend to be exhaustive and has been written to provide that general studious reader with an account of the principal strains of heterodox the right of "Those Preaching Women" and the answers that the orthodox worked out in opposition to them.

I began with a brief definition of Women in Ministry and ended with a brief Critical analysis of the texts of scripture interpreted in our constitution and as is taught by our Church. Since it is very difficult to give a brief definition, and a brief critical analysis of the texts discussed in this writing, I have done my best to cram all I can in the space allotted.

GETTING OUT THE FLAKES

It is no secret that "Women in Ministry," especially "Pastoral Ministry", attract more than its share of flakes. The author of this paper takes seriously the responsibility of filtering out the flakes as much as possible and building an accountability system, which will help keep me, and those who are in this particular study with me, from becoming flaky ourselves. We are striving to lay biblical, theological, and ecclesiologically sensitive ministry foundations for "Women in Ministry" with excellence, sobriety, and integrity. We will probably make mistakes ourselves, but hopefully, when we do we will learn from them and promptly correct them.

WHY THIS PAPER

For the past 20 years, in the providence of God, He has been raising up a fairly sized group of women who have actually been doing effective ministry as pastors aril leaders. These women have accumulated a wealth of experiences which they ha e shared with other pastors, men included, who have highly benefited from the

I believe that more than any other writing I have written, this one emerged from the immediate leading of God. I had planned on doing a series of three books on Systematic Theology Illustrated all three are for the purpose of seeing our church with a strategic and targeted contribution in the world of Christian Education. But God, through our Chairman, interrupted me and I strongly sensed that I was to do this work on Women in Ministry because He (God) wanted church leaders to have a practical guide for implementing what the Spirit is saying to the churches about **His Maidservants**.

When .1 begin to raise objections that I did not want the repercussions that went with such a publication, God seemed to become more specific. Those of you who read these pages I hope will sense the pain and sincerity under which I went as I wrote what the Lord said about **His Maidservants**.

IS WOMEN IN MINISTRY BIBLICAL

Several of our Bishops address, in their states, the issue of biblical basis for Women in Ministry. It is not our purpose here to reiterate their arguments except to say that all of us who contribute our understanding to a work such as this see ourselves as biblical Christians and none, that I know of, would so much as consider recommending an area of biblical truth to the Church of God in Christ if we were not thoroughly convinced that what we are teaching is the will of God and does not in any way violate scriptural teaching. We are personally and individually convinced that Women In Ministry, like that of men, is biblical and is proceeding from that premise.

At the same time, I am not ignorant of the fact that other brothers and sisters of high Christian integrity will disagree with me and those who are in this study with me. Several have recently expressed their utter disdain for "A Preaching

Woman" and especially "A Pastoring Woman" and have spoken to me personally about it also. I thank God for my informed critics and bless them. For one thing, they have brought up some very important issues, which they espouse and that are in opposition to the findings I write about. For another thing, we feel that even our less informed critic keeps us on our toes and help us sharpen what we say and what we do. In no case do we have a desire to enter into the polemics and attempt to refute our critics. We have no inclination. to make ourselves look bad, and you will find none of that in this writing.

We are acutely aware that women as Pastors are a relatively new innovation being introduced to the Church of God in Christ. We happen to feel that we are being led by the Holy Spirit, but even so, well-known social scientific laws of diffusion of innovation inexorably will be in effect. Any innovation typically draws early adopters, then middle adopters, and finally late adopters. In many cases, some refuse ever to adopt the innovation. They would rather fight than switch." Women in Ministry as Pastors are currently in the early adopter stage and it is the stage that, predictably, stimulates the most heated controversy. The knee-jerk Christian Leader's reaction when opposing any innovation is to say, "It is not biblical," as some did when the Sunday School and Young People's Willing Worker was first introduced and as some did for the abolition of slavery.

We have come to now to the time where there are so many examples of Women in Ministry in the Word of God, and history, as I said at the outset of this paper, that it would take a much larger work than is at hand, to critical analysis of any text of scripture is very important when it comes to the proper or right interpretation of it. Far too many heretical teachings are produced by improper interpretation of Scripture. We must understand that in order to properly interpret any text or document, we must follow the **8-Laws or Rules of interpretation**. These Rules are followed in Courts of Law, and by Etymologist, Linguist, and Semanticist. If these rules of interpretation are not followed, then the "Rules of Misinterpretation" are. l will first give you the **Rules of Interpretation** and then my understanding of the **Rules of Misinterpretation**.

HETERODOXY AND ORTHODOXY

The reason for following these rules of interpretation, very carefully, is that they keep us from entering into Heretical teachings, "earnestly contending for the Faith that was once delivered to the saints" (Jude 1:3) and bound to the Fundamental Orthodox Christian Faith. None of us would like to realize that the teaching we espouse was outside the parameters of Jesus, the Apostles, or the Fathers of the Church.

Heresy! When have we heard that word? It seems that it goes with ecclesiastical torture chambers, and zealous witch-hunts. It smacks of intolerance and rigid, Nielding dogmatism. The real "Kill you if you're not right" syndrome seems to go along with it. The relativistic world and church, somehow or other, have managed to out give its (Heresy's) function. Heresy trials are virtually nonexistent in the contemporary church. However, I do not feel that we ought "throw the baby out with the bath", that is, we should not throw the fundamental stand against heresy out with the torture chambers. There is a position or stance that the apologist and the interpreter of Scripture must take with those who are teachers of any heresy.

Historically, the church has distinguished between "heresies" and "errors," indicating a difference in degree rather than in kind. That is, though all heresies are errors, not all errors are elevated to the rank of heresy. The heinous word heresy is reserved for an error of a most severe sort. All errors of truth matter, but not all errors threaten the very substance of the truth. When the error does not interfere with the Basic tenants of the Orthodox Christian Faith, there can necessarily be no spiritual harm done.

Error invades the thinking of every Child of God. None of us is infallible. None of us is Omniscient, not only because we are sinners, but because we are human beings, inherently limited and finite. "The finite cannot understand or comprehend the infinite." There is only one "KNOW-IT-ALL", and that's God. Omniscience (All-knowing) is a divine attribute of God alone. God does not and will not impart it to us. We all concur with the adage "To err is human, and to forgive is Divine."

Our error, however, is not limited to our human boundaries of finite limitations as human beings. Errors are also a real and often deadly result of our sin. We wonder, for example, why there are so many diverse views as to what the Bible teaches. God is neither the author of confusion nor of error. The fault does not lie in Him nor with the Bible, but with us. We are the ones who are guilty of distorting what the Bible teaches. To distort the Word of God is no small matter. It does violence to the very Author and Spirit of truth.

PRIVATE INTERPRETATION

You might at this point wonder, "How then do we know what the proper interpretation of any text of scripture is?" "How do I arrive at the proper interpretation of the Bible Text?"

One of the essential elements in the Protestant Reformation was the principle of private interpretation of the Bible. That is not to say that the view was never articulated before Martin Luther, but the Reformation did emphasize the position. The concept of private interpretation is subject to much confusion. It suggests to some a license for subjective and relativistic interpretation: "What is God telling me in this passage?" or, "Well, there are a number of ways to read the text." How often have we heard and or made, innocently and or ignorantly, of course, these idealized comments of the most important document in the history of mankind. This alone should readily show us that of all the written material in the world the Bible should be, and rightly so, the most carefully interpreted text of all times. Therefore, it is necessary to come up with or find a rule or set of rules which solidifies or concretizes the kind of interpretation we give to any document.

There are several ways of arriving at a philosophical, and conclusive interpretation of a document; 1. The Hegelian Thesis, Antithesis, and Synthesis, 2. Montgomery's Bibliographical, Internal evidence, and External evidence and 3. The Institutions of Law's 8-Laws of Interpretation. I think for the benefit of those who are teachers the latter of these is most feasible.

277

Some materials or documents can exist within a particular society without any kind of protective scrutiny. Because they render no apparent danger to the society found to which it was written. (i.e, Shakespeare's Comedies, Plato's Iliad and Odyssey, Byron, Shelly and Keats Poetry, etc.,) If these are misinterpreted, we will only get a wrong line in the prose, or a wrong statement in philosophical thought. However, if we misinterpret Scripture; (1) we get the wrong message from God, (2) we give the wrong message to the people, (3) and we may end up in the wrong place.

In order to avoid such atrocities, it is incumbent upon every Teacher/Preacher to use the 8-Rules to avoid any Private Interpretation. The right way to interpret may cost more time and study, but the results are always correct and fulfilling.

Now let us walk together through this study prayerfully, studiously, and carefully.

OVER INTERPRETATION

Technically speaking, there is no such thing as Over Interpretation. Wrong interpretation, in any form, is Heresy. When a text is taken out of context and is made to be the only focal point of doctrine, I call that Over Interpretation. For example, the Pentecostal Assemblies Of The World's (PAW) interpretation of Acts 2:38 and St. John 3:5; is, "that salvation comes when one is baptized in water" saying the name Jesus in a baptismal formula, supposedly "for the remission of sins" and includes as a matter of fact that "the blood is applied in the water baptism." While very little or nothing is said about the "shedding of blood for the remission of sins", consistent with Old Testament Atonement. Members of other Pentecostal families interpret Deuteronomy 22:5, as a reason for women not to wear pants, while it is all right for them to wear blouses, or pajamas which is the woman's counter to the man's shirts and pants. That kind of interpretation is, in my estimation, an over-interpretation and yet is biblically heretical.

To get a text that is alone, without any supporting text, is also an over-interpretation. For example; The Holy Spirit is referred to as "It" in many

Pentecostal or Holiness Circles, when there is only one scripture in the entire Bible that uses the word "it", the rest says He.

The Eight Rules Of Interpretation

1. The Rule of Definition
2. The Rule of Logic
3. The Rule of Historical Fact
4. The Rule of Precedent
5. The Rule of Usage
6. The Rule of Unity
7. The Rule of Context
8. The Rule of Inference

Women in The Bible

Let us look now at scripture that supports the ordination of women (giving legitimacy to the female's "call"). There are 64 women in the Bible by name and there are many others of them without a name. Those Women whose names are not mentioned are listed in texts such as in Paul's letter to the Romans, Chapter 16:13 NKJV. "Greet Rufus, chosen in the Lord, and his mother and mine." Terms like Sisters, Daughters, Mothers, Girls and Women are all indications of unnamed women in the Bible:

Of these women in the Bible, there is a vast number of them were Leaders. Some were Judges, Queens and Prophetesses. I would like to take with you a closer look at the rights, privileges and authoritative positions these women held in the Old Testament with or without the authority of God and the persons over which they served.

Judges

A Judge in the Old Testament was an official who was authorized to hear and decide cases of Law. A History in Scripture; Family Head...Gen. 38:24-27, Established by Moses...Exodus 18:14-26, Deut. 1:9-17, Rules for... Deut. 16:18-20, 17:2-13, Circuit...1Samuel 7:6, 7:15-17, Levites assigned... And were also those who lead Israel during their Great Spiritual decline and we read of all of them in the Book titled for them.

The Hebrew title is Shophetim, meaning "judges," "rulers," "deliverers," or "saviors." Shophet, not only carries the idea of maintaining justice and settling disputes, but it is also used to mean "liberating" and "delivering." First, the judge delivers the people; then they rule and administer justice. The Septuagint used the Greek equivalent of this word, Kritai ("Judges"). The Latin Vulgate called it Liber Judicum, the "Book of Judges." This book could also appropriately be titled "The Book of Failure."

Position of Women in The Bible Before Jesus Came

Among these Judges who Ruled Israel, was Deborah the Prophetess, Wife and Judge. Judges 4:4. Let us take a close look at her <u>GOD GIVEN</u> responsibilities:

In Judges 4:5, She judged the children of Israel, 4:6-7, She had authority OVER men, under the direct supervision of God and God alone, 4:8, Men depended on heir for their decisions, 4:9, prophesied that God would give glory to a woman, 4:14, commanded the Armies of Israel, 4:23, Deborah was totally used by God, 5:1-31, shows that she was a leader and mother in Israel.

Another Ruler in Israel was Queen Esther. In Esther 4:3,10,11,15 she commanded and ordered men, 9:29, she wrote with the full authority of God and the King. Queens in the days of Esther were next in command when the King was absent.

Position of Women in The New Testament

Position of Women in the Church

How Women Are Made Missionaries/Teachers and Not Preachers/Pastors

The Church of God in Christ has licensed and appointed qualified women to the position of Missionary/Teacher for a number of decades. This position involves conducting revival services for local congregations, where she 'Teaches" the Word of God in the same mannerisms as does the man. Paul's letter to Timothy has been the crux of the contention of most of those who deny the preaching role of the woman in ministry. (This text will be discussed in full under the subject How scripture is used for proof-text against Women in Ministry)." Some of these worsen use the same type of delivery that is used by the men of our church. We call this type of delivery "Hooping and/or Moaning". These terminologies are used to describe the preaching method/style of most Afro-American Preachers, mainly in and of the Traditional Holiness Church. Hooping was first practiced in the late 1800s. It was the Freed Slaves harmonious "Call and Answer Ceremony" as he worshipped the God of his Salvation in songs and sermons. This influence of this

African tradition upon the Afro-American religious ritual, as used by men and worsen, was more evident in the Church of God in Christ than in any of the other churches. Therefore, it was a common practice for the men or women to "Hoop" when they sang songs or delivered a sermon.

Some women who have learned to hoop well remain in the category of 'Teacher', while a brother who may not be able to hoop as well, nor have the theological clarity which that woman has is called a "Preacher". This kind of method which we have chosen to distinguish between the two is, in my estimation, quite unfair. I, as well as some of my colleagues, ask the question, "If since they "Teach," they have learned to perfect it to the same Preaching satisfaction, why their method of delivery is met with less satisfaction as men on the same level.

The Two Most Misunderstood Text About Women in Ministry
"I suffer a woman not to teach or usurp authority over a man."
"For it is not lawful for a woman to speak in the church."

Husbands and wives in service is quite different from a ministry in service, "a woman is a woman no matter where she is" is a correct statement. However, in the Lord, in church, in ministry, or in the church, "there is neither male nor female" there is quite a difference "in God using a person" and administrative order. The Pastor is over me in the Lord, however, he does not take that authority in the home or on the job. "A male is a male is a male." However, the deacon's responsibility to a single woman is not the same responsibility of a father to that same single woman. The difference is, "there is a spiritual law in church and there is a physical law." The physical law is that man is the head of the woman and the spiritual law is "there is neither MALE nor FEMALE, BOND nor FREE, JEW nor GENTILE, but we are all one in the Spirit.

Biblical Authority and The Ordained Ministry

INTRODUCTION

Any serious attempt to understand scripture involves more than simply understanding vocabulary. The old preacher who when asked what a particular text meant, responded, "It meant what it said and it said what it meant!" may have been very effective in his evangelistic results, but his tools of biblical interpretation were clearly lacking. Or, again, the Christian who sought to justify committing suicide by referring to certain "proof-texts". His justification was, Matthew 27:5 says of Judas that he "...departed, and went and hanged himself." And Luke 10:37 says, "... go, and do thou likewise." The attempt to give meaning to a text not intended by the writer and without regard to the context in which a verse may be found, is to do serious injustice both to the word of God and to the hearer. The twin dangers of faulty interpretation and the temptation to "proof-text", are pitfalls to be cautiously avoided.

You may know what words mean while the ideas behind the words are yet foreign. This is particularly true when a study is made of the very difficult passages in the writings of the Apostle Paul that relate to the role of women at home and at church. The literary form must be noted, the context of the particular passage in the issue, problem or circumstance being addressed, the theological perspective of the writer and what he hoped to accomplish by the writing, the mores and values of the culture in which the reader lives as the work of other disciplines, and the impact they have on the lifestyle, any writings by the same author that may further amplify or clarify the text in question.

With regard to those passages written by Paul, the Apostle to the gentiles, they are deemed to be difficult to interpret because there is, in fact, no absolute, singular interpretation. There are varying and, indeed, opposing interpretations of the same scripture texts. Since we cannot put ourselves in a time capsule and go back 2,000 years and place ourselves in the mind of both writer and reader, we must, with intellectual honesty and with the expository and interpretive tools at our disposal, do the best we can to discover the meaning of the text to the first century reader, and only then lift from that meaning an application or principle that has meaning and relevance for us today.

One does not have to be a scholar to understand the process of biblical interpretation as described above is not an attempt to discredit scripture, but is rather an aid in comprehending it. The book of Nehemiah tells us of Ezra's effort to explain the words of the Law in a way that made it understandable. They "caused the people to understand the Law. So they read in the book of the law distinctly, and gave the sense, and cause them to understand the reading" (Neh. 8:7-8). Interpretation was necessary to understanding and application. Even those persons who claim to let the Bible speak for itself, as soon as they open their mouths, are in fact interpreting what the writer said, to what he meant, to how it is to be applied to my life, except over the very difficult and often hazardous route of biblical interpretation, just a theology is the bridge between revelation and application. It is with that understanding that the writer will look at several passages from three of the letters of Paul. 1 Corinthians, Galatians and 1 Timothy with the hope of lifting meaning for our discussion of women and biblical authority for the ordained ministry.

Before looking at the New Testament Pauline texts, however, there is an important question that needs to be asked and answered that requires at least a cursory look at Genesis, chapters 1-3. The question being, what is God's will for human life, generally, and woman in particular?

GOD'S PURPOSE FOR MAN

There is no proper understanding of self without first understanding God's purpose for man as is revealed in Genesis Chapter 1

"And God said, Let us make man in our image, after our likeness: and let them have dominion over the fish of the sea, and over the fowl of the air, and over the cattle, and over all the earth, and over every creeping thing that creepeth upon the earth. So God created man in his own image, in the image of God created he him; male and female created he him. And God blessed them, and God said unto them, Be fruitful, and multiply, and replenish the earth, and subdue it: and have dominion over the fish of the sea, and over the fowl of the air, and over every living thing that moveth upon the earth." Genesis 1:26-28.

Observe, that the book of Genesis does not only tell us of man's beginning but, rather, goes back prior to the beginning of the throne room of heaven, the council chamber of the Almighty. It is there that God counsels with himself, his triune self, and declares his intention to do two things: to create man in his image and likeness and to give him dominion (rule) of the whole of creation.

Two questions come naturally to mind. How is man to be defined and what does it mean to be created in his image and likeness? It would seem that Genesis 5:1-2 clarifies Genesis 1:26.

> "This is the book of the generations of Adam. In the day that God created man, in the likeness of God made he him; Male and female created he them; and blessed them, and called their name Adam" Genesis 5:1-2.

In these two verses, the same Hebrew word is translated into English in two different ways. In verse 1, we see, "In the day that God created man..." In verse 2, the identical Hebrew word for man used in verse 1 is translated Adam. "...and called their name Adam..." Adam or man, both are correct. The point to be made is that Adam is defined as male and female.

In Genesis 1:26, "Let us make man (the same word as used in 5:1 and 5:2) in our image, after our likeness..." can be just as correctly translated "Let us make male and female in our image and after our — likeness..." Man, or Adam, is defined, then, as male and female created in the image and likeness of God.

What is meant by "the image and likeness of God?"

Ordination for the majority of our church's population; our mothers, sisters, wives. and daughters, has been opposed or supported through the use of scripture. Those who oppose ordination (giving legitimacy to the female's "call") repeatedly use the following Scripture for their argument. Let's begin with 1 Timothy 3, a female cannot be an Elder, an Elder must be the husband of one wife, an Elder cannot be a novice. Also, one must make a distinction between an office and a gift. A gift is the spiritual ability that God gives to every believer to function effectively and efficiently within the "body of Christ". Pastoring is a gift. Many Christians believe that although God Cals to the ministry whomever He wills, it is biblically clear that the pastoral or overseeing ministry is limited to men. Another passage that is used to oppose ordination of women is (1 Timothy 2:11-15) The woman is to "learn in silence and bear children." Since that by the time of the Pastoral Epistles, a distinct organizational church had taken place in the local assembly. The apostle seems to be making the following statements: (1) When teaching the assembly is to be done, the qualified overseer or elders are to do it. (2) In the Episcopal Church, the Bishop or overseer has the authority of leadership over the assemblies, and the priests (Elders) in the parish churches are under him.

The passage in 1 Corinthians 14:33-35 seemed to be diametrically opposed to 1Corinthians 11:2-16. The previous one talks about women praying and prophesying. Here women are admonished to keep silent. Over the years scholars have attempted to solve the seemingly contradiction. First, these verses are said to be an interpretation. Second, the activities of verse 1 Timothy 2:11-15 are merely mentions, not condoned, and they are disallowed in 1 Corinthians 14:34. Third, praying and prophesying is not the same activity as speaking or teaching and therefore allowed by Paul. They do not challenge the authority or leadership of men so they are not restricted. Fourth, there are two types of service: a public service for all and a private service for believers only, Paul allowed women to participate in the latter but not in the former. Finally, the problem of 14:34 deals with a specific difficulty in the Corinthian situation, namely with the tendency of the women to interrupt the dialogue section in the service with wide, edifying questions. Paul refused to allow this activity in this situation but does not give a blanket refusal to women's participation in the service.

The two most misunderstood texts about women in ministry "I suffer a woman not to teach or usurp authority over a man" and "For it is not lawful for a woman to speak in the church." Husbands and wives in service is quite different from ministry in service." A woman is a woman no matter where she is" is a correct statement. However, in the Lord, in church, or in ministry, "there is neither male nor female" there is quite a difference "in God using a person" and administrative order. The pastor is over me in the Lord. however, he does not; take that authority in the home or on the job. "A male is a male is a male." However, the deacon's responsibility to a single woman is not the same responsibility of a father to that same single woman. The difference is, "there is a spiritual law in church and there is physical law." The physical law is that man is the head of the woman and the spiritual law is "there is neither MALE nor FEMALE, BOND nor FREE, JEW nor GENTILE, but we are all one in the SPIRIT.

Some Christians believe that Paul would stand in opposition of female ordination and would substantiate that claim giving this twofold relationship.

a. Adam was formed before Eve (2:13) a reference to God's established order in creation and the principle of headship (Gen. 2:21-12). There is a proper kind and order of leadership in the new creation, as well as in the old, prior to, and following the Fall.

b. Eve was genuinely deceived by Satan; whereas Adam was willfully disobedient to God's command (2:14). She acted on her own initiative and was deceived. Paul did not wish Eve's error to be repeated in the church. Thus, a woman--no matter how gifted or capable--is not "to have authority" (not just "to usurp authority," KJV) that properly belongs to a man in this sphere. This is simply God's established order. Paul did not mean that a woman is inherently less intelligent or more easily deceived than a man and so cannot teach or lead. Male headship itself has not preserved the church from heresy. Neither did Paul mean that sin in the human race is the fault of a woman (cf.Rom.5:12-21).

Despite her equal standing in Christ, a woman should not despise the key role assigned to her--childbearing and child rearing--and should use it as an opportunity to glorify God. Her unique ability to bear and nurture life is evidence of God's favor upon her. In so doing she will work out her salvation in God's ordered plan and will reap eternal reward (2:15).

Though women are forbidden to teach men in corporate worship, they can always teach women and children (Titus 2:2-5) and give instruction to men as well, at least privately, as Priscilla and Aquila did with Apollos (Acts 18:26).

Last but not least, those Christians in opposition of female ordination says that "scripture affirms a basic pattern of functional order applicable to the church in which men are given headship, the task of leadership, and women are to e subject to this leadership (as are men who are not designated leaders)." Therefore, we will circle this section on this note, THE MAN'S HEADSHIP; THE WOMAN'S SUBMISSION.

We have seen from 1 Corinthians 11:3 that the man is the head of the woman, and in Ephesians 5:23 that the husband is the head of the wife. The husband is directly responsible to Christ to take that place of headship. The husband is never told to force his wife into submission. Rather, wives are told to be subject to your own husbands as to the Lord--as the church is subject to Christ, so also the wives ought to be to their husbands in everything" (Eph.5:22-24). "You wives, be submissive to your own husbands so that even if they are disobedient to the Word, they may be won without a word by the behavior of their wives as they observe your chaste and respectful behavior" (1 Pet.3:1-2). Peter then gives the example of Sarah, Abraham's wife, who "obeyed Abraham, calling him 'lord', and you have become her children if you do what is right" (3:6). "Let the wife see to it that she respects her husband" (Eph.5:33).

Many women have proven they can do just that! They have proven themselves to be able business managers, mayors, lawyers, judges, engineers, congress-persons, etc. The godly woman does not take the submissive role in the home and assembly settings on the basis of inferiority but on the basis of the Word of God. She does it "as to the Lord" even if better educated and smarter than her husband. Being one, hey of course counsel together. The wife submits her will to God and to her husband because he is her head. She respects him for the role. picturing Christ, that God has given him.

Peter gives essentially the same instructions as Paul: they both were apostles and God-inspired their words as recorded in scripture. However, Peter adds another good reason for wives to submit. Their ungodly husbands who disobey (Greek "apeitheo" disobey: refuse to be persuaded), whether saved or not, can see a sermon every day as they carefully observe the godly behavior of their wives. God holds out a promise, although perhaps not an absolute one, that the husband can be and will be won (saved or restored) by a wife who does not compromise her Christian principles. She obeys her husband when it doesn't counteract obedience to Christ, her ultimate Head. She doesn't nag. She shows him cheerfulness. love, chaste behavior and reverence. She, of course, prays for him. He thinks, "why is my wife acting this way? I don't deserve it. There must be something to this Christianity." God may work His mighty work of salvation in his heart and then what a wonderful home it will be. God may teach the wife patience through the trial, but we can lay hold of His promises in His own time if we uphold our end of the bargain.

"For as many of you that have been baptized into Christ have put on Christ. There is neither Jew nor Greek, there is neither bond nor free. There is neither male nor female: For ye are alone in Christ Jesus." And if ye be Christ's, then are ye Abraham's seed, and heirs according to the promise." (Gal.3:26-29) The ministry of women in the New Covenant Local Church.

Jesus Christ suffered on Calvary's cross. He died on that cross to bear away our sins. according to the scriptures. He was buried and rose again the third day. according to the Scriptures. After His resurrection. He showed Himself alive and appeared to His disciples for forty days. At the end of the forty days, Jesus Christ said to them: "Thus it is written, and thus it behooves Christ to suffer, and to rise from the dead the third day. "And that repentance and remission of sins should be preached in his name among all nations, beginning at Jerusalem. And ye are witnesses of these things. And, behold, I send the promise of my Father upon you; but tarry ye in the city of Jerusalem, until ye be endowed with power from on high." (Luke 24:46-49)

These words of Jesus are what the church general calls the "Great Commission" It is the commission to the disciples of Jesus to preach the gospel and evangelize the world. Now. to whom does this commission apply? Only to the eleven Apostles of Jesus Christ? Oh. no! It is quite evident from the scriptures that this commission was given to a great host of believers, 120 of them accepted the opportunity.

The Bible record is very clear that those who were to be commissioned to preach and teach the gospel and evangelize the world were to "tarry (wait) in the City of Jerusalem until they received the promise of the Father (the outpouring of the Holy Spirit)."

The first chapter of Acts gives us the answer. In verse 13 the James of the eleven apostles of Jesus Christ is mentioned. Then, in verse 14, we read: "These (the eleven) all continued with one accord prayer and supplication, WITH THE WOMEN, and Mary the mother of Jesus. and with his brethren." So, we see there was a company of, people, apostles and men, and women--waiting for the outpouring of the Holy Spirit on the Day of Pentecost. When the Day of Pentecost arrived. They were all in one accord and one place."

The "gift of the Holy Spirit" was now received by Jew and male and female. and eventually would be given to both bond and free. Now, if this great gift of the Holy Spirit was given so freely to all. (and this great gift is also known as the "baptism of the Holy Spirit"), then the "lesser" gifts of the Holy Spirit are also meant for Jew and Gentile, bond and free, male and female. These lesser gifts mentioned in 1 Corinthians 12, are these: the word of wisdom, the word of knowledge, the discerning of spirits, faith, working of miracles, healing, prophecy, tongues, and the interpretation of tongues.

Again we repeat: "IF THE GREAT GIFT OF THE HOLY SPIRIT IS FOR MEN, AND WOMEN ALIKE. SO ARE THE LESSER GIFTS OF PREACHING AND TEACHING." Let us turn our attention to some of the more prominent women mentioned in the New Testament. The first preachers of the resurrection were women. Jesus told Mary Magdalene and the women, "Go tell my disciples and Peter that I have risen from the dead and that I am going to Galilee and there they shall meet me." In Acts, Philip. the deacon (later the evangelist) went to

Samaria ministering the Word of God. Surely one minister was enough in a family, but four virgin daughters Philip had also prophesied. Five people in Philip's family had a New Testament ministry—the father and his four daughters.

The apostle Paul based his teaching on the roles for women from the Creation and fall narratives of Genesis 1-3. He does this in this passage and others; 1 Corinthians 11:7-12; 1 Timothy 2:11-15; and Corinthians 14:34. Genesis 1:26-28 demonstrates that man and woman are in the image of God. Thus, it would seem like Paul, in Galatians 3:28, is emphasizing the unity of male and female.

If one looks at the context of Galatians 3:28, he/she will discover that Paul is discussing the nature of justification and how one may be included in the Abrahamic Covenant. The entrance into the covenant is by faith and not by works. Faith is the great equalizer. All believers; Jew/Gentile, slave/free, male/female are justified by faith and are made heirs of the promise. In Christ's offer of salvation, there is no distinction. It seems that Paul is arguing that no kind of person is excluded from the position of being a child of Abraham who has faith in Jesus Christ. In essence, every woman is equal to every man. When it comes to our equality in the kingdom of God, men and women are equal but they do not have the same function. There is a functional difference. No woman should have to ask for equal rights, she has them automatically. She has God ordained equality. Every woman is equal to every man. Galatians 3:28 asking a fundamental theological statement about the equality of man and woman in their standing before God and not about how male/female relationships should be conducted in society. Second, there is a distortion of the biblical worldview. God is the source of the very concept of authority and hierarchy (Rom.1:18-32).

In 1 Corinthians 11:2-16. Paul has an interesting and perplexing discussion about women praying and prophesying. The passage presents three thorny problems because of the combination of theology and practical exhortation. The issue centers around whether or not the commands are "culturally universal" or "culturally limited." Some religious groups-interpret them to be universal and therefore insist on women wearing hats or handkerchiefs. Others see them as relating to the particular day in which Paul lived with certain theological overtones for today

Last but not least is Phoebe, a minister of the church at Cenchreae, her position as "deaconess" is in the masculine, thus no linguistic or theological grounds can be distinguished between male and female as we consider her as "minister" substantiating the text round in Gal. 3:28 "in Christ, there is neither male nor female."

In our understanding. Paul assumes in his considerations of this woman by his presentation of her; that there would be no problems accepting her as a minister (giving legitimacy to her "call") for she was honored and aided by the Romans. This would thus lead you to believe that Phoebe was not an "isolated phenomenon Phoebe's ministry" produced recognized fruit, as a clear sign of the call of God as He blessed and increased her ministerial efforts. Her ministry is not confined, she ministered beyond her own congregation. She was known throughout the world, to the Greeks, Romans, and Barbarians. This implies that she propagated the Gospel everywhere. It is believed that she was the one who took Paul's letter to Rome as she ministered even unto him.

So then, we must admit that Jesus Christ exchanged His life for our life. We must all learn to iv the new life. Galatians 2:20 reads "I am crucified with Christ; nevertheless I live; yet not I, but Christ liveth in me; and the life which I now live in the flesh I live by the faith of the Son of God who loved me and gave himself for me." In other words, the rules have changed. We live by the rules of the believer's life. Galatians 3:25-27: "But after that faith is come we are no longer under a schoolmaster."

Jesus came to make a difference, to set all mankind free. Events throughout the Scriptures let us know that Jesus broke with institutionalism and traditionalism.

THE FOUR GOSPEL WRITER'S PERCEPTION OF WOMEN

Since the members of the Christian community claim to be followers of Jesus in some way, it is logical that the scriptural accounts of the attitudes of Jesus toward Women should play a major part in shaping their views. The writers of the four gospels have provided Christians with the memory of the life of Jesus. In studying these books, it is possible or probable that the Gospel Writers were not trying to give us a completely objective, accurate. and detailed account of Jesus' work on earth. Rather, they used stories and teachings in a selective way to make a statement about the meaning of Jesus' life for men and women. As these Gospel Writers (Matthew, Mark, Luke, and John) followed Jesus, could it have been that their perception stemmed from their own intolerance predicated on misogyny that was prevalent in that day.

NO RESPECT OF PERSON

Over the period of years of Bible study, one often wondered with amazement how (4) writers who were so close to the events and activities of Jesus delivered to us somewhat different interpretations. Though they were similar in nature, there were differences in timing, and scenic descriptions. This can be construed as something minor in substance; however, it is to point out the human nature that bears inherent flaws. The bottom line question is; were these men writing under the authority of the spiritual truth of Jesus' attitudes toward women. or did they interject their own prejudices. Throughout Biblical history, we find such behavior. This separatism, racism, and nepotism was illustrated in Acts 10:1-5 where Peter, who was a Jew, preached to Cornelius who was a Gentile. Racial partition had kept these factions at odds for centuries. Jesus even encountered this brand of racism in St. John 4:9 as he journeyed through Samaria, and finding a woman at Jacob's well. Due to years of fighting, she could not understand why Jesus who was a Jew would ask her for a drink of water. Traditionally, Jews had no dealings with Samaritans. There are many other Bible references with which we can find examples of this behavior. Could women have been victims of similar atrocities in the New Testament?

Resolved: That the Bible Supports The Ordination Of Women

COMMENTS BY DR. H. TUCKER WATKINS
FEBRUARY 22, 1994
ATLANTA, GEORGIA
C H. Tucker Watkins

Throughout its history, the Church of God in Christ has tried to be consistent with God and His Word. We have made mistakes, but we recognized and corrected them. For instance, as the late Bishop J. 0. Patterson preached in his last sermon general Church, we once prohibited our members from wearing dentures and eyeglasses.[1] But we've come to understand that the Bible contains no prohibition against these.

We have been a progressive Church. Progressive in the sense that we have tried to grow in Grace. As we have learned more about the Word, we have incorporated changes to reflect our understanding. I am convinced that the Church of God in Christ desires to be consistent with the Word. We used to teach that the Bible was its own best commentary. I submit that careful study of and right dividing of the Word will bring us to the understanding that God has spoken on this question and that His Word is clear: THE BIBLE SUPPORTS THE ORDINATION OF WOMEN!

The only legitimate authorities to address this question are God and His Word.

Speaking to the prophet Micah, God declared that He chose the three Exodus leaders: Moses, Aaron and Miriam! God chose a woman to be one of the three leaders of the Exodus. Can we honestly say God didn't know what He was doing? Can we say God didn't mean what He said to Micah?

In the Church of God in Christ, we have a history of showing a connection between the Old and the New Testaments. In the Old Testament God, through the prophet Joel, declared that He would pour out His Spirit on all flesh. He would pour His Spirit on sons and daughters. In the New Testament on the Day of

Pentecost, God through Peter declares that the falling of the Holy Ghost on the 120 men and women in the upper room was that which the prophet Joel had declared in the Old Testament.

The Church of God in Christ readily accepts Paul's pronouncement that in Christ there is neither Jew nor Greek. Since the majority of our members are African Americans who are descendants of slaves, we welcome the news that in Christ there is neither bond nor free. We have read that in Christ there is neither male nor female, but we have not come to understand and appreciate this liberating truth.

In the Old Testament, we have the history of the Levites - men who were priests by virtue of their birth. The Old Testament also contains the history of the Nazarites-men and women who were ministers by virtue of God's call. The Bible informs us that the Lord spoke to Moses and instructed him that when "either man or woman" shall separate themselves to vow a vow of a Nazarite, they were to be separate unto the Lord. Here again, we have an Old Testament pattern that is continued in the New Testament. Men and Women, sons, and daughters are part of the ministry. In the Old Testament Miriam, Deborah, and Esther are examples of women leaders. In the New Testament, Lydia, Phoebe, Priscilla, and Euodias and Syntyche are women who were pastors.[4] These and other women labored with Paul in the Gospel just as the men with whom Paul was associated. In Christ, there is neither male nor female.

We have long used Paul's word to exclude women from full rights and responsibilities of ministry. But careful study and scholarship have shown that Paul's was a ministry of inclusion. Paul included women among his supporters and colleagues. The Bible substantiates that there were a number of women prophets, or preachers, in both the Old Testament and the New Prophecy or preaching is one of the gifts of the Spirit. Can anyone argue that the gifts are not available to all believers?

Many of us confuse tradition with what is right. Tradition is an important part of a stable society. Accordingly, there is some virtue in doing things the way our parents did them. But, we must recognize that man is fallible and that we must go to God to seek truth and right. In the first scriptural reference to women petitioning for, and winning rights, the daughters of Zelophehad came before Moses the priest, the princes and all the congregation. The law and tradition had dictated that only men could inherit from their fathers. But these sisters argued that they had no brothers and that they should be entitled to their father's possessions. "And Moses brought their cause before the Lord." The Lord proclaimed that the daughters "speak right."[5] So it is today. It is time to make a decision based on the Word, not based on tradition. Jesus warned the leaders of the church about the danger of tradition:

> Howbeit in vain do they worship me, teaching for doctrines the commandments of men. For laying aside the commandment of God, Ye hold the tradition of men... And he said unto them, full well ye reject the commandment of God that ye may keep your own tradition. Mark 7:7-9

We are now at a place where we can no longer plead ignorance. We know much; therefore, much is required. I remember when the Church of God in Christ frowned on advanced education. Seminary graduates were highly suspect. Now we have our own seminary. We have admitted and graduated our sons and daughters. I remember when the first woman graduate of the Charles Harrison Mason Seminary was ordained, about twenty years ago. She was ordained in a private ceremony. She was not supposed to talk about it. She was to acknowledge her ordination professional reasons only: to serve as a United States Army chaplain. She was not to think of her ordination as a license to participate in ministry within the Church of God in Christ. What does this mean? In the law we call this a fiction. To be ordained by the Church of God in Christ should mean that the person is able to carry out the normal duties of a minister in the Church of God in Christ. It is embarrassing at best and hypocritical at worst to say the Church of God in Christ will ordain women to work as ministers outside the church but prohibits these same women from serving as ministers inside the Church. This is more than an inconvenient dilemma. This is a problem of major proportions.

When we look to the Scripture for guidance we find a similar situation with, Peter and the other apostles. After Pentecost, they were arrested three times in rapid succession for teaching in the name of Jesus. Though they had performed many miracles the Sanhedrin Council forbade them from teaching in the name of Jesus.

Then Peter and the other apostles answered and said, we ought to obey God rather than men. We are his witnesses of these things; and so is also the Holy Ghost, whom God hath given to them that obey him. Acts 5:29, 32.

The Sanhedrin decided to kill the apostles.

> Then stood there up one in the council, a Pharisee, named Gamaliel, a doctor of the law, And said unto them, Ye men of Israel, take heed to

yourselves what ye intend to do as touching these men.... And now I say unto you, refrain from these men, and let them alone: for if this counsel or this work be of men, it will come to naught: But if it be of God, ye cannot overthrow it; lest haply ye be found even to fight against God. Acts 5:34-35 and 38-39.

Thus, the effort to limit the content of the Apostles' ministry failed.

The following syllogism seems appropriate:

1. Only God ordains.[6]
2. God is no respecter of persons.
3. Therefore, God ordains both men and women.

The Church of God in Christ ordains women for ministries outside the church. In so doing the church seeks to limit the Word of God as preached by women. In practice, the church recognizes that God fills women with the Holy Ghost and calls them to preach. But, the church does not officially recognize the calling of women by its attempt to confer limited ordinations.[7]

Nevertheless, man is powerless to limit those whom God has called, and mad cannot constrict the reach of the Holy Ghost. Peter and the other apostles rightly refused to restrict their teaching by omitting the name of Jesus. Should women who are called agree to limit those with whom they can share the Gospel? The church's current policy is that ordained women cannot fulfill the call of their ministry inside the church. This limitation would restrict the Word of God. This policy would prohibit those within the church from hearing God's Word through a female preacher.

We must take an honest look at "accommodating" tradition. To say these ordinations are lawful but must continue to be unrecognized because they are not expedient does not leave us in the same posture as Paul.[8] Ordination is more important than dietary concerns. The Church of God in Christ must reject the tradition of man and hold to the commandment of God.

I believe the Church of God in Christ wants to be honest. I believe the Church wants to be in compliance with God and His Word. I believe that once we seek

Him for direction, as Moses did and as Dad Mason did, we will reject the tradition of man and follow the commandment of God. When Zelophehad's four daughters came to Moses after their father's death, Moses listened to their petition. Moses brought their concern to the Lord; the Lord told Moses the women, "speak right". When Moses told the leaders what the Lord said, they immediately revised their law and rejected their tradition so these four women could inherit.

I believe the Church is trying to do the right thing. I believe it is time for the Church of God in Christ to go to God, as Moses did. I believe God will say the women and men who support the open, honest ordination of women, speak right.

We have enough guidance. We have the Old Testament and the New Testament. We have our own church history. How many women have preached in our churches for the Church of God in Christ? How many Church of God in Christ women now serve as pastors? We have no legal barrier. The Church of God in Christ Manual doesn't prohibit the ordination of women. The Manual lists only four requirements for ordination: 1) moral fitness, 2) spiritual fitness, 3) attested loyalty to the Church, and 4) completion of any prescribed course of study.

I believe the Church of God in. Christ will seek God, will reject the tradition of men, and openly ordain women.

---

1. November 12, 1989
2. Micah 6:4
3. Numbers 6:1-2
4. Read Romans 16:1-5, Acts 16:14-15, and Philippians 4:2-3
5. Read Numbers 27:1-8
6. The church recognizes this ordination with a ceremony.
7. As noted above, there are ordained women pastors within the Church of God in Christ. However, their presence is something of an open secret, unmentionable in official church circles. When these women are referred to by church officials they are called Administrators, Shepherdesses, Mothers.
8. Ordained women who are not pastors are called Speakers, Evangelists, or Missionaries. This is hypocrisy because we know what these women really do despite the disguised titles.
9. See 1 Corinthians 6:12 and 10:23

MEN'S ORDINATION: PRIESTS, PASTORS, MINISTERS, RABBIS
http://www.religioustolerance.org/when-woemn-ere-first-ordained.htm.
Seminary-Louisville, Southern Baptist Convention, and the *Westminster Seminary.*

The Louisville seminary is notable because they carry the discrimination of women to an extreme position. They enforce doctrinal purity by refusing it to members who favor the ordination of women.

Other Religions:

Liberal Jewish groups, including *Reform Judaism,* have had female leaders.

The theology of most <u>Neopagan</u> groups has always emphasized the genders; a few give their priestesses greater power than priests.

<u>Native American</u> traditional religions have recognized both male and female.

Women have been accepted as ministers within the <u>Unitarian Universal Church</u> for decades.

When Some Denominations Started to Ordain women

We are unaware of any denomination in recent history which has stopped their ordaining women. However, many have gone in the opposite direction. Partial approximate dates of either: the approval of female ordination in principle or the ordination of their first women clergy appears below. We are attempting to add to this list and firm up the dates shown:

1852: Antoinette Brown was ordained by the Congregationalist Church with others to create the United Church of Christ.

1865: Salvation Army is founded and ordains both men and women.

1889: Cumberland Presbyterian Church

1914: Assemblies of God is founded and ordains first woman clergy.

1920's: Baptists

1920's: United Reformed Church in the UK

1936: United Church of Canada

1939: United Methodist Church (African Methodists had ordained women previously)

1942: Anglican communion, Hong Kong. Florence Li Tim Oi was ordained basis; may have been in 1943)

1948: Evangelical Lutheran Church of Denmark

1949: Old Catholic Church (in the U.S.)

1956: Presbyterian Church (USA)

1960: Evangelical Lutheran Church in Sweden

1971: Anglican communion, Hong Kong. Joyce Bennett and Jane Hwan regularly ordained priests.

1972: Reform Judaism

1972: Swedenborgian Church

1970's: Evangelical Lutheran Church in America

1974: Methodist Church in the UK

1974: Episcopal Church (11 women were ordained in Philadelphia before it changed to allow this)

1988: Evangelical Lutheran Church of Finland

1992: Church of England

1992: Anglican Church of South Africa

1995: Seventh-day Adventists (Sligo Seventh-day Adventist Church in Takoma Park ordained three women in violation of the denomination's rules)

1998: General Assembly of the Nippon Sei Ko Kai (Anglican Church in Japan)

1998: Guatemalan Presbyterian Synod

1998: Old Catholic Church in the Netherlands

1999: Independent Presbyterian Church of Brazil (ordination of clergy and some Protestant churches have allowed women to become bishops:

1980: Methodist Church

1989: Episcopal Church in the U.S.

1992: Evangelical Lutheran Church in Germany

1996: Lutheran Church in Sweden

1997: Anglican Church of Canada

Unknown: Evangelical Lutheran Church of Denmark

Unknown: Anglican Church of New Zealand

1998: Presbyterian Church in Guatemala

1998: Moravian Church in America

Reference: When churches started to ordain women (religioustolerance.org/when-woemn-were-first-ordained.htm)

RESEARCH TOPIC BIBLIOGRAPHY

"The Ordination of Women"

Submitted To

Dean Oliver Haney

By

Ms. Michele Jacques

For

COGIC Policy

The Interdenominational Theological Center

Atlanta, Georgia

April 13, 1992

THE ORDINATION OF WOMEN
Presentation Notes

My portion of the presentation today has to do with the issue of women's ordination. It is in specific answer to the statement on Women in Ministry (p14) in the Official Manual of the Church of God in Christ. The manual states that we, the COGIC, do not ordain women because there is no mandate in scripture to do so. Neither does it accept the use of certain other scriptures as mandates for the ordination of women or men. The church's position, with regard to the ordination of women, raises many questions. Particularly, because it indicates fundamentally, that ordination is primarily and ostensibly a matter of choice.

A cursory reading of various literature with regard to the interpretation of the 1 Timothy scripture could tend to be confusing. Some writers state that the scripture in Timothy is an apologetic for the duties of bishop and deacon. The indication that it is a desirable thing", is something which could have been said to engender interest and enthusiasm and evoke pride for one who serves and to recruit, as it were, others to serve in these capacities. Apparently, these were considered undesirable duties and a corrective to this was needed. Writers also indicated that the word bishop is untranslatable. There has been tremendous confusion about what the word really means and whether in this passage it even refers to such a thing as an office. It is most properly analogous to superintendent, manager and only is one definition--ruler--valid in the most extreme case or sense of the use of the term. Further, there is difficulty with distinguishing between a bishop and a presbyter. Thus, we may conclude that the word bishop itself points very possibly to "lay leaders in the church as well as to clergy." (IDB p410) There is no static, fixed, or absolute translation of the word. At any rate, it was a position where the lay leaders (not just ordained folk) had the say in the election process. Another source indicated that the text assumes the presence of both male and female presbyters. Our Timothy verse is an indication of this, specifically with reference to the qualifications of deacons.

There is also an indication that there was no apparent hierarchical relationship between bishop and deacon. Some say this text also infers that one may move from the position of deacon to bishop, but still, no hierarchical implications may be based on even this.

Biblical scholars further conclude that one would be hard-pressed in the early church to find any uniform organizational structure. The experience of the early church gives us no other formula for church organization than this one proffered by B.H. Streeter in the IDB:

> Whatever else is disputable, there is, I submit, one result from which there is no escape. In the Primitive Church, there was no single system of Church Order laid down by the Apostles. During the first hundred years of Christianity, the Church was an organism alive and growing—changing its organization to meet changing needs. Clearly in Asia, Syria and Rome during that century the System of government varied from church to church and in the same church at different times. Uniformity was a later development... It is permissible to hint that the first Christians achieved what they did because the spirit with which they were inspired was one favorable to experiment. In this--and perhaps in some other respects--it may be that the line of advance for the Church of today is not to imitate the form, but to recapture the spirit, of the Primitive Church. (p408)

The commentary, however, in these same sources goes on to discuss the text without reference to these other variables of the presence of women or the continuing difficulties with the translation of terms. This posed a serious problem for me in trying to understand the text in question. Indeed, what they seemed to have done was to transpose upon their commentary the current state of organizational affairs in the church.

This brings us to the basic problem of translation of any text from one language to another. The Greek for instance may have approximately seven tenses to a particular word. The English translation of a similar word may have only three tenses. These are the same problems we have faced for instance with the translation of the text in the

Song of Solomon, where it reads, "black *but* comely" in the WV, but after the argumentation and research from Doctors Gopher and Bailey, in the NRSV the text was changed to read more appropriately-black *and* beautiful." Thus, the negative connotation with the use of the word but was removed and the text can now be read more accurately. And these kinds of issues in the translation are yet a continuing problem.

With particular reference to this scripture, the issue of translation was a difficult one Fortunately, I could turn to one of our colleagues with a solid background in Greek and who had done research on this area to assist me: the Reverend David I. Cassidy.

The following will provide another framework for us through which to look at these scriptures and develop a better understanding of the possibilities which lie in the text as they impact upon the ordination of women.

SUMMARY STATEMENT:

The word cheirontoneo often translated ordained or refer to some activity which what we now call ordination is somewhat obscured by the way it is used within certain translations of the bible especially the Ka-V. One particular passage of scripture (Acts 14:23) translates the word cheirontoneo (ordained), while in other translations (NAS, NRSV & HIV) the word is consistently translated appointed. The process, as the word indicates, involves an election or selection to a particular task or office by raising hands. In this particular instance by the presbuteros or apostles, but in other instances chosen by the congregation (2 Cor 8:19). Even though the word eeiontatheis is translated appointed by better translations even when this word is used in reference to men, the word in and of itself carries no gender limiting connotations and therefore does not by itself exclude women when it is used. The word that is most often translated 'ordained', but in reality is 'appoint', prepare, to set, to become, judge and separate and has no representative word in Greek from which we derive as a. definition: a sacred God-given and/or process for investing with the office of minister, priest or rabbi anyone of either sex. (Vines Expository Dictionary of Old and New Testament Words, 1981)

Presbuteros: When one refers to women ministers in the COGIC one is constrained to use the term missionary as a ministerial designation. Women are not allowed to use the term elder, bishop or pastor, nor reverend because it is believed that these terms refer only to male ministers. However, when one examines the Greek word that is translated elder, (presbuteros), it is a word that is not exclusively used in connection with male ministers. The word is often found as Dresbuteroi (as the nominative vocative masculine form) in Acts 2:17; 1 Peter 5:55 carries a double meaning which can be translated as to the older people, but at the same time elders. The concept of being old is the dominant theme, not maleness. If the term Dresbutos is used in connection with male ministers, then the feminine counterpart Dresbutera older women in 1 Tim 5:2 should be similarly associated with femaleness or as a designate for female ministers. If Dresbutero (the dative singular masculine) in 1 Tim 5:1 is a male minister, then also is the woman who is also referred to as presbuteros (accusative plural feminine) in verse 2, a female minister. This accusative form/use of presbuteros implies that a question has been asked or anticipates the question: what about the women? For the accusative answers, questions like: to what extent, in what direction, and to what purpose? In verse 14, the term there is presbuteros. The two prominent translations of verse 14 are the elders who direct the affairs of the church (NIV) and the elders who rule well (NAS, RSV 81 UV). This text indicates that there were elders who rule in ways other than in the area of preaching and teaching doctrine.

Those who labor in preaching and teaching are especially worthy of double honor, while those who just rule are not. The term here then does not supply evidence for a gender-specific androcentric rendering of the presbuteroi in reference to men only, but more than likely as indicated by the context from which it is an extension does include female elders who also rule well. Thus there is a strong possibility of female elders who are appointed by special groups, apostles, and others by their congregations.

Further, the word deacon is frequently used in the NT to designate those who minister (that at least 18 times in the KLIV alone) in the doctrine and preaching

307

of the word: Acts 20:24, 2 Cor 4:1, 2 Cor 6:3, 11:8, 1 Tim 1:12 Also, Paul so designates himself as diakonon in a figurative way and in reference to his apostolic ministry. Eph 4:12 is a clear example of ergon diakonias, which means work of the ministry. The emphasis here then is on the word itself and not the person, in the sense of what is done and not who is doing it. Therefore, the term deacon describes what is the essence of all ministry. The idea of servanthood, rather than a slave: master (which in the greek is doulos) relationship is the foundational consciousness from which all who desire to be diaknoi tou euanggaliaon (which means ministers of the gospel) are to approach ministry. We must not fail to mention that where the word deacon is used in reference to a male or a female it is always in its masculine form. It is literally a generic term. Therefore, within the biblical text there is no such separate designation technically as a deaconess or female deacon. [Gender is not the issue where a deacon is concerned, ministry is.]

Contrary to the Official Manual of definition on (p141) diakanos does not denote the service or ministration of a bondservant (doulos). But according to Vines Expository Dictionary; (diaknos) views a servant in relationship to his [or her] work (diakonia). While doulos (an adjective that indicates involuntary servitude), views a servant in relationship to the master (despotes or despot). Therefore, a deacon is not a type nor an indication of a second class subservient, but a fellow worker in the gospel.

CONCLUSION:

What statement then can we make about the question of the ordination of women?

1. There is no apparent biblical mandate for ordination generally.

2. Ordination is both an elective and selective process.

3. The elective process is one in which the entire congregation, at times, may participate depending upon the particular congregation.

It is a (elective and selective) process in which both lay leaders and/or clergy participate. The positions of elder, bishop, presbyter and deacon were characterized by both female and male persons.

The Early Church had no uniform prescriptive structure for the organization of the church.

Thus, the COGIC's stance with regard to the ordination of women poses both theological and ethical issues. This stance rests most firmly on a theological perspective which is undergirded by the acceptance of the basic inequality of women. Further, it is (after research and study) a matter of the choice. The COGIC has no biblical grounds on which to deny the right and privilege of ordination. The Church is obligated to participate with God in God's calling of an individual to ministry. The research also implies that there is no hierarchical sense in which women can be denied ordination. Women were interactive in all areas and at various levels of church organization. Two quotes from Jarena Lee and Sojourner Truth give us a credible perspective and commentary on this issue. They say...

> How careful ought we to be, lest through our by-laws of church government and discipline, we bring into disrepute even the word of life. If the man may preach, because the Saviour died for him, why not the woman, seeing he died for her also? Is he not a whole Saviour, instead of a half one, as those who hold it wrong for a woman to preach would seem to make it appear? (Jarena Lee)

> I feel that if I have to answer for the deeds done in my body just as much as a man, I have a right to have just as much as a man there is a great stir about colored men getting their rights, but not a word about the colored women; and if colored men get their rights, and not colored women theirs, you see the colored men will be masters over the women and it will be just as bad as it was before. So I am for keeping the thing going while things are stirring: because if we wait till it is still, it will take a great while to get it going again. (Sojourner Truth)

The words of these two women would indeed call for a Church Council the alarm of importance with regard to this issue. When things get stirring and stir toward the goal of justice why not confront all existing injustices?

BIBLIOGRAPHY

1. Buttrick, George Arthur. The Interpreters Dictionary of the Bible, Volumes I, II and III. Nashville: Abingdon Press, 1962.

2. The Interpreters Bible, Volume XI. Nashville: Abingdon Press, 1955.

3. Cassidy, David M. "The Ordination of Women" (Class Presentation). Atlanta: The ITC, COGIC Polity, 1989.

4. Griffin, Arthur D. By Your Traditions. Chicago: Black Light Fellowship, 1989.

5. Jamieson, Robert, A. R. Fausset and David Brown. A Commentary Critical, Experimental and Practical on the Old and New Testaments, Volume VI.

6. Grand Rapids: William B. Eerdmans Publishing Company, 1945.

7. Jewett, Paul. The Ordination of Women. Grand Rapids: William B. Eerdmans Publishing Company, 1980.

8. Lock, Walter. The International Critical Commentary A Critical and Exegetical Commentary on The Pastoral Epistles (1 & 2 Timothy and Titus). Edinburgh: T. & T. Clark, 1952.

GLOSSARY

A DEFINITION OF TERMS

PURPOSE

It is the purpose of this paper to present a concise definition of the following theological terms: PREACHER, PASTOR, PROPHET, PROPHETESS, and MISSIONARY

PREACHER

A preacher by definition is simply a person who preaches; a clergyman; a minister; one who speaks publicly on a religious subject, delivers a sermon, proclaim something, or give earnest advice.

The term "preacher" occurs eleven times in Scripture, seven in the Old Testament and four in the New. The Old Testament references are found in the book of Ecclesiastes, the remainder in the in Romans, 1 and 2 Timothy, and II Peter. In the Old Testament, "preacher" is a translation of one Hebrew word QOHELETH, to convoke, or to call together, or summon to assemble; it is the verb form of the noun convocation. The root meaning of QOHELETH is an assembler, like a lecturer for example.

In the context of Ecclesiastes, the term "preacher" is ascribed to Solomon. It is as if he called an assembly and addressed the subject matter he considered important. The idea suggested is that a preach r is an assembler and a proclaimer. The NIV translates the word a teacher; others translate it as a proclaimer, speaker, or spokesman.

The Living Bible Paraphrase renders Eccl. 12:9,10 like this:...Because the Teacher was wise, he went on teaching the people all he knew... Verse ten reads, "For the preacher was not only a wise man, but a good teacher; he not only taught what he knew to the people, he taught them in an interesting manner". The preacher was wise and skillful as a teacher, communicating what he knew in an interesting manner that aroused a desire or curiosity in those who heard him.

When we come to the New Testament, the "preacher" is not defined in the context in which it appears. So we look again at the root meaning. In Romans 10:14, it is the translation of the word KERUX, the one heralding, bringing news, or announcing divine truth (the gospel). This is the role that Paul declared that he was ordained to fill (2 Tim.1:11).   Peter ascribes the same to Noah as a "preacher of righteousness (II Peter 2:5). A preacher, then, is one who preaches the gospel as a herald, bringing good news or glad tidings from God, "...in demonstration of the Spirit and of power".

PASTOR

By definition, a pastor is "a minister in charge of a church". The concept, borrowed from animal husbandry, has its roots in the Old Testament. There it appears only once in the book of Jeremiah (17011). The writer does not define it, so we check its root meaning. From Hebrew, Latin, and Greek, the common term for pastor is shepherd. From a Hebrew word it means to "tend a flock": and figuratively "to rule". From New Testament Greek, the concept comes from another word which is used metaphorically of Christian "pastors" as noted in Ephesians 4:11.

In the Ephesian passage, the office of the pastor is listed as one of the gifted ones given to the church with very specific responsibilities—"For the perfecting of the saints for the work of the ministry, for the edifying of the body of Christ:..." or "to prepare God's people for the works of service.

Harold V. Bennett
Resource Person
Commission on Women in the Ordained Ministry
Bishop George McKinney, Chair
February 24, 1994

ORDINATION: Public affirmation of calling to and readiness for ministry, wherein authorization to guide the affairs of a religious body happens, so that properly trained persons may function in particular capacities. The clearest example of this process appears in Acts 14, namely Acts 14:23 where the Greek term χειροτονέω, (stretching forth of hands) appears.

DEACON: διάκονος (a waiter, server) Official of a religious body who has the task of serving in the assembly. Ministry of the word is no particular function of this office.

MISSIONARY: (No biblical term discovered) One who is sent on a mission or a specific assignment.

BODY OF CHRIST: (σομα Χριστὸν) collectivity of persons who accept Jesus, the Christ as their personal Lord and Savior. 1 Corinthians 12:27 and additional places in scripture contain this phrase.

MINISTRY: (διακονοα) Meeting the needs of humankind. Attestation of these terms is in Numbers 4:12 and 2 Chronicles 24:14 in the First Testament, and several places in the Second Testament, of which Acts 1:17 is an example.

THE CHURCH: (ἐκκλησία) Gathering of persons for religious purposes. This term appears in several places in scripture, namely Matthew 18:17, Acts 5:11; 8:3; and 1 Corinthians 4:17.

SOURCES

Baler, Walter. A Greek-English Lexicon of the New Testament Chicago: University of Chicago Press, 1952.

Brown, Francis, editor. The New Brown-Driver-Briggs-Gesenius Hebrew and English Lexicon. Peabody, Massachusetts: Hendrickson Publishing Company, 1979.

The following definitions are taken from Strong's Greek/Hebrew Dictionary.

SEDITION appears in the Bible 5 times: In Ezra 4:15; Ezra 4:19; Luke 23:19; Luke 23:25; and Acts 24:5. In Ezra the root word comes from the Aramaic ('eshtadduwr) and means rebellion. In Luke and Acts sedition comes from the Greek (stasis) that means a standing (properly, the act), i.e. (by analogy) position (existence) by implication, a popular uprising; figuratively, controversy. In the KJV it means dissension, insurrection, uproar.

HERESY appears in the Bible only once--in Acts 24:14. The Jews accused Paul of heresy and Paul uses this word himself in presenting his defense to the governor, Felix. It is from the Greek word hairesis that means properly, a choice, i.e. (especially) a party or (abstractly) disunion. In the KJV it means sect. A sect is a group of people who hold a particular view, such as Sadducees, who were called a sect in Acts 5:17. The same Greek word is used, hairesis.

TRADITION does not appear in the Old Testament. This precise word appears in the New Testament 11 times. The root word is the Greek word paradosis and means transmission, i.e.(concretely) a precept; (specifically, the Jewish traditionary law. In the KJV it means ordinance, tradition. You may want to look at Matthew 15:2, Mark 7:7-9 and I Pet 1:18 for examples of how this word is used in the New Testament.

PREACHING appears one time in the Old Testament — in Jonah 3:2 and is derived from the Greek qweiyah, which means a proclamation. It appears in the New Testament 26 times. Six different Greek words serve as the basis for this word in the various New Testament verses. in Mt 3:1, for instance, the Greek word kerusso which means to herald (as a public crier), especially divine truth (the', Gospel). In the KJV this word translates to preacher, proclaim, publish. In Acts 8:4 the Greek root word is euaggelizo and means to announce good news ("evangelize") especially the gospel. And in the KJV it is translated declare, bring (declare, show), glad (good) tidings, preach (the gospel). In Acts 11;19 the Greek word is 'ale° and means to talk, i.e. utter words. In the KJV this word is translated preach, say, speak (after) talk. In Acts 20:9 the Greek word is dialegomai and is the middle voice; to say thoroughly, i.e. discuss (in argument or exhortation). In the KJV it is translated dispute, preach (unto), reason (with); speak. In Romans 16:25 the Greek word is kerugrna and means a proclamation (especially of the gospel; by implication the gospel itself. in 1 Corinthians 1:18 the Greek word is logos and means something said (including the thought); by implication a topic (the subject of discourse) also reasoning (the mental faculty) or motive; by extension, a computation; specifically with the article in John the divine expression (Le. Christ).

Footnote:

'I researched only the precise word the Task Force requested. For instance, I researched "woman", but not "womankind" and "woman's" which also appear in the Bible.

WOMAN appears in the Bible 361 times. When God speaks and compares Himself Israel, Zion, or Jerusalem to a woman there is no word in Strong's dictionary to define the word woman. This happens in scriptures such as Isaiah 13:8, 21:3, 26:17; Jeremiah 4:31, 6:2, 49:24; Lamentations 1:17. Where the word refers to a human woman the Greek word most often used is 'ishshah which means feminine; a woman. In the KJV is translated [adulter]ess, each, every, female... However, in Acts 9:36 where Dorcas is described as a certain disciple in Joppa: a woman full of good works, there is no word in Strong's dictionary to define it. In other verses, such as Romans 1;27 the Greek word is thelus which means female, woman.

MOTHER appears in the Bible 244 times. In most places the Greek word used is 'em and means a mother (as the bond of the family); in a wide sense (both literally and figuratively) like father. The other word used is meter which means a mother (literally or figuratively, immediate or remote and means mother.

THE CALLED: this phrase appears in the Bible 2 times — both in the New Testament, Romans 1:6 and 8:28. The same Greek word is used--kietos which means appointed, or (specifically) a saint; and in the KJV means calling.

USURP: To seize and hold (as office, place, or powers) in possession by force or without right. To take the place of by or as if by force.

SUBMISSION--Legal agreement to submit to the decision of arbitrators. The condition of being submissive, humble, or compliant. An act of submitting to the authority.

BLASPHEMY--Insulting, showing contempt or lack of reverence for God. Act of claiming attributes of diety; irreverence towards something considered sacred or inviolable.

HERESY--Adherence to a religious opinion contrary to church dogma. Dissent or deviation from a dominant theory, opinion. Practice an opinion, doctrine, or practice contrary to the truth or to generally accepted beliefs or standards

SEDITION--Incitement of resistance to or insurrection against lawful authority.

PROPHET/PROPHETESS--One to whom God speaks. One whom listens and obeys. one whom says, "Thus says the Lord!" "Simply a mouthpiece for God." p 136

RULER--One that rules; specifically Sovereign.

DOCTRINE--Something that is taught. The teachings or principles or position of a body of principles in a branch of knowledge or system of belief.

DOGMA--a principle of law established through past decisions.

A Definition Of Terms

by

Dr. D. R. Williams,

Pastor of Williams Temple COGIC-Gainesville, Florida

Presented to

THE DOCTRINAL REVIEW COMMITTEE

Bishop George McKinney, Chairman

November 10, 1993

Memphis, Tennessee

In Paul's farewell address to the elders of the Ephesian church, le suggests that these men, serving as pastors, were appointed or ordained by the Holy Ghost (Acts 20:28b). From this we can conclude that pastors are Spirit-filled shepherds, or elders, or overseers of the church, who exercise watchful care over the flock of God.

Consequently, a pastor is "responsible for teaching, feeding, healing, wounds, developing unity, helping people find their gifts, and doing whatever else is necessary to see that they continue in the faith and grow in their spiritual lives." When we read Paul's words to Timothy, we understand more of what a pastor is. "Let the elders that rule well be counted worthy of double honor, especially they who labor in the word and doctrine." Here the pastor is seen as one who works hard in teaching the word and setting forth doctrine or the foundational truths of the Scripture. A similar idea is expressed in I Thessalonians 5, where Paul exhorts the brethren to "know them which labour among you and are over you in the Lord, and admonish you...."

What is a pastor? A pastor is one who cares for the people of God, the flock of God, the church, nurturing it to spiritual maturity. Jesus, Israel's Shepherd, demonstrated this concept like no one else. He demonstrated that a pastor should be a good shepherd, give him elf in the interest of the sheep, relate to them closely, and provide for their spiritual growth and progress.

THE PROPHET AND PROPHETESS

The concepts of "prophet" and "prophetess" are both Old and New Testament terms. The word "prophet" is from a Hebrew word NABIY, an inspired man; NIBTYAH, an inspired woman. Both words are derived from a primary root word NABA, to prophesy, or to speak or sing by inspiration, whether predictive or simple discourse. The inspired man or woman is one who receives a message directly from God and addresses it to a specific people for a specific purpose, in a specific situation. The message they bring can warn of some future or impending destruction, or can address a situation in the present time. All the Old Testament prophets (and prophetesses) addressed the situations of their contemporary scene, as well as predicted coming events.

When we come to the New Testament, the prophet and prophetess were men and women who "spoke forth or openly of the mind and counsel of God".

According to Vine's dictionary of New Testament Words, we read that prophecy is "the declaration of that which cannot be known by natural means; it is forth-telling of the will of God, whether with reference to the past, present; or the future." As a gifted man, the prophet's purpose in ministry was to "edify, to comfort, and to encourage the believer" (1 Cor. 14:3). In the same context, Paul shows that the message of the prophet not only speaks to the believer but also to the unbeliever.

In addition to the major and minor prophets of the Old Testament, there were others who were inspired to proclaim the message of God orally. We are familiar with figures such as Samuel, Nathan, Elijah, Elisha, Miriam, Deborah, Huldah, John the Baptist, Agabus, and Anna. Thus, from these brief references, we can conclude that the prophet or the prophetess were those who were inspired by God to speak the message of God to a given people for a special purpose.

Prophet (a) from prophetess (1) the mouthpiece for God; (2) knew they were called at a certain moment, sometimes contrary to their own desire; (3) prophetic formulae indicates the fact of the prophets consciousness of bringing a God-inspired message; and (4) failure to understand their own message proves it came from without and not within their own consciousness. (Manual, p136-8)

(b) Prophet from prophetes meaning foreteller; a man who is inspired by God to speak
Prophetess-(a) No reference found in the Manual
(b) Prophetess from prophetis meaning foreteller; a woman who is inspired by God to speak

THE MISSIONARY

The term "missionary" is not an Old Testament concept. by common definition, a missionary is "a person sent on a religious mission.". Broadly speaking, a missionary is a person who works to advance some cause or idea. by implication, apostle Paul is said to have gone on several missionary journeys. But the Scriptures do not refer to him as a missionary. He himself declared that he was ordained or appointed a preacher, apostle, and teacher (1 Timothy 1:11).

He never referred to himself as a missionary. Luke writes that the Holy Spirit commanded the prophets and teachers at Antioch to separate to Him Barnabas and Saul for a special work (Acts 13:2), but they were not called missionaries.

In the Church of God in Christ, there are those who are designated as missionaries, but they are not sent forth on a religious mission by the church. They are primarily women who affirm that they have been called by God to be a missionary. Usually, they do not say that they are called to India, or Haiti, or Jamaica, or China, or Africa etc. They usually serve in some capacity in the local church, or on the district, or state level, advancing some cause or fostering some kind of program, such as feeding the hungry, visiting the sick, caring for children and elderly people. They care for the homeless and the dying. Some however, do affirm that they are called to preach or to serve as evangelists. As such, they function primarily in ministering the word. (See Official Manual, p.p. 149-150)

PASTOR (a) from poimen, meaning helper or feeder of the sheep. Now refers to minister over a congregation; was always an elder (one of seniority); appointed to hold office in the church and exercise spiritual oversight of the flock, inferred that ones appointed were Elders. (Manual, p139-40)

(b)Pastor from poimen, meaning a shepherd (lit. or fig.) used of sheep herders, of Christ and leaders in the church, closely linked with teachers (IDB)

ELDER OR PRESBYTER (a) from presbuteroi, meaning older ones; referring mainly to a person; were most likely a council of advice for local churches. The early church "was evidently unaware of the distinction between elders and bishops. (Manual, p139-140) (b)Elder or Presbyter from presbuteros (male minister) presbutera (female) the feminine counterpart for female ministers or older men and older women who are not ministers, but doing ministry (Cassidy).

BISHOP (a) from episkopoi, meaning overseer; emphasizes what the elder or presbyter does: oversight of the flock to provide for, govern and protect it. No trace of official ordination in hierarchical sense of elder to bishop in apostolic times. (Manual, p139-40)

(b) Bishop from episkopay/episkopos from the root of epi meaning over, upon or on behalf of or to watch

HEAD (1 Corinthians 11:3) (a) No reference found in the Manual

(b) translated "source' or "origin" not connoting the idea of rule over or lording over another (Jewett); in reference to the Genesis 2 creation narrative with woman being made from man (verse 8) and so men from women and both from God referring to verse 12; related also to Gen 3:16, a teaching from the Law speaks to an order of creation (IDB) upon which rabbi's based argument of subordination of woman to man.

AUTHORITY (1 Timothy 2:12) (a) No reference found in the Manual

(b) Authority from authenteo meaning a worker acting of oneself or dominate: usurp authority over (Strongs); this Greek verb is obscure in its meaning may mean interrupt (Dibelius) or dictate to (Moffat) or contradict, or women are to have no administrative positions in the church (IDB); reference to Gen 3:16/Gen 2, rib creation narrative which says Adam (translated human being) was created first then Eve and that it was deceived not Adam and broke God's law. No mention of Genesis 1 creation narrative is made where male and female are created together in God's image. (Stagg)

Definition Of Women, The Bible, And The Role Of Women

WOMAN (Heb. 7, 6). Woman, with man, was 'made in the image of God': 'male and female he created them' (Gn. 1:27). She is man's helper (Gn. 2:20).

From the Heb. laws we see that the mother-was to be honored (Ex. 20:12); feared (Lv, 19:3) and obeyed (Dt. 21:18ff.). She was to be reckoned with in her household, naming the children and being responsible for their early education. The same sacrifice was offered for cleansing, whether the new-born child was male or female (Lv. 12.5f)

She attended the religious gatherings for worship; and brought her offerings for sacrifice. The Nazirite vow was taken by her as she sought to dedicate herself specially to the worship of Yahweh (Nu. 6:2).

The woman was exempt from sabbath labour (Ex. 20:10), and if sold as a slave was freed like the man in the 7th year. If there were no male heirs, the woman could inherit and become a landowner in her own right.

Young men were exhorted to marry within the tribe lest their womenfolk wooed them away from their service of Yahweh.

Monogamy was regarded as the ideal state, although polygamy was common, and the relationship of Yahweh and Israel was often "compared with that of a man and wife.

There are many examples of women of stature paying their part in the life of the people, e.g. Miriam, Deborah, Huldah, and being in a direct personal relationship with Yahweh. On the other and, one sees the tremendous influence wielded against Yahweh by women such as Jezebel and Micah.

As time went on there was a tendency, under rabbinical teaching, to make the man more prominent and to assign to women an inferior role.

Of greatest importance in the NT is our Lord's attitude to women and his teaching concerning 'Mary, the mother of Jesus, was described as Blessed among women' (Lk. 1:42) by her kinswoman, Elizabeth. Anna. The prophetess at the temple recognized the baby's identity (Lk. 2:38). 'There was much concerning her

Son that Mary did not understand, but she 'kept all these things. pondering them in her heart' (Lk. 2:19), until the time to make public the details of his birth and boyhood. As he was on the cross Jesus commended her to the care of a disciple.

The Gospel narratives abound with instances of Jesus' encounters with women. He forgave them, he healed them, he taught them, and they in their turn served him by making provision for

his journeys. by giving hospitality, by deeds of love by noting his tomb so that they could perform the last rites for him, and by becoming eyewitnesses of his resurrection.

Jesus included them in his teaching illustrations. Making it clear that his message involved them. By thus honoring them he put woman on equal footing with man, demanding the same standard for both the sexes and offering the same way of salvation.

After the resurrection, the women joined in prayer and supplication' with the other followers of Jesus, in entire fellowship with them (Acts 1:14). They helped to elect Matthias (Acts 1:15) and received the power and gifts of the Holy pint on the Day of Pentecost (Acts 2:1-4, 18). It was the home of Mary, the mother of John; Mark, which became a center of the church at Jerusalem (Acts 12:12). Paul's first convert in Europe was the woman Lydia (Acts 16:14). Priscilla with her husband taught the great Apollos the full truths of the gospel. The four daughters of Philip 'prophesied' (Acts 21:9). Many others, for example, Phoebe, were active Christians, wholly engaged in the service of the gospel. Paul dealt with the local situation in the churches by requiring that the conventions of the time be observed. Meanwhile, he laid down the principle that 'God shows no partiality and that in Christ there is neither male nor female since. Christians are all one in Christ Jesus (Gal. 3:28).

Bibliography: K.D. Stendahl. The Bible and the Role of Women. 1966: P K Jewett. Man as Male Female. 1975.

Doctrinal Review Committee

Women in Ministry

Bishop George McKinney, Chairman

Dr. T.A. Body, Secretary

For

EXECUTIVE COMMITTEE OF THE GENERAL
ASSEMBLY

Church of God in Christ

November 14, 1993

Notes from Chairman's Interim Report at AIM 1998
Los Angeles, CA

Issue: Shall the COGIC ordain women as Elders with all the rights and privileges including the eligibility to serve as pastors?

1. Basic Findings:

A. The COGIC has always recognized women in ministry as missionaries.

B. evangelists, teachers, church planters

C. The COGIC has recognized and affirmed women in ministry by licensing through the Department of Women.

D. During the past 30 years, several Bishops have, without the official sanction of the National Church, ordained women as Elders-some of whom have served as Pastors, Administrators, Chaplains in the military and hospitals and other institutions.

2. Areas of Controversy:

A. Interpretation of Scripture

B. Importance of Culture, manners, and custom related to status and role of women in New Testament times.

C. What is the influence of women's liberation or feminist movement?

D. Is God's order for biological family analogous to God's Divine Order for the Church?

E. Would God bestow gifts on women which He did not intend for them to use?

Headship-Genesis 3:1536... "He shall rule over thee"
Does this mean that man is **head** when a queen is on the throne?

1ˢᵗ Corinthians 11:3... "The head of every man is Christ; the head of woman is the man; the head of Christ is God"

Bishop W.W. <u>Hamilton</u> had some concerns regarding the participation of women in governance. He told the story of a newly saved man who was after 2 years ordained and had ss to the General Assembly and could vote. He compared this man to women who have 10, 20, 30 years in ministry and are unable to vote. He suggested that we consider admitting all District Missionaries to the General Assembly.

The First Meeting

of "The Doctrinal Review Committee"

on "Women In The Ministry"

at the Hyatt Regency Hotel (Austrian Room)

Atlanta, Georgia

July 28, 1993

MINUTES OF THE MEETING

Bishop George McKinney, Chairman

Recorded by

Dr. T. A. Body, Secretary

Hyatt Regency Hotel (Austrian Room)
Atlanta, Georgia

Wednesday

July 28, 1993, 6:45 PM

The meeting was called to order by our Chairman, Bishop George McKinney. Prayer was then was offered by Supt. Carl E. Howard of Oakland, California.

The Chairman asked introductions of each committee member Attendants were:

Bishop George McKinney of San Diego, California,

Dr. T. A. Body of Stone Mountain, Georgia

Eld. Ronald Hoston of Rochester, New York

Eld. James A. Parson, Sr. of Baltimore, Maryland

Bishop W. W. Hamilton of Seaside, California

Supt. Carl E. Howard of Oakland, California

Dr. Oliver Haney of Atlanta, Georgia

Lt. Col. Dianna McNiel James of Columbia, So. Carolina

Dr. D. R. Williams of Gainsville, Florida

Dr. Robert Lee Asberry of Dallas, Texas

Eld. Sherman Davis of Tacoma, Washington

After the introductions, Chairman McKinney explained the awes me responsibility of the mandate given us by the General Assembly. He said; "there will be a need to have concerted effort in prayer and dedication to the Lord as we are go about fulfilling the mandate set before us to ramify the Church Of God in Christ's true doctrinal position on 'Women in the Ministry.'

He asked the committee of elaborate on the way we should go about organizing the strategy of our investigation. He expressed his desi e to see that each committee member was totally involved and would have personal responsibility in this awesome task. This, if worked diligently, would enable the committee's temporary findings to be presented to the General Assembly by April of 1994.

After prayerful consideration and extended deliberation, we decided that the specific areas of investigation and assignments, for the committee, should be as follows:

1. A defense for the position of Official COGIC Doctrinal Manual.

2. A defense for the women who are already pastors, etc.,

3. A definition of terms, Preacher, Pastor, Prophet, Missionary and Prophetess.

4. A Historical review of Women in the Old Testament.

5. A Historical review of Women in Ministry the New Testament and in the Early Church History.

6. A Woman's view of Women in Ministry from the Tradition view and the Feminist view including the New Feminist Bible.

7. A Biblical answer to the Questions "Who Calls to the Ministry?" And "How is a person Called?"

8. A view of Male domination and headship in scripture and the concepts of Ministry about Ruling and Serving.

The Chairman then expressed his appreciation for the writing of "An Apology For Women In Ministry" by Dr. Body. He asked Dr Body to share briefly with the committee the paper he had written. Dr. Haney commented that there were also others who had written a vast array of books on the subject of "Women in the

Ministry," and that there was a wonderful group of these books in the Library of our Inter-Denominational Theological Center (ITC) He stated that the Library and these materials were made available for our perusal at any time. The Chairman then suggested that, we would need a 'meeting of minds' before the November '93 Convocation, and having a need to review the materials in the ITC Library, we also could meet and bring our assignments there in September. We unanimously agreed and Dr. Haney welcomed us.

Dr. Haney also suggested that we use some of the experts in the Church of God in Christ who were graduates and are Old and New Testaments Scholars and would be *able* to present us the *"Texts"* liberal and a fundamental point of view. There was no specific suggestions as to how we would acquire the help of these experts.

The Chairman asked Dr. Haney if it was possible to get some of these materials in the Library copied and sent to the members of the committee. Dr. Haney said that it was possible and he would be responsible to get them to us expeditiously. However, he said that this effort would be very costly and asked if there were any funds available for the expense of it. We suggested that the Chairman go to the Chair of the General Assembly and ask for funds. We also asked Bishop Hamilton, the Genera Secretary, if there were any funds available in the national treasury for our use and there was no comment. It was suggested that we would undergird the responsibility given to Dr. Haney ourselves. We all accepted it as usual.

Chairman then asked for comments and questions from the committee in reference to our method and message of presentation to the General Assembly.

Bishop Hamilton asked, "How are we going to go about presenting a practical, livable approach, of the matter of Women to our brothers and sisters who have a traditional in Ministry, value system of it or nominal theological understanding of the scriptures in question?" The committee complimented Bishop Hamilton for bringing this question to focus, especially at such a crucial time in the History or our church. We summarized tissue he presented and decided that, in order to meet the nee of the coming generations in our church, and for the theological soundness we must give to our pastors and student-preachers, in the Church of God in Christ, it was of cardinal importance that our Study and Findings be **well sought out hermeneutically scholarly, ecclesiologically, and theologically.**

The Chairman felt that we should make the choice of what our particular and individual responsibility would be in the investigations and assignments we had suggested. As we chose our work, the chairman elucidated the responsibility of each one and the assignments were as follows:

1. A defense for the Official Doctrinal Manual of the C.O.G.I.C. Assigned to: Elder Robert Lee Asberry, Elder Sherman Davis and Lt. Col. Diana 11. James

2. A defense for the women who are already pastors, etc.

3. A definition of terms, such as Preacher, Pastor, Prophet, Missionary and Prophetess.

   Assigned to: Elder Ronald J. Roston and Dr. T. A. Body

4. An Historical Review of Women in the Old Testament. assigned to: Elder Ronald J. Roston and Dr. T. A. Body

5. An Historical review of Women in the New Testament and in Early Church History

   Assigned to: Bishop W. W. Hamilton

6. Woman's view of Women in Ministry from the Traditional view the Feminist view including the New Feminist Bible. assigned to: Mother Parthenia T. Crudup

7. A Biblical answer to the Question "Who Calls to the Ministry?' And "How a person is called?"

8. A view of Male domination and headship in scripture and the concepts of Ministry about Ruling and Serving.

   Assigned to: Dr. James Parsons

After viewing our responsibilities, Chaplain Diana James suggested making a report of these findings by September may not give us enough time to do it thoroughly and that a better time would be when we came to Memphis for the '93 Convocation. The Chairman got the wishes of the house, and it was unanimous that we should meet in Memphis during the Convocation, instead of coming to ITC in September and bring our completed assignments there.

A motion was made to adjourn by Dr. Williams and seconded by Dr. Body. The meeting was adjourned. The next meeting was set for Wednesday Morning,

November 10, 1993, in the Cafeteria at Mason's Temple. The time will be announced later.

Submitted by: Dr. T. A. Body

The Second Doctrinal Review Committee Meeting
Notes on the Meeting
Held
November 8, 1993 8:AM
Mason Temple Cafeteria Lounge

Chairman McKinney and a few of the committee members met this morning in the Lounge of Mason Temple's Cafeteria. This meeting was set during our last committee meeting held in Atlanta, Georgia. The attendees today were Dr. Joseph Clemmons, Bishop W. W. Hamilton, Elder Charles Stevenson, Supt. Norman Harper, Supt. Carl Howard, Elder Sherman Davis, Jr., Robert Asberry, Elder Ron Hoston and Dr. T. A. Body.

Chairman McKinney suggested, that since there were only a few members present and that it is of utmost importance that a better forum of members be present during our deliberations, that those members who were present would give brief summations and have a brief 'round the table dialogue on their individual reports. Bishop McKinney further stated, this kind of dialogue was very necessary so that we could have a feel of what most, if not all, of the committee members were doing or have done.

The meeting was informal and very deliberative. The first report was given by Bishop Hamilton He gave a very brief overview of the things which he and Dr. Hunt had done together and individually on the subject of "An Historical Review of Women in the New Testament and in the Early Church." He stated that his particular interest was towards the Women in the New Testament, while Dr. Hunt's area was specific interest towards a broader view of the Historicity or Women in the Early Church. Conclusions of their findings were not yet given because he (Bishop Hamilton) needed to confer with Dr. Hunt. Their paper is forthcoming.

Next was Supt. C. A. Stevenson on the subject of "Who calls to the ministry?" And "How is a person called? He said in his paper he discussed how various people were call and concluded that all persons who were called by God, got their call from the very same source. He said he also discussed how both men and women were called in Scripture. He concluded that although God calls whomever He wills, the use of Pastors in the book of 1 Timothy excludes women in office. He also concluded that there is room for women in the ministry but not after the ethical codes of the feminist movement's influence on or in the COGIC.

Then Dr. Asberry gave a brief review of his subject The Traditional View or The Defense for the Official Doctrinal Manual of the C.O.G.I.C. as it sees the role of the women in ministry. He stat that "The crucial issue in our church is women in leadership and in what capacity of leadership. Some of the influence of the feminist movement has rubbed off on us. In our consideration Women in Ministry we must consider the evangelical point of view. The whole of our study to come down to the interpretation of scripture. The question of Ordination is, How far should we go?" He added that he had discussed it with Dr. Hoehnor (I might have the name misspelled), who is a respected Theologian of Dallas Theological Seminary, and his (Dr. Hoehnor) conclusion was women can minister to women only and maybe even Harold Hoehnor Shepherd them in small groups. He also referenced another Author, Vicky Craft of Northwest Bible Church, Dallas, TX, said that women should carry cut their work with women.

There were various refreshing moments of dialogue on whether there was a difference between the Pastoral office and the Gift of Pastoring. Including the Appointment and or the Call to the Office of the pastor.

Dr. Clemmons in his brief summary on "The Authority and Rule" was "What is the interpretation of and scripture on the person who leads and how much authority is given that person. He also went through definitions of interpretive rules we must follow to come to the same or nearly the same conclusions that will make sense to our hearers.

Elder Davis, in his presentation, concurred with those findings of Dr. Asberry and those who hold to the additional view of our manual. He said that Feminist Movement has had enough influence in the world and it was not right for the church to lower its standards to succumb to its whims.

Dr. Clemmons brought to our attention that a lot of the problems we face with our dissolving, resolving and solving problems, which exist in our Doctrine, is "We don't have a Mission Statement. What is our purpose and what is our goal? The committee concurred and Chairman McKinney said that we will put that on the agenda for very near future consideration. We all felt that if we had a Mission Statement we would have the proper goals set for future generations.

Bishop McKinney summarized our discussion with the mandate the church has placed upon our shoulders and said that we should be as sincere about the responsibility of each of our assignments. He continued, "There is a lot of Tension here in the work that is set before us. Our conclusions must Godly and something to be given to our posterity. There was continual conversation about the how of our conclusions and how we must deal with the issue at hand to let the church have the opportunity to take a definite position in and of what we do with and for the Women who are in the Ministry of the Church of God in Christ.

Dr. Boy discussed the meaning of terms and the work that has been done in the title "Missionary and Preacher." After hearing from Dr. Body, it was suggested that Dr. Body write about the Abuse Eind Misuse of Women in Ministry of the C.O.G.I.C. in the past as well as the present, etc.

The meeting was concluded with prayer by our chairman.

The next meeting is to be held at Mason Temple Cafeteria Lounge Thursday 11/11/93 at 7:00 AM

Dr. George McKinney, Chairman

T. A Body, Secretary

Doctrinal Review Committee Report #1

November 11, 1993
To the Executive Committee of the General Assembly
Dr. Frank Ellis, Chairman
Hyatt Regency Hotel
Mark Twain Conference Room
Memphis, Tennessee

Mr. Chairman:
Members of the Executive Committee:

The Doctrinal Review Committee received its assignment, with a great sense of dedication, sincerity and anticipation. We knew also that the task was not an easy one, but all the members Pro and Con were very grateful to you and our leaders for your selection and appointment. Brother Chairman, we knew that your reason for the design and the appointment of such a commission was to investigate every possible avenue of scriptural and historical knowledge to settle once and for all times in the Church of God in Christ the innumerable questions of "Women in Ministry."

Our first meeting was held in Atlanta, Georgia during the Sunday School and Musical Convention. You had the privilege and opportunity to meet the eight members of the Committee who met. Our session was a planning session of how we would go about developing a rational argument for and against Women in Ministry. Present in that meeting was an even distribution of those who were diametrically opposed to Women in Ministry and those who were totally for them. This session was very communicative. There was one lady present in our session and we listened to her tearful plea to consider her plight as a woman raised in the COGIC, trained in our Theological Seminary, maintaining a membership in the COGIC and is the highest-ranking officer in the United States Army of the COGIC serving as Chaplain.

Some of the men whose ideas about women in ministry, by their own confessions, became refocused and they exhibited greater signs of sincerity for our assignment. They understood as we began our plight, that a precedent had been set by our Church. It was not just simply the argument of total exclusion of women in the ministry, but that of inclusion. This precedent has been set by the Church of God in Christ, consciously or unconsciously, in our Seminary and in our local ministries.

We were able to assign to each person or several persons one of the eight steps of approaching this subject. The areas of investigation were as follows:

1.   A Defense for The Official Doctrinal Manual of the Church of God in Christ

2.   A Defense for the Women who are already Pastoring in our church.

3.   A Definition of terms, such as preacher, pastor, prophet, missionary and prophetess.

4.   A historical review of Women in the Old Testament.

5.   A historical review of Women in the New Testament and in early church history.

6.   A Woman's view of women in ministry from the traditional and the feminist view including the Feminist Bible.

7.   A biblical answer to, Who calls to Ministry and how a person is called.

8.   A view of male domination and headship in scripture and the concepts of ministry about ruling and serving.

In order to keep a firm hold on all the efforts of each committee member, our chairman was insistent on our communicating with him and the other committee members by fax, mail and telephone. We were also able through one of the members of the committee, Dean Oliver Haney to gain access to the well-facilitated library of ITC. We will meet three days in December for a perusal of the minds and works of the experts in the field of Women in Ministry from every religious and theological perspective.

Our next meeting was held at Mason Temple's cafeteria lounge where we received about eight reports from the aforementioned steps of perusal. As the reports were made we then began to see the tension that we face in our investigation. The arguments became very intense but we remained under the control of the Chairman who kept us focused on our mission.' It will not be an easy task because the scholars on this commission are searching with diligence for an apologetic or defense for their position whether it be pro or con.

We were able to have two other meetings, while here at the Convocation, where new materials were presented and more reports turned in for each member to read and personally investigate.

Each member of the committee wishes to thank the Chairman of the General Assembly for his prayerful and scrutinous selection of the persons with whom were working. We, also, would like to express to the Chairman of the General Assembly that it is with joy and great anticipation that we accept the challenge of eying the opportunity to serve our church in the capacity of Doctrinal Reviews. Because we understand that our findings, if passed by the General Assembly, will affect the documents and doctrine of our church for us and our posterity.

Bishop George McKinney, Chairman

Dr. T. A. Body, Secretary

ACKNOWLEDGMENTS

We appreciate and thank God for all of the hard work the Doctrinal Review Committee members contribute to this work.

Doctrinal Review Committee Members
Of The General Assembly
of The Church of God in Christ, Inc.

Elder Charles Quillen,
Elder Charles Stevenson,
Bishop Clarence Sexton,
Elder A. Hunt,
Dr. Joseph Clemmons,
Elder James Holton,
Dr. D. Williams,
Dr. Oliver Haney, Jr.
Elder Sherman Davis,
Elder James Stovall,
Dr. Robert Asberry,
 Elder James Parson, Jr.,
Lt. Col. Dianna James,
Mother Parthenia Crudup,
Bishop W. Hamilton,

Elder Walter Bogan,
Bishop William James,
Bishop Wesley Sanders,
Elder Jessie Denny,
Dr. Norman Harper,
Elder Clyde Young,
Dr. Aliene Gilmore,
Supt. Carl Howard,
Dr. Thomas A. Body,
Mrs. Michele Jacques-Early,
Elder Steven Johnson,
Bishop George D. McKinney, Jr.,
Ph.D.

www.ingramcontent.com/pod-product-compliance
Lightning Source LLC
Chambersburg PA
CBHW080227270326
41926CB00020B/4169